God's Grand Design

Blessed Mother Mary Directly Speaks

Our Heavenly Father Speaks to You, His Sacred Child, About This Book and Its Author

This book is written for you by my special favored son. He is my sacred child, like of all of you are. But listen to what he has to say for I approve of His words in this book. He has worked very hard to bring you advanced truths of my creations. Richard is completely right when he describes that the spiritual realm, and the physical universe are indeed created so all of my sacred children may return to me after the rebellion of Lucifer and the fall of Adam and Eve as is described in your Christian Bible.

Listen to Him with both your ears, for Richard has a unique and true understanding of things that are not available to those who believe in me by other means. I your Father in Heaven, have asked Richard to do something that I have never asked any others of my children. Listen to Him for he is my Messenger, and he will help lead you back to me so we may together enjoy eternal life in a paradise that each of you can barely imagine. Yet, it is waiting for you.

Richard is one of my special children even before he was born on the Earth. If you listen to what he has to say and read what he has written, that will lead you back to me without fail. I love all of you so very much from the bottom of my Heart. Pray to me. Ask me questions about your lives. I will answer you. Be prepared to listen to what I have to say for it will be for your eternal goodness and salvation.

I love you.
Your Loving Divine Father

God's Grand Design

Blessed Mother Mary Directly Speaks

Her Apparitions & The End Of Times

Richard Ferguson

Richard Ferguson

God's Grand Design: Blessed Mother Mary Directly Speaks
by Richard Ferguson
Copyright © 2024 by Richard Ferguson
All Rights Reserved.
ISBN: 978-1-59755-809-9

Published by: ADVANTAGE BOOKS™
                Longwood, Florida, USA
                www.advbookstore.com

All Rights Reserved. This book and parts thereof may not be reproduced in any form, stored in a retrieval system or transmitted in any form by any means (electronic, mechanical, photocopy, recording or otherwise) without prior written copyright law, permission of the author, except as provided by United States of America.

Unless otherwise indicated, Scripture quotations taken from The Holy Bible KING JAMES VERSION (KJV), public domain.

Scriptures marked (NKJV) are taken from the Holy Bible NEW KING JAMES VERSION®. Copyright© 1982 by Thomas Nelson, Inc. Used by permission. All rights reserved.

Library of Congress Catalog Number: 2024946291

Name:	Ferguson, Richard, Author
Title:	***Blessed Mother Mary Directly Speaks – Apparitions & The End of Times***
	Richard Ferguson
	Advantage Books, 2024
Identifiers:	ISBN: Paperback: 9781597558099
	eBook: 9781597558204
Subjects:	RELIGION: Christian Life – Inspirational

Lead Contributor and Lead Editor: Evangeline Ferguson

Second Printing: January 2025
24 25 26 27 28   10 9 8 7 6 5 4 3 2

Table of Contents

1: INTRODUCTION 9

2: BLESSED MOTHER MARY 11

3: BLESSED MOTHER MARY'S REVELATIONS NEVER HEARD BEFORE 14

    BECOMING GOD'S ANOINTED MESSENGER 17
    MY ANOINTED MESSENGER HISTORY. WHO EXACTLY IS YOUR AUTHOR OF THIS BOOK? 17
    SATAN ATTACKS ME VICIOUSLY THREE TIMES 19
    THE BEGINNING OF MY CHRISTIAN SPIRITUAL WARFARE 20
    THE UNEXPECTED ARRIVAL OF JESUS CHRIST AND BLESSED MOTHER MARY 22
    WHY ME LORD? 25

4: ALL ABOUT OUR BLESSED MOTHER MARY 30

    HOW DOES BLESSED MOTHER MARY SPEAK WITH ME? 31
    THE SACRED PROCESS 31
    THE REASON MOTHER MARY SPEAKS TO ME 32
    THE BEAUTIFUL VOICE OF MOTHER MARY 35
    MOTHER MARY, THE LINK BETWEEN EARTH AND HEAVEN 36
    MOTHER MARY'S LOVING THOUGHTS TO ME YOUR AUTHOR 40

5: THE FIVE APPARITIONS OF BLESSED MOTHER MARY 41

    MOTHER MARY SPEAKS TO ME ABOUT ALL HER APPARITIONS 42
    LA SALETTE 47
    LOURDES: MIRACULOUS HOLY EVENTS OCCUR 66
    GARABANDAL: THE MULTIPLE APPARITIONS OF BLESSED MOTHER MARY 73
    THE GIRLS STATE OF ECSTASY 73
    THE POWDER COMPACT STORY 74
    MANY PEOPLE WERE SKEPTICAL OF WHAT THEY SAW 75
    THE VATICAN CHOSE TO DISBELIEVE OUR BLESSED MOTHER MARY'S APPARITIONS AT GARABANDAL 75
    ZEITOUN – THE MANY APPARITIONS 93

6: THE CATHOLIC CHURCH IS NO LONGER WHAT YOU THINK IT IS 96

    THE AFTERMATH OF THE POPES REFUSAL TO RELEASE THE THIRD FATIMA SECRET AND NOT CONSECRATE RUSSIA 102

THIS WAS THE EXCHANGE BETWEEN FATHER MALACHI MARTIN AND ART BELL....................... 104

7: THE ANTI-CHRIST IS NOW IN THE VATICAN. 107

MALACHI MARTIN: END OF TIMES - THE ENTHRONEMENT OF LUCIFER IN THE VATICAN 110
POPE FRANCIS, A MODERN DAY SATANIC THEOLOGICAL TYRANT 113
POPE FRANCIS WANTS TO DESTROY THE CHURCH AND CATHOLICISM. 114
POPE FRANCIS WANTS TO COMBINE OUR BELOVED CATHOLIC CHURCH WITH MANY OTHER
RELIGIONS SUCH AS ISLAM, BUDDHISM ETC.. 115
POPE FRANCIS REVEALS THAT JESUS'S DEATH IS NOT WHAT WE ARE BEING TOLD 120

8: BLESSED MOTHER MARY HERSELF TOLD ME THIS 125

9: NEW HORRORS FROM CARDINAL BERGOGLIO AKA. POPE FRANCIS 130

10: THE HERESIES OF POPE FRANCIS 140

FRANCIS' HERESIES ON ATHEISM AND ATHEISTS: 141
A STATEMENT RELEASED BY THE VATICAN DECEMBER 18, 2023.. 143
MALACHI MARTIN AND THE SATANIC INFILTRATION OF IMPURITY IN THE CHURCH 144
EVIDENCE THAT THE END OF TIMES IS UPON US 144

11: MOTHER MARY SPEAKS FREELY ABOUT THE WORLD SITUATION TODAY WITH EMPHASIS ON THE UNITED STATES OF AMERICA 148

STATE OF THE CHURCH:.. 149

12: MOTHER MARY DESCRIBES FATIMA 1, FATIMA 2, AND FATIMA 3 152

A FUNDAMENTAL DESCRIPTION OF ALL THREE FÁTIMA REVELATIONS 152
FATIMA APPARITION 1 157
FÁTIMA APPARITION 2 160
FATIMA'S SECRET APPARITION 3 161
WHAT IS A RELIABLE CATHOLIC CHRISTIAN CATECHISM. 162

13: THE WIDESPREAD THEOLOGICAL CRIME OF THE VATICAN TO KEEP THE REAL FATIMA THIRD SECRET FROM GOD'S SACRED CHILDREN 164

THE STORY OF SISTER LUCIA OF FATIMA AND THE VATICAN'S IMPOSTER WHO REPLACED HER . 164
SISTER LUCIA 1 AND SISTER LUCIA 2.. 165
DOCTOR CHOJNOWSKI CONCLUDED THE FOLLOWING: 166
SISTER LUCIA 1 VS. SISTER LUCIA 2 166

14: POPE FRANCIS LIES ABOUT THE 3RD SECRET OF FATIMA 170

15: FROM BLESSED MOTHER MARY: THE REAL 3RD SECRET OF FATIMA SPOKEN DIRECTLY TO ME, FATHER'S ANOINTED MESSENGER 174

    A MAGNIFICENT DIALOG 174
    THE SKY WILL BLACKEN LIKE IT HAS NEVER DONE BEFORE. 175
    OUR BELOVED CHURCH 176
    SATAN WILL PLACE HIMSELF ON THE THRONE OF PETER IN THE VATICAN 177
    SATAN'S EARTHLY POWER 177

16: THE LONG-AWAITED CONSECRATION OF RUSSIA TO THE IMMACULATE HEART OF BLESSED MOTHER MARY 179

17: WHY ALL THE DESTRUCTION, PAIN, AND AGONY DEAR MOTHER MARY 181

    BELIEVERS WILL BE PAINLESSLY SNATCHED OUT OF OUR PHYSICAL BODIES 182

18: A FURTHER DESCRIPTION OF THE TORMENT, PAIN, AND AGONY COMING DURING THE END OF TIMES TO THOSE WHO REJECTED OUR LOVING FATHER . 186

19: SATAN'S PLAN FOR WORLD CONQUEST 188

    THE END OF TIMES BEGAN IN THE 1960'S. 188
    POPE FRANCIS IS THE ANTI-CHRIST 189
    WILL BELIEVER BE TREATED DIFFERENT THAN THOSE WHO CONTINUE TO REJECT GOD? 190

20: A LAST-MINUTE ADDITION FROM OUR LORD, JESUS CHRIST 199

21: THIRD SECRET OF FATIMA CONTINUES 203

    THE FOLLOWING IS BY FATHER MALACHI MARTIN WITH ART BELL 208
    WHAT FATHER MALACHI MARTIN TELLS US ABOUT THE THIRD SECRET OF FATIMA 209

22: POPE BENEDICT: THE TERRIFYING REVELATION IN FATIMA'S 3RD SECRET .. 212

23: EXISTENTIAL MORALITY AS DEFINED BY ALMIGHTY GOD 221

24: A ONE-WORLD GOVERNMENT IS COMING 223

    POPE FRANCIS APPROVES 223

25: THE DEMOCRAT PARTY WITHIN BIDEN'S SATANIC MORAL DISASTER 226

    ABORTION 230

26: CURRENT DEMOCRAT POLITICS PROMOTES THE END OF TIMES 234

My Personal Editorial on The Democrat Party and It is Malignant Dangers to American Citizens 234
Joe Biden 237
More Racial Hatred Sowed 238
In our schools 239
Sexual Perversion 239
Tyrannical Control of our language 239
Our Now Destroyed Southern Boarder 239
Covid Lies 240
Rumors That a Chinese Army Is Forming Within Our Country 240
Joe Biden is by far the most tyrannical president this country has ever seen. 241
President Of United States Joe Biden said: 244
So, What Is a Loving Christian Voter to Do? 246

27: THE CATHOLIC CHURCH 247

28: THE END OF TIMES ARE HERE! 252

Worldwide trends 252
The Conclusion 256
Beyond Human Politics and The Mess, It Causes 258
The Above-Described Disasters Will Indeed Happen 261
Pain and suffering that are to come 261

29: THE LAST WORDS FROM OUR BLESSED MOTHER MARY 263

30: BLESSED MOTHER MARY'S CLOSING THOUGHTS 265

APPENDIX: 267

1

Introduction

This introduction contains vital information regarding how this book came to be and the people involved in writing it. Unless you read others of my books, this will be the only sacred book besides the Bible that is in your possession. There are especially important points that must be made in this introduction so you will be able to understand the miracle that you are holding in your hand.

1. 100% of everything you read in this book is completely true and is approved by your Almighty Father in Heaven. He is with me 100% of my life and knows all my thoughts and my emotions and so on. I've been gifted enormously by our Heavenly Father. I am able to speak with not only Him, but also our Lord and savior Jesus Christ, the Holy Spirit, which proceeds from them and our Blessed Mother Mary. I am able to carry on conversations with the Trinity and Mother Mary. If I tell you something theological you can rest assured whatever I say is completely true. I have had a **Covenant of Truth** with our Heavenly Father for the past 40 years or so. I will not and cannot tell a falsehood in any of its forms.

2. Your author Richard Ferguson is indeed your **Heavenly Father's Anointed Messenger.** I was chosen by our Father for many reasons that are described later in this book. One of the reasons dates back to a conversation I had with our Heavenly Father while I was still in the Heavenly Kingdom before I was born to earth.

3. It was a monumental pleasure to have many different discussions with our Blessed Mother Mary in the writing of this book. We have come to know each other extremely well. To the point where at times I already know what our Blessed Mother is going to say. I wish all of you could hear her most unique and loving soft voice I have been gifted to hear in the writing of this book.

4. But when the writing of this book comes to an end, I will still always be able to speak with her and that gives me some peace of mind.

5. Lastly, contained within this book is detailed information about me and my spiritual life long before our Heavenly Father asked me to write, **God's Grand Design of All Creation for Your Redemption.**

I owe it to you to document my spiritual history and abilities to reassure you I am very capable of performing the tasks our Heavenly Father asked me to perform on your behalf. Of this theological material out of my deep love for the Trinity and Blessed Mother Mary and especially for ***you***, God's sacred children. Your Heavenly Father never makes mistakes, and he chose me to do this. I am completely honored and humbled he chose me.

6. I will not fail our Heavenly Father and I will not fail you his beloved sacred children.

7. One thing you should know, Satan has attacked me throughout my life. And while I am writing these theological materials your Heavenly Father wants me to; I am forced to perform spiritual warfare every day due to his attacks against me. Satan is a real pest.

There are other details about me and my life in both the spiritual and physical realms later on in this book. In conclusion, the bottom line is I am a sacred child of God just like you. But in my case our Heavenly Father has chosen me to do some extraordinary things for the benefit of all others of his sacred children. And so, I will.

I love all of you sacred children ever so much,

Rich

2

Blessed Mother Mary

May 14, 2024
Blessed Mother Mary

Oh, my dearest of sons, how can I possibly thank you enough for working so very hard? And revealing to your Heavenly Father's sacred children ever so much of the content of what I have been trying to communicate to His children for the last 500 years or more. It has been for me extremely difficult and frustrating to bring forth the messages that our Father wants His sacred children to know about. As I have told you earlier, I have really had 375 apparitions each of which were intended to bring the love of your Almighty Father and the Trinity. But also tell this vitally essentially information, it is ever so sad for me to also have to bring the terrible warnings to God's children on earth.

As you know my dear son, God's sacred children on earth are exposed purposely to Satan and all of his falsehoods and temptations. Each of you came to the earth to take what is known in the Heavenly Kingdom as the "Earth Test." This test has two features to it. The first is to experience your Heavenly Father in ways that go beyond what can be experienced in the Heavenly Kingdom. You will come to know your Heavenly Father in a far deeper and unique way than if you had chosen to stay in the spiritual realm in your home in the Heavenly Kingdom.

The second feature is you will be exposed to physical hardships and suffering on earth so as to evaluate your dedication and love for your Heavenly Father. Additionally, you will be exposed to so many different Satanic temptations that will include putting yourself above others of God's sacred children and even God Himself. Yes, you know dear son, this will lead people to their ultimate destruction in hell.

My dear son you have become far stronger within the spiritual Kingdom because of all the suffering you have gone through. And now you are God's

Anointed Messenger to bring His message of peace, love, understanding and acceptance of the Godly rules that exist on earth. Also, dearest son you have done magnificently to explain to God's sacred children precisely how all of creation works and how it is tied together for the benefit of His sacred children.

Since I was born human on earth 2,000 years ago, I am able to bring much needed information to God's sacred children on earth. My messages of love can be found in my apparitions like the one at Lourdes. But even though it breaks my Heart, your Father asked me to bring messages of warning to His children on earth. This is because the large majority of His children have succumbed and given in to Satanic temptations. Most of them have abandoned Jesus Christ who is the way the truth and the life. No one goes to the Father except through Him. Over a period of time, the children on earth have rejected increasingly the one true God. And have fallen for physical sensual pleasures, adoration of Pagan Gods and given up true Godly morality replacing it with their imaginary rules that are invented so as to bring physical pleasure only. Once my dear son you have described the country you live in as a modern-day Sodom and Gomorrah.

You are so right dear son. Ever so sadly dear son, you are also so very right when you said that your Democrat party is the political arm of Satan. If only people could stand back and look at what has been happening to your society through them and where the tragic events will continue to occur because of them. The destruction of your southern border is one example where tremendous pain and suffering is now just starting to happen to your society. Such that your country will become unrecognizable from every other sad country in the world just like what your former President Barack Obama has wanted. I remember dear son he said, "I see no reason why America should be any better than all the other countries in the world." Look to Canada and the tragedy unfolding there, which is what will happen to your country if you do not turn to God.

It is for these reasons that I have come to earth. And appeared to many people 375 times so as to plant the seeds of Godly love to everyone who is willing to listen and live their lives accordingly. Because of my efforts and the unwillingness of people today to spread my words of love and importantly of the warnings of what will come. If they continue to turn their backs on the one true God, there will be many catastrophes from many different directions on earth.

Dear son, you have documented my warnings very well inside this book. And all the time and the efforts and the suffering you have gone through. To bring this book to God's sacred children the same milestone of love of you for your Heavenly Father and the Kingdom of Heaven.

The only last thing I can say is I look forward so much to hug you and thank you upon your arrival within the Heavenly Kingdom.

I love you ever so much,

Your Blessed Mother Mary

Thank you, dear Blessed Mother Mary! I love you too ever so very much! We will always continue our discussions.

3

Blessed Mother Mary's Revelations Never Heard Before

As <u>Spoken Directly to Me</u>, Our Father's Anointed Messenger [1]

Note From Your Author Richard Ferguson:

Yes, our Blessed Mother Mary does indeed speak directly to me regarding the topics in this sacred document. Over the many years since the life of our Lord and savior Jesus Christ, Blessed Mother Mary has spoken to many people. There have been many apparitions to a wide variety of people in the years since then. In fact, Mother Mary has appeared 375 times to various people across the world, far more than you have been led to believe. She has also had an ongoing relationship with Pope John Paul II as seen another example. Our Blessed Mother Mary will always choose to speak with selected dedicated Christians that love the Holy Trinity and of course Blessed Mother Mary herself.

Our Blessed Mother Mary has chosen to speak to me because your Heavenly Father has asked me to be His Anointed Messenger. My mission is to bring His sacred children His message of love, peace, acceptance, and advanced theology that brings far deeper understandings of not only the Trinity, but also His creations and why they exist. You can find that information in another book I have written last year in 2023 titled, <u>God's Grand Design of All Creation for Your Redemption.</u>

---

[1] Note: My dear sacred child of God, this book you hold in your hands is a <u>Sacred Document</u>. It is so because it contains the direct words of our Blessed Mother Mary. All sacred words contained within will always be presented in bold and italicized print. My words as author and <u>Anointed Messenger</u> of our Heavenly Father will always be in regular Times New Roman text.

My dear sacred children of God, <u>this book you are holding in your hands is no ordinary book. It is a sacred document.</u> Why? It is approved by God Our Heavenly Father and Blessed Mother Mary. It is sacred because it contains the direct words of our Almighty Heavenly Father and our Blessed Mother Mary. The contents of this book are in perfect alignment with our holy Bible. There are no incompatibilities. It centers around the magnificent apparitions of our Blessed Mother Mary and her messages to all of God's sacred children on earth. In very many ways Mother Mary is the link between the Heavenly realm and the physical realm on earth.

This book contains a selected number of Mother Mary's apparitions that apply very directly to the End of Times that the earth has entered into. Signs of the End of Times are all over the earth if anyone cares to pay attention. This book will explore the prophecies made by our Blessed Mother Mary and how at this time they are increasingly being fulfilled. There have been all too many charlatans in the media claiming they know what is going to happen. A very few holy people do but the vast majority just want to sell you something. The very first part of this sacred document we'll focus on Mother Mary's apparitions at Fatima Portugal.

It is her apparitions at Fatima, especially the third secret, that directly apply to the state of the world we are experiencing now. It is her apparitions from Fatima the Catholic Church tried to keep secret. This is because the truth of what Mother Mary had to say revealed awful Satanic things about the Catholic Church. Other apparitions we will discuss support Mother Mary's words in Fatima.

All sacred words of Blessed Mother Mary contained within this book will always be presented in bold and italicized print. My words as your faithful Anointed Messenger and author will always be in regular Times New Roman text.

On page 2, you have read the exact words of our Heavenly Almighty Father spoken to me as a message to all of His sacred children. This means you. Not only does this book bring the message from Almighty God, a message of love, of understanding, acceptance, and advanced theological understandings as revealed by our Blessed Mother Mary.

15

The contents of this sacred book will indeed shock many of you. Much of the content of the secrets of Fatima is very upsetting yet we have been living in the beginning of the End of Times since 1960. Lately Pope Francis claimed he "finally revealed the entire contents of the third secret of Fatima" <u>Pope Francis is a damned Satanic liar</u>. Included later within this book are the Pope's so called total revelation word for word. After that are the exact words of our Blessed Mother Mary who revealed the third secret to the three shepherd kids at Fatima. Sister Lucia is the child who wrote down Mother Mary's words. They DO NOT match with Pope Francis at all. More on that later.

Most Christians think of our Blessed Mother Mary as the Mother of God and who appears on occasion in apparitions with children emphasizing the need for prayer, sacrifice, penance and praying the rosary.

I am fortunate enough to be one of the people our Blessed Mother Mary wishes to talk to. In my case it is for writing the books that contain the messages of our holy Father in Heaven, our Lord and Savior Jesus Christ and of course our Blessed Mother Mary.

As our Father's Anointed Messenger, it is my holy mission to bring God's truth of all creation to you His sacred children. I will do this until as Jesus Christ told me, until I rejoin Him in the Heavenly Kingdom. The following text explains in some detail how I became our Heavenly Father s Anointed Messenger. The process of becoming the Anointed Messenger started before I was born to this earth.

Now, in everything I say and write, the question will always remain why I should believe this author and what he says Mother Mary told Him. The answer to that question is really quite simple. I ask you to pray directly to Our Heavenly Father our lord and savior Jesus Christ and the Holy Spirit which proceeds from them. Ask them if what you are reading is true and correct. I am God's Messenger not God's sales associate. All I can do is to tell you the truth about the Trinity and Mother Mary says. I am not here to try and convince you of anything. Our Heavenly Father gave you free will and a magnificent capacity for logic, reason, and faith. If you use the tools our Heavenly Father gifted each of us with, you will come to understand everything within this book and the others I have written are true.

I am our Father's Messenger, and I will not engage in Christian apologetics. From the sacred words I bring, you will either come to a higher level of understanding and faith, or you will reject it. I always remember what Saint Thomas Aquinas said many years ago:

If You Have Faith and You Believe, No Proof Is Necessary

If You Don't Have Faith and Disbelieve, No Proof Is Possible

If you have questions or are confused about something within this book, I strongly encourage you to pray to Almighty God about that. It is in this way you can never ever go wrong. Remember, as I described in the first book of this series titled, "God's Grand Design of All Creation for Your Redemption," our Heavenly Father loves each of us so very much. So much that when we were created in the blink of an eye billions of years ago in the Heavenly Kingdom, he left part of Himself within our personal spiritual being. It is in this way our Heavenly Father knows everything about us and will always hear every prayer we ever say. He has promised each of us he will always answer every one of our prayers and questions.

Becoming God's Anointed Messenger

I think it is necessary at this point to document for you who I really am. I cannot go into tremendous detail because this book is about our Blessed Mother Mary and not me. It is only fair I reveal to you not only who I am but also my background and my activities throughout the life I lead. This also includes some personal items and my educational background as well.

My Anointed Messenger History. Who Exactly Is Your Author of This Book?

I was born to earth as an only child. I was not wanted by either of my parents. To them I was just an irritating obstacle. My father was a violent man, and my mother never lifted a finger to stop Him from beating me for the slightest transgression as a small little boy. Years after leaving home, Jesus Christ told me my father was there to do everything he could to stop me from fulfilling my life's mission. The mission as was agreed to between me and our Almighty Father in Heaven. Satan wanted to destroy me through the cruelty of my own Father. Satan failed and my father is now in hell because of what he did to me and many other horrible things. Even if you have not had experiences like this do NOT make the mistake, they are not true. I went through public school then got accepted to Santa Clara University where I got my bachelor's degree in chemistry and physics with minors in philosophy and theology. I had a job pumping gas at a gas station in San Jose so I could pay for half my tuition. Later I got a job at IBM doing computer maintenance.

Upon graduation I had a choice to make. Since I had a commercial pilot's license I obtained on the side, I could have a wonderful career with the airlines. Or I could have a more settled life working for NASA as a research scientist at the Ames Research Center. I ended up working for NASA as a scientist exploring upper atmospheric particles that arrived at the earth from interstellar space. This gave me enough money to pay the tuition to get a master's degree in business. Loving flying as I do, I was a flight instructor on the side. Over the years I've owned three different airplanes along the way.

Over the years I found myself developing a small real estate investment company that allowed me to retire in my 50's.

During my late 40's I started to feel and ever-increasing yearning in my life to know God far better than I did. Every day I felt this increasing emptiness within me I knew only our Heavenly Father could fulfill. By then in my life a number of spiritual events have already occurred. This supported my growing need through fundamentally "come to God." At the time I worked in corporate computer marketing for Hewlett Packard corporation. I had a travel schedule worldwide. This conflicted with my class schedule. But the university was very accommodating, and this gave me the opportunity to work extremely hard to receive another master's degree in pastoral ministry and theology. My chosen minor was spirituality. Over the coming few years after graduation, I wrote six Christian spiritual books. You are reading book 9.

When I started to write book number seven, something miraculously occurred after I got through the text to page 20. <u>My world completely changed at that point</u> I had absolutely no idea of.

By then in my life, I already had numerous spiritual experiences. I did not know it at the time, but I was already on Satan's radar screen. This is because there are no secrets in the spiritual realm and my identity is known to everybody in the spiritual realm. This includes Satan. Satan also knew of my previous discussion with Our Heavenly Father before I was born to the earth. Because of Satanic influence it is my father who did everything he could when I was growing up to destroy me. He wanted to mold me into His own Satanic image. It did not work. A last note on him, my father is indeed in hell. I know this as he tried to come up from under the floor to me four times. And each time, I told him to go back to hell where he belongs in the name of our Lord and Savior Jesus Christ. Speaking of this, all Christians should know you have authority over Satan. Just tell them to go back to hell in the name of our Lord and savior Jesus Christ. And then say one Our Father and Hail Mary and thank our Father in Heaven for your power over Satan.

I later found out from Jesus I had a conversation with our loving Father in the Heavenly Kingdom about my coming life on earth. That discussion determined my life theme when I was born to the earth. My life theme is amazingly simple. I wanted to put every other one of God's sacred children ahead of me and I would serve them. I would serve others of God's sacred children by bringing advanced understandings of our Father's creations to them. However, Jesus Christ pointed out to me this is one of the most difficult life themes for sacred children coming to earth. Satan hated this. One point of education for you about the spiritual realm is there are no secrets whatsoever. Everybody knows everything about everybody else. Please ponder this.

Satan Attacks Me Viciously Three Times

This is something Satan hated terribly about me, and he would want to destroy anybody that has such a loving God centered theme in their earthly life. <u>The one most terrible experience I had was when Satan attacked me three times in the middle of the night</u>. This occurred on three separate occasions. There was a loud crash within the house as if a car crashed through my home and into the living room.

When Satan invaded our bedroom, and my two children sleeping in the next bedroom, I thought all hell broke loose with the most horrific crashing sound I imagine in the middle of the night. When I looked up toward the foot of the bed there stood Satan Himself. Remember Satan can be only one place at a

19

time. And there he was standing at the foot of our bed staring at me with his glowing red eyes.

There is no doubt it was Satan. To picture what he looked like, start with the Star Wars character Darth Vader. His voice had a certain deep quality to it with horrific anger and rage that just cannot be duplicated by any human being. He stood about seven feet tall. He outstretched His arms to almost 90° with His attached blackest of black cape that covered a lot of material. Standing at the foot of my bed he bent over, and his hooded eyes and head were staring right at me. By the way, His eyes are indeed a very bright terrifying red.

With that and his body bent over such I had to look up almost vertical to see his head and red eyes. Then he yelled at me these words, at the top of his ugly voice he yelled at me three times. He said, "**I will get you! I will get you! I will get you!" After yelling this at me with his booming loud voice when his head was no more than two feet from my nose, he leaned backward to straighten himself. He continued to stare at me for some more seconds. Then with the audible whoosh he departed my bedroom to the left. He went straight through the wall as if it did not exist. Silence and peace returned to our bedroom.**

Yes, I was completely frightened by this. But I did not pee my pajamas. Okay. That's a manly thing. However, in the succeeding weeks and months I learned about spiritual warfare. I learned Satan and his demons can be controlled by true Christian believers. It is not hard, and they must obey. Since then, I have been forced to conduct spiritual warfare every day.

The Beginning of My Christian Spiritual Warfare

Since then, Satan has harassed me every day of my life. While engaging in the sacred writing of the books Our Heavenly Father wants me to write for His Anointed children to read, Satan would be there throwing rotten thoughts into my brain. So as to distract me and conduct harassment. I was forced to conduct spiritual warfare.

I must tell you this dear sacred child of God, to battle Satan is not as hard as you think. Is it scary? Yes at least at the beginning. But after a while it gets to be routine. If you are on good terms with our loving Father, our Lord and savior Jesus Christ and the Holy Spirit which proceeds from them it is relatively easy. Every time when I am writing and Satan tries to interfere, I just simply stop what I am doing calmly then I say one Our Father and one Hail Mary. Then I command Satan to leave me, to depart me and go back to hell where he belongs in the name of our Lord and savior Jesus Christ and our Blessed Mother Mary. Satan must obey otherwise he will get chopped up into a fine powder by one of God's archangels. One time the Angel who appeared to do this asked me if I wanted to watch. I said yes.

At the beginning I saw Satan and then the Angel started to do his work with his sword. Shortly thereafter all I saw were tiny bits of Satan's body strewn all around the place. His body color is also a red maroon kind of tint to it. The Angel said it would take him a long time to reconstruct himself. Frankly, me being me, I wanted to set fire to that pile of body fragments and perhaps have a weenie roast. Nonetheless this gives you an idea of my life as I pursue with love, deep love and devotion to the Holy Trinity and our Blessed Mother Mary. Satan is not to be feared but do not get careless either. I would rather he be ordered to go back to hell where he belongs. For he must obey the commands given to him by a sacred child of God in the name of our Lord and savior Jesus Christ.

What I just told you also applies to non-Satan personages as well. My father was a very cruel person. And he would at times after he died, rise up from the floor and in a very harsh tone of voice say to me, "I want to talk to you." My response was simply, "go back to hell where you belong in the name of our loving savior Jesus Christ." He had to obey, and I could physically see him descend back down through the floor and then the episode was over. My father being in hell is exactly where he should be.

That being said, a summary of my life as told to me by our Lord and Savior Jesus Christ started when I was still in the Heavenly Kingdom before born to this earth. I had a conversation with our Heavenly Father. After I was born to the earth to two parents that did not want me, I made it through bachelor's degrees and then master's degrees in business. At NASA I enjoyed interacting with the U2 spy plane which carried particles filters up to 80,000 or 85,000 feet where they could collect upper atmospheric particulate matter to determine the constitution of interstellar particles. After that I had a normal career in corporate computer marketing at Hewlett-Packard corporation. I raised three children before my late wife died of cancer. However, now I am so happily married to a beautiful woman that one point in her life taught theology at the university of Santo Tomas in Manila Philippines.

This book is a must read for all Christians and all people who believe in Almighty God. It is perfectly consistent with our beloved Biblical literature. However, it explores advanced theology our Father wants all of His sacred children to understand. Additionally, it brings to everyone His message of love and acceptance. He wants ALL His sacred children just how much He loves them and wants to pursue them so they will say "yes, I want to go back into the Heavenly Kingdom from where I came."

This book is number 9. Number 8 is a book about creation in all its details. Both of these books are based on our existing Biblical literature and information articulated by our loving Lord and savior Jesus Christ and our Blessed Mother Mary. Everything I write is completely consistent with both the Old Testament and the New Testament. But they go far beyond the Biblical understandings and bring magnificent more detailed understandings of how all of God's creation works together which includes all of His sacred children living within His creations. More booklets are to come expanding everyone's deepest understandings of so many distinct aspects of Almighty God and His creations and how they all fit together for the benefit of you His sacred children.

The Unexpected Arrival of Jesus Christ and Blessed Mother Mary

When I was approximately 70 years old, I was meditating after I got up and then swung my feet over the side of the bed. I noticed something very strange occurring about forty feet away in front of me. There were two spiritual entities there just standing there and looking at me. It was easy to see one was a male with brown hair and white robes. The other person was definitely female with blue and white robes and a blue hood over the top of her head. She was shorter than the male. The first time I saw this having been experienced at seeing other spiritual beings, it was not that big a deal to me, but it got my attention. After a few seconds I went about my business for the day. The next day I woke up and I noticed these same two spiritual persons looking the same but being a little closer to me than the previous day before.

Well, that got my attention. Something was up but I had no idea what it was. But I had things to do, and I resumed my daily activities. Waking on the third day and swinging my feet over the right side of the bed these two spiritual persons were still even closer to me than the previous night and the one before that. They still remained silent but now I knew something was really up, but I did not know what. On the fourth day they were no more than five or six feet from me in front and to my right side. Strangely I was almost certain I knew who they were at this point, but I did not daresay anything, at least not yet. I was beginning to think these two spiritual people were Jesus Christ and our Blessed Mother Mary. Naw, that cannot be or so I thought.

Now the fifth morning arises. It was a morning like no other in my entire life. When I woke up laying down and staring at the ceiling, I did not see them. I wondered where they went. Soon I was to find out in a matter of seconds. In the act of swinging my legs over the side of the bed, my eyes caught the unmistakable image of our Lord and savior Jesus Christ and our Beloved Blessed Mother Mary. They were silently standing right next to my right shoulder. Perhaps 4 to 6 inches away from me. This shocked the heck out of me. I did not know what to do, I did not know what to say, I did not know anything to do in any way. I was completely stunned. There I was, my feet hanging over the side of the bed with two Biblical sentient spiritual beings standing right next to me on my right side.

I started to go into a state of shock. But I had enough presence of mind to ask the following question in a telepathic way I have used many times before speaking with spiritual beings: I asked, "**are you who I think you are?**" Jesus answered with these exact words, "***Yes, It Is I***." Instantly I thought it strange he did not say "it is me." Because that is the incorrect English everybody uses. Proper English is exactly what Jesus said." ***Yes, It is I***."

With that response from Jesus, everything and I mean absolutely everything within all of my senses turned completely white. All my surroundings in the bedroom completely disappeared. They were gone. I no longer felt I was sitting on the edge of my bed. There was no sensation at all. The ceiling was gone, the floors were gone, the bed I was sitting on was gone. The only things that existed were my consciousness, my identity, and an awareness of who I was with and where I thought I was but apparently not anymore. Instantly, the only awareness I had was I existed, and our Lord and savior Jesus Christ and Mother Mary were close by my right side. There was nothing else. There was absolutely no fear.

The next thing I heard was dear Lord Jesus telling me to put my feet back up on the bed and just rest and remain calm as much as I can. I did that but in the process of doing it I did not see my legs anymore. I don't remember feeling them either, nor did I see the rest of the bed or the rest of the bedroom for that matter.

It was just me, our loving Lord Jesus Christ, and our beloved Mother Mary. Nothing else!

After an unknown time resting on the bed. Jesus told me to just keep laying down and listen to what he wanted to tell me. He said Mother Mary and He are there to help me with the coming things our Heavenly Father wants me to do for the rest of His sacred children on earth. I do not remember His exact words but that is the central idea.

Jesus also told me both He and Mother Mary would stay with me by my side forever more. They will never leave me. I felt wonderful hearing that.

After this encounter, our Lord, and Savior Jesus Christ and Our Blessed Mother Mary were indeed at my right-hand side 100% of every waking moment of my life. I can see them in full living color. They are with me always, and they know absolutely everything about my existence, including what I was thinking, what I was feeling, what was happening to me and everything else directly associated with my existence. Today they remain indeed always with me by my side. There was never a moment in which I could not see them. But rather I can always see Jesus with our Blessed Mother Mary in her blue and white robes, and our Lord and savior Jesus Christ. To this day as I write this sentence, I can clearly see both of them standing no more than six inches from my right shoulder.

Frankly at first this whole thing was quite unnerving. But after a while I started asking Jesus a lot of questions about so many different theological topics. He is always ever so happy to answer anything I wanted to know. It is through this personal tutoring of our Lord Jesus I learned ever so much about creation and about all the details related to how creation works together through its individual facets of existence.

Hint: All aspects of our Heavenly Father's creation work together like all the parts of a fine Swiss watch. They mesh together perfectly for one reason and one reason only. All of creation exists for the sole purpose of God's sacred children making their way back to the Heavenly Kingdom from where they came.

Secondly, it is to provide His sacred children the opportunity to choose either our Father or Satan. We make this choice by how we conduct our lives.

It is through the private tutoring of our Lord and Savior Jesus Christ along with our Blessed Mother Mary that has given me the most magnificent information. Information about all of creation both in the spiritual realm and the physical realm that allowed me to write the master book **"God's Grand Design Of All Creation For Your Redemption."** I didn't rely on any resources like online or YouTube. Why would I ever do that when Jesus Christ is the one who did indeed create the entire physical realm that we call the universe?

Why Me Lord?

During the time that I was writing that book, this question came to me. After a while I began to wonder, "why me?" Why did our Heavenly Father choose me of all the others of God's sacred children within the universe to ask of all people to be the Anointed Messenger and write this ever so important book? The most important book that will become recognized as a sacred book in the eyes of the Christian community along with the Old Testament and the New Testament.

I asked Jesus that exact question. **WHY ME?** Jesus once told me sometime last year that our Heavenly Father chose me to be His Anointed Messenger because of something I said to Him. First dear sacred children of God, all of you were in the Heavenly Kingdom BEFORE you came to earth. All of us could talk with our Heavenly Father. Well, that really got my attention. What on earth could I possibly have said? And the other thought I had was, "oh good grief, me and my big mouth!" Sometimes I tend to do that.

Yep. That was my instantaneous thought when Jesus told me that. After I gathered myself a little bit, I asked our Lord what did I say? Jesus told me before my upcoming earthly life I told our Heavenly Father I wanted to put other people ahead of myself while I was in my upcoming life on earth. This would be my lifetime theme as all of us do have a life theme. Jesus then told me this is a particularly difficult life to live. Boy, was he right! Maybe I will write an article about that. At this point though I think I should terminate anymore thoughts about how I became our Heavenly Father's Anointed Messenger. I have already spent too much time away from our Blessed Mother Mary.

There is one thought I wish to leave you with. Regarding my lifetime on earth as a chosen one, I know our Heavenly Father is within me just as he is within every sacred child of His on earth. This means YOU! Yes, you, as everybody are a sacred child of Almighty God. All sacred children are made in the image of God. This is why Satan hates every one of us. If you were a rabbit, he would not care. In another book I will write I will describe in great detail the trials and tribulations in my life. All of them were caused by hateful Satan against me because he knew our Father chose me as His Anointed Messenger.

Regarding our Blessed Mother Mary, it was she and our Lord and Savior Jesus Christ that approached me some years ago now. They told me they would be with me forever by my side. My dearest sacred children of God, I cannot tell you how beautiful and magnificent it is to say Lord and Savior Jesus Christ and Blessed Mother Mary right beside me slightly behind my right shoulder. And yes, dear sacred children I can see them in living color.

This is why at certain points centering upon our Blessed Mother Mary, you'll read her saying things pointing to her instantaneous knowledge of how I am physically feeling. Also, how tired I can get and many times becoming exhausted. Even though our Mother Mary is now a pure spiritual being, she retains the ability to know and understand my feelings within my physical body.

Question: Dearest Mother Mary, during the time you and Jesus were approaching me for the first time would you comment please on what it is you were thinking about all of that? Jesus did do all the talking and I would really like to know what your thoughts were as a you and my savior approached me for the first time.

Answer: *Of course, my dearest son, I felt this certain amount of trepidation because we did not know exactly how you would react. We know your love for your Heavenly Father and Jesus, the Holy Spirit and me was very great. But we needed to be very gentle with you because the last thing we wanted was to in some way as you would say "scared the pants off you." You have had many spiritual experiences in your life already before we approached you and that was an exceptionally good thing. Because of your experiences that ranged from the elders on the cruise ship praying for your late wife Marilyn to Satan Himself trying to scare the living daylights out of you. There were so many other incidents that we felt this would be one more spiritual experience for you that would not damage you in any way. This is what we were very afraid of with any sacred child of God still living in their physical body.*

It was your love for God and for me that made me feel you are the only right person. With all your experiences academically with your degrees in chemistry and physics and being a pilot which demands certain amount of perfection and discipline. And the way that you brought up your children within the Catholic faith and their education and that you are the leader of your family bringing them up in the right way. Along with then you are getting your master's degree in ministry and theology we knew that you had all the necessary qualifications to do what it is your Heavenly Father has asked you to.

I felt strongly that you would say yes to your Heavenly Father. So too did Jesus my son. I will never forget before Satan attacked you those three times when you were yelling at Him for making a mess on earth that you repeated those terrible swearwords aimed at Him. It showed us that you were just not afraid, and you were a fighter. When our Heavenly Father joined you on the airplane when you were halfway across the Pacific Ocean. And He told you that he was happy you were a fighter right after Satan attacked you in your airline seat, you just reconfirmed everything we thought that you would become. And you have become everything we wished for plus a lot more.

It is particularly good that you asked me this question. Because all these sacred children of your Heavenly Father when they read this will understand just how close all of us are together. Which includes everyone of God's sacred children also as you have demonstrated throughout this book many times. I love the fact that you speak your mind in truly clear forceful terms. And in addition to you being a fighter you also have all the protections of the Heavenly realm right by your side.

My dearest of sons, I love you so very much. And, in a way, I hope that we can just keep writing and writing and writing this book, but I know it must come to an end sometime soon. But I will always be with you right by your side along with my son for that is timeless and will never end.

I love you dear son.
Your Mother Mary

Point of Learning

Each of us are really two parts. The physical part and the spiritual part. The physical part is what dies after 70 or 80 years. The spiritual part is eternal. The reason our Blessed Mother Mary could keep track of how I'm feeling during the writing of this book is because my spiritual part is connected to my physical body. And that is how our spiritual Blessed Mother Mary knows how I am feeling, what I am thinking and how tired I get at times. We both have a deep spiritual connection with each other. My dear sacred children of God, I cannot begin to tell you how wonderful that is.

For me, the same connection is also true with our Lord and Savior Jesus Christ. Needless to say, this also includes our Almighty Loving Father. Both Jesus and I along with our Heavenly Father do speak with each other as we wish. If you want to learn more about these sacred connections, my first booklet titled "God's Grand Design, Booklet 1, Creation".

If anybody tells you you're nothing more than a pile of chemicals that started out in some stupid swamp somewhere has Satan embedded in their brain and they should know better. It is these kinds of people who have rejected the Holy

Trinity, (God), and believed Satanic garbage. Garbage that is always available for those sacred children of God that prefer to believe in only what their eyes tell them. That is the express lane to Hell.

4

All About Our Blessed Mother Mary

I know very well most of you will reject what I have just written. This rejection has been proven over many years considering how the message from our Lord and Savior Jesus Christ was received 2,000 years ago. Surprisingly to me the same thing happened to our Blessed Mother Mary over hundreds of years with her loving apparitions. She told me she appeared 375 times, but we know of only a few. She laments about this. People were either scared, disbelieving, or unwilling to tell other people what Mother Mary told them. Let us take her apparition at Fatima. That became a Vatican political football where the Church officials became horrifically political and now Pope Francis just last month as this is written TOLD FALSEHOODS about the third secret. He bold face TOLD a FALSEHOOD that the third sacred has been fulfilled and Russia has been consecrated to the Immaculate Heart of Blessed Mother Mary. NO! Francis is a liar! He made it look like that, but he did not say the proper words as shown in another part of this book.

Another roadblock was the Catholic Church itself. The general attitude of the Church was deep skepticism, disbelief, and outright hiding things from our Father's sacred children. This last action by the Church is what they did to the third secret of Fatima as told by our Blessed Mother Mary. They did so because the third secret was extremely powerful and made the Catholic Church look really bad. As you will see herein, you will read all the contents of the third secret and judge the Church for yourselves.

Without a lot of detail, our Heavenly Father through Jesus Christ and Blessed Mother Mary asked me to write a book. A book that delivers our Father's message of love, peace, understanding and acceptance to His sacred children on earth. Additionally, Father provided advanced theological information that addresses advanced existential understandings of how all His creation is designed, how it works and where we as Father's sacred children fit into things. Everything in these advanced theological understandings is completely consistent with our Blessed Holy Bible. The title is: <u>God's Grand Design of All Creation for Your Redemption.</u> It begins by answering the question of what exactly you are. The answer is magnificently beautiful.

Remember, each and every one of you is a sacred child of Almighty God. You are a spiritual being living on earth for specific reasons that I will not go into now. I have written a booklet titled, "<u>God's Grand Design Booklet I Creation</u>." It is here I have written everything your Heavenly Father wants you to know about your existence. Everything written there is completely consistent with our Christian Biblical literature.

We will start with La Salette, then continue with Garabandal, Lourdes, Zeitoun and finally to Fatima. But first I feel it is very revealing and appropriate I describe what our Blessed Mother Mary's voice sounds like. In a nutshell it is beautiful.

How Does Blessed Mother Mary Speak with Me?

The manner in which Mother Mary's thoughts wind up in a sacred book like this is actually pretty simple. Given that our Heavenly Father appointed me as His Anointed Messenger, which brings with it the ability to speak with the Holy Trinity and our Blessed Mother Mary. Yes, that last sentence is absolutely true but also exceedingly rare.

At the direct request of our holy Almighty Father, I wrote a book that contained what our Father wants all of His sacred children to know. The title is, "<u>God's Grand Design of All Creation for Your Redemption</u>." Now I am writing this book about the End of Times with the help of our Blessed Mother Mary. Blessed Mother Mary has a lot of amazing information for all of God's sacred children.

The Sacred Process

When it is appropriate, I will cloister myself in an incredibly quiet room within my home. I must create the physical conditions necessary so my prayer for all attention centers on our beloved and Blessed Mother Mary. I have to pray the Our Father and Hail Mary. Additionally, I will pray as much of the rosary as is necessary to completely eliminate any distracting earthly thoughts that may have been bothering me. There are times when I have to conduct spiritual warfare against Satan. He hates me more than you can imagine.

Nonetheless, I am protected. And when I am peaceful within my thoughts and my attention drifts to our Blessed Mother Mary, I am then ready to ask her the questions. And I invite her to tell me anything she wants all of God's sacred children to know about.

This is such a beautiful and sacred thing to do, preparing to speak with actually not only our Blessed Mother Mary but also our Lord and savior Jesus Christ. Additionally on more rare occasions I will want to ask our loving Heavenly Father a question or two. But what usually happens is I will be engaging in some activity and our Heavenly Father starts talking to me at His will not mine. I remember one time I was away from my computer and our Heavenly Father started to speak with me. I was forced to respond by saying, Father, please wait a moment until I can get my speech to text software up and running. This way I could make sure everything you say will be preserved for all your sacred children.

While I was preparing the computer and turning on the software, I thought to myself, "good Lord, Richard, do you realize what you just did? You actually ask the creator of all that is seen and unseen to wait a minute for you? How awful can you get? But our loving Father waited for the minute or two and then I said, "dear Father I'm ready please tell me anything you wish." And within a fleeting moment that's exactly what He did. I will never forget that moment as long as I live and actually for all the eternity when I am back in the Kingdom.

The Reason Mother Mary Speaks to Me

The reason is so important that I tell you how all this came about. That my position with the Trinity and Blessed Mother Mary is because everything, I mean everything, that has been published with regards to our Blessed Mother Mary's apparitions is always second hand and thirdhand. And loaded with opinions that many times are completely misguided and based upon only partial information. This does a terrible service to God's sacred children which is YOU!

Additionally, the Catholic Church at all levels is preventing God's sacred children from hearing firsthand and accurately the contents of the messages our Blessed Mother Mary has bestowed upon us at her various apparitions. This is especially true with Fatima. I will complain about this more later in the book.

What you hold in your hand has NO INTERFERENCES from the Catholic Church or any other people who wish to manipulate the words of our Blessed Mother Mary. One case in point. Mother Mary asked the third secret of Fatima be delivered to all of God's sacred children in the year of 1960. That never happened. <u>Why? It is because the third secret does indeed reveal terrible things that will happen to the earth unless mankind repents. But importantly the third secret reveals the vast corruption, apostasy, blasphemy, sexual perversion, and even Satanic worship within the Vatican. Yes, you read that correctly!</u>

I have included other apparitions within this sacred document because of two reasons:

1. Mother Mary asked me to.
2. The content of these separations all fit together to produce a picture of the future of God's sacred children on earth. That future is referred to as "The End of Times."

This will all be discussed openly and plainly within this book. Jesus Christ Himself said, "I am the way the truth and the life and no one goes to the Father except by me." Well, the Church has been fighting the release of the truth Blessed Mother Mary has been trying to deliver to God's sacred children for many hundreds of years. The Church has gone so far astray for example as to create a fake Lucia of Fatima so as to drastically water down the true message of Fatima. At least this is what significant evidence shows along with experts that have scientifically proven the lady posing as Lucia today is not the real historical Lucia.

This book contains the authentic words of our Blessed Mother Mary as she wants everyone of God's sacred children to hear firsthand. Many priests, nuns, bishops, and Cardinals have all been sworn to secrecy. So, they have been muffled by the Vatican and other Church powers to prevent you from hearing about what you should know. I HAVE NOT TAKEN ANY OATH OF ANY KIND! So, this book will deliver all of Blessed Mother Mary's messages through her apparitions to God's sacred children, YOU! Fundamentally this means the words of our Blessed Mother Mary are going directly from her to you through the printed words in this book.

She will do this directly. How? It is because your Heavenly Father has asked me to be His Anointed Messenger. As His Anointed Messenger I have been gifted to be able to talk with Blessed Mother Mary directly. Yes! I have been magnificently gifted by our loving Father in Heaven to be able to talk directly with our Blessed Mother Mary and our Lord and savior Jesus Christ. Additionally, our Heavenly Father speaks to me very clearly about assorted items that come up regarding the publication of the books he wants to be written and published for your benefit.

Previous to this book, I have written a small book titled, "<u>God's Grand Design, Booklet I Creation.</u>" I suggest you get a copy. Our Father wants you to know what is contained there. Regarding this book, there is no intermediary. Whatever Blessed Mother Mary tells me directly, I transcribe it directly to my computer where a text file is generated. This text file contains the exact words of whatever Blessed Mother Mary tells me.

<u>There are no filters, no priests, bishops, Cardinals or any other Church related people that will get in the way and pervert and modify and twist the truth of what Blessed Mother Mary has said.</u> She wants everybody to know about the coming times and especially the End of Times which are upon us right now. Since approximately 1960 the world has entered the End of Times. More on that later in this book.

So, what you are about to read is the unfiltered, untwisted, unedited and unmodified words of our Blessed Mother Mary. It is the messages she has been trying to get out to all of God's sacred children. Therefore, you must realize this book is sacred from the first page to the last period on the last page. It is sacred truth as said directly by our Blessed Mother Mary, the Mother of God, the Mother of our Lord and savior Jesus Christ.

The Beautiful Voice of Mother Mary

I have never seen a description of what Blessed Mother Mary's voice sounds like throughout all my research from many diverse sources that claim to have heard what she says in her apparitions. I don't know why this is because her voice is remarkably distinctive and divine. I have had the beautiful experience of hearing her melodious language many times during the course of writing this book. If you were to imagine a loving human based Heavenly Angelic female voice in your mind, you would be describing Blessed Mother Mary. A voice full of love and gentleness for each and every one of God's sacred children.

I can describe her voice as ever so feminine and gentle speaking slowly and softly while caressing a sincere love that projects a magnificent divine quality to what she says. Her voice with its softness and its ever so caring tone of love really does gently sooth my mind and it makes me feel so wonderfully loved.

Her divine love for me feels like it is contained in every word she says. When she speaks of warnings to all of God's sacred children like the third secret of Fatima, there is a tone of urgency and deep concern in her voice. One beautiful characteristic of how Blessed Mother speaks is when she wants to emphasize a word, she's stretches out the word more than the others. For example, if she wants to say, "that is a real problem," it will sound like she is stretching out that phrase a little longer than normal. Poetically speaking her voice is like a soft breeze rustling through the trees with a love that defies description. Her loving and lilting voice is like a divine touch to my soul. Oh, how I wish each of you could hear with your own ears our Blessed Mother Mary. But, one day you will after you enter the paradise, we call the Heavenly Kingdom.

She is never at a loss for words and when she explains something she also includes related thoughts that amplify what she means. She knows me ever so well. There have been times, actually many times, when I suffer from my chronic migraine headaches and am in a lot of pain when I want to speak with her. She knows how I feel and many times she suggests we delay our conversation and I need to have rest for a time. I take my strong pain medicine and after a while I feel better, and Mother Mary knows that and then we continue what we intended to begin with.

There have been times also when I have been very tired many times from headache pain and even though the pain is gone, I'm just exhausted and even Mother Mary knows this too. And even then, she suggests I rest. She has told me to rest so many times because our Lord and Savior Jesus Christ told her I work too hard especially when I was sick for two months early in the year 2024.

Mother Mary, The Link Between Earth and Heaven

Most people believe Mother Mary is the Mother of Jesus Christ and was raised up to Heaven by God. Some people know she has had apparitions that are miraculous. Beyond that people do not know much. The fact is Mother Mary is extremely active in her sacred attempts to bring redemption to all of God sacred children. You will be amazed at everything she has done and is currently doing to bring about a heavenly future for as many of God's sacred children on earth as she possibly can.

I bring you the below information because its message is twofold and enormously powerful. Most Christians think of our Blessed Mother Mary as the Mother of God and who appears on occasion in apparitions with children emphasizing the need for prayer, sacrifice, penance and praying the rosary. Our Mother Mary plays an active role in helping those of goodwill to avoid catastrophes on earth.

Her importance goes far deeper than just that if that isn't enough. Our Blessed Mother Mary also maintains holy friendships and communications with people who were still on earth. The below story about Pope John II talking with her and abiding by what she asks Him to do. This is so powerful and goes way beyond apparitions. Remember please, it is our Blessed Mother Mary that will put an end to Satan by virtue of her magnificent love and her Immaculate Heart! It is our Blessed Mother Mary's Immaculate Heart that will crush the head of Satan. How? It is by her Immaculate intense love.

I am fortunate enough to be one of the people our Blessed Mother Mary wishes to talk to. In my case it is for writing the books that contain the messages of our holy Father in Heaven, our Lord and Savior Jesus Christ and of course our Blessed Mother Mary. This book is completely dedicated to our Blessed Mother Mary.

March 14, 2024
Spoken by our Almighty Father's Anointed Messenger

My dear sacred child of God, this book you hold in your hands is a <u>Sacred Document</u>. It is so because it contains the direct words of our Blessed Mother Mary. All sacred words contained within will always be presented in bold and italicized print. My words as author and <u>Anointed Messenger</u> of our Heavenly Father will always be in regular Times New Roman text. Why is it this way? It is because Blessed Mother Mary is far more important than me, God's Anointed Messenger.

Here is the first of many things Mother Mary will say within this Book.

April 17, 2024
Our Beloved Blessed Mother Mary:

My dearest son Richard, you have worked so extremely hard to bring the truth of our Holy Father to His sacred children on earth. You are so very correct that our Father's sacred children have now entered into <u>***The End of Times***</u>***. As you have observed, dearest son. That falling away from the love and the rules of life that our Father has put forth for the benefit and the happiness of His children on earth has been under increasing attack by Satan. As you have said, you have observed the crumbling away of God's manner of living on earth so as to return to Him in the Heavenly Kingdom for all eternity.***

Especially, dear son, your book titled <u>***God's Grand Design of All Creation for Your Redemption***</u>***, is a magnificent piece of Biblical literature that you have written in common everyday language so everybody can understand. It is slowly gaining in popularity and will continue as such. I am honored dear son, dear Anointed Messenger of our Father, to be with you writing about my apparitions throughout the many years until now.***

One thing I want your readers to know is that in your research you have found that there have been about thirty-four apparitions of me, mostly to little children. I have chosen little children because they have not been in the world long enough to become jaded, and their minds are still fresh, close to their Heavenly Father and honest. But in some cases, as you have found

out like La Salette in France, the children became afraid due to the elders that surrounded them. Maximin could not stand the pressure and revoked saying that he told a falsehood. He did not. Both you and I know this.

Another thing that people do not realize is that I have appeared to many others since my son was on the earth. In actual fact, my dear son, I have appeared many times more than the 34 apparitions that have been published to be read by God's sacred children in the Church. Most of the time the children that I appeared to after a time became exceedingly frightened and did not tell anyone of what occurred. My message to everyone is always ever so simple. It is basically love, peace, penance, sacrifice and to always say the Holy Rosary.

People continue to not understand the Almighty power of what I have just mentioned. Why is this so? It is because doing these things strengthens enormously people's love and connection directly to the Trinity and me. This strong connection destroys Satan's ability to cause agony, pain, suffering in the world. Basically, the closer you are to your Heavenly Father, the farther away Satan becomes. Satan's violence and destructive temptations do not stand a chance against prayer, sacrifice, penance, and the Holy Rosary.

This is why in doing these things great spiritual power comes to all those who listen to what I have to say. With this spiritual power across many people in the world, ever so many wars in the world would be avoided.

However, the time of Satan is at hand. To you my dearest Anointed Messenger of our Holy Father, what you have said is that the world has now entered into the preliminary stages of the End of Times. You have also stated that you know Satan is working within the Vatican and yes, my dear son, Pope France is under the control of Satan and is the last pope. Frightening as this may be, things will get worse before they get better. In another part of this book you are writing, I will expand upon my prophecies all of which will come true before my son returns to earth.

A horrific number of lives and souls will be lost in the coming years. Dear son, I suggest you at this time document all the wars in the world right now. It is heartbreaking yet I knew all of this would happen and so now you too.

Let us, you, and I, now proceed with far more details in this magnificent Book and I want you to center upon my apparitions that talk about the End of Times.

I love you ever so much my dearest son. You are protected and always in my prayers.

Your Blessed Mother Mary

Question dear Mother Mary: If you don't mind being quantitative? Could you put a numerical figure on just how many times you appeared to different children in separate places on earth to deliver your messages and your warnings?

ANSWER: *Oh, of course, dear son, I will. You may be surprised but remember I also appeared without saying anything to anybody. It is my image of love and peace that appears to people to remind them of not only me but my messages of love, peace, sacrifice, prayer, the mass, and the powerful Rosary. These are too numerous to mention because ever so many thousands of people see my image but then my effect on their prayer life slowly fades away.*

But regarding the times in which I have spoken to selected ones of God's sacred children and have not been reported. The number you are looking for is 375 times that I have spoken to the sacred children of God. My appearance almost always produces fear among the children. Many times, they do not report what they saw because of their fear of getting into trouble with the elders. Other times elders ignore what they say thinking they are just making up fanciful stories. Even when the children describe my appearances. To the parents and local elders all along with in the contents of what I have said, the event gets tangled up and confused by people in the Church.

Many times, even the local priests and bishops accused the children of lying and this is what happened at La Salette. They reported what they saw and what was said. One of the children disappeared from the scene and the other, Maximin simply denied our encounter and said he told a falsehood. However, there are particularly important and shining examples of when things mostly go right and the legitimate appearance of mine reaches the higher authorities in the Church. But even then, due to the honest content like in Fatima, the Church hierarchy decides to hide my words of prophecy because they think it makes the Church look bad. Lastly, Garabandal, Akita and Medjugorje are good examples of things going properly and I would like you to emphasize these in this magnificent book you are writing.

People, God's sacred children must know what is coming and that things have already started that are part of the End of Times. This is not the end of the world; it is the End of Times which will be horrifically painful in so many ways that I will tell you later in this terrific book.

Mother Mary's Loving Thoughts to Me Your Author

Today on Sunday, February 18, 2024, when I woke, Mother Mary was immediately on my mind. Even though I was praying the Our Father as I always do first thing in the morning as my feet hit the floor but still sitting on the edge of the bed. It was intuitively obvious to me our Blessed Mother wanted to tell me important things that are on her mind and I can do my research later. Our Blessed Mother wanted me to do today exactly what I am now doing, which is to document what she wants to tell all of God's sacred children. This will be published in the second book with the title," <u>God's Grand Design, Blessed Mother Mary Speaks Her Apparitions and The End of Times</u>."

I perceive a strong sense of urgency in creating this book. And so it will be that I will devote 100% of my efforts in fulfilling anything and everything our Blessed Mother wants me to say and to do.

As a reminder, our Blessed Mother's words will be transcribed directly from what she tells me from the spiritual realm. And I will repeat word for word what she says to me in the computer software I have that is speech to text. In this manner 100% of everything you read within this booklet are Mother Mary's direct words.

5

The Five Apparitions of Blessed Mother Mary

For the purpose of this book written when the world has already entered the End of Times, Mother Mary decided there will be a total of five of her apparitions there will be documented here. Remember, Mother Mary has appeared 375 times to various people on earth. But for quite a number of reasons what she had to say was never distributed to all of God's sacred children as was intended. Mostly those she appeared to become very afraid and were scared to tell anyone.

These five apparitions are not in chronological sequence. The reason for this is because.

The five apparitions contained here are as follows:

1. La Salette 1846: Mother Mary discusses her sufferings in order to hold back chastisements due to our Father's sacred children's grave sins and lack of prayers. She talks about the increasing chaos and confusion leading up to World War 1 and World War 2, very prophetic and very accurate!

2. Lourdes 1858: Mother Mary wants God's children to know they can turn to their heavenly Father for healing in preparation for the coming chaos. As well as world wars that will start in the next 50 years and will decimate France along with many other countries.

3. Garabandal 1961: Many apparitions to four children that invoked sacred transes to these children while Mother Mary was present. Known for the miracle of the host. Like all apparitions Mary's message is of hope, conversion, love, prayer, penance, and sacrifice with great emphasis on the rosary. This is the formula to end all wars. The rosary is the most powerful sacred force on earth.

4. Zeitoun 1968: This celebrates the place where the Holy Family fled to from Jerusalem due to the persecution of Herod killing all babies under age 2. Also, she wanted to demonstrate the Holy Trinity is for everyone because Zeitoun is in Islam Egypt. This is the only apparition where Mother Mary did not speak.

5. Fatima 1, 2, 3. 1917: I saved this for the last because the three secrets of Fatima especially the third with our modern-day times and the fact we now have already entered into the End of Times. This also includes the anti-Christian Satanic actions of the Vatican and especially Pope Francis. This is discussed with proof and great detail. Horrific to say but true. The last thing the Vatican wants is for our Heavenly Father's sacred children to have the full truth of the third secret of Fatima. That is discussed in great detail here directly from Mother Mary herself.

Mother Mary Speaks to Me About All Her Apparitions

Question: Are the apparitions on this list the only ones you appeared in or are there more? Knowing how things go, I strongly suspect there are a lot more.

Answer: *Yes, my dear son there are many many more. Oh, how I wish that all the others would be made public as well. There are many reasons for the existence of unpublished apparitions. People to whom I have spoken to get very afraid to share their experiences not only with their friends and family but especially with the Church hierarchy. They fear they will put the spotlight on them and be accused of being many negative things all of which are not true. I thank you my dear son for having the courage to publish my words of love and concern for my children on earth.*

The other reason for apparitions not reaching the general public is the Church itself. It categorizes my appearances in such a way that most of them are automatically eliminated because priests, bishops and cardinals are very skeptical and tend to not believe what my children tell them. The other reason is what has happened with what I said to the three Shepherd children in Fatima. A lot of what I said makes the Church look bad in its own eyes. They have gone to great lengths to keep the important parts of the third secret away from God's sacred children.

My dear son, what you uncovered in your investigation is true. The Church became very dishonest and substituted the real sister Lucia with an imposter. The scientific investigations that you uncovered proved that in no way could the imposter woman in the pictures be the real sister Lucia. They went to such great lengths to keep the truth of my apparitions away from the faithful. They will pay a heavy price for that when their time comes. When we get to the section of the third secret of Fatima, I will tell you everything knowing that you will indeed have this published. Once and for all to the entire world which was my intent to begin with to have it released to the world in 1960. Because of your wonderful efforts my dear son the delay in releasing my prophecies will be only 64 years and not so very much longer.

As far as the number of prophecies and apparitions that I have appeared in that are not released to my children in numbers in many hundreds. I am incredibly sad to tell you this, but this is very real. And I cry for my children because they have been kept away from the sacred truths that they must know to help turn around the terrible path people on earth continue to be on. My warnings have been largely avoided for all the above reasons.

Remember always that the most powerful forces on earth are prayer, penance, sacrifice, and the rosary. In 1962 we came close to consecrating Russia to my Immaculate Heart to prevent so much ugly wars that have happened since then. It is said that such few people in high places can cause so many deaths among God's children.

Question: Which of these apparitions do you feel are the most important based on where we are now in human History?

Answer: *Thank you for asking me this my dear son. I think you already have a very good idea of what I'm going to say. In order they would be Garabandal, Our Lady of Success, our Lady of La Salette, our Lady of Lourdes, our Lady of Fatima and lastly our Lady of Akita. It is this last apparition on October 17, 1917, that is by far the most important and upsetting to people who have read it. It was necessary that my prophecy in the third secret be released to the laity within the Church immediately after my appearance. But Pope John XXIII read it and said,*

"It was not for that time."

He was wrong. It was very ready and in accordance with my will and the will of your Father and your Savior Lord Jesus Christ.

Thank you so very much my dear Blessed Mother Mary. It is these apparitions I will now cover in depth according to my research. And most importantly your comments to confirm or correct what has been already written about these apparitions on what has been already published for each one.

Dear Mother Mary, His or any other comments you would like to make at this time, or would you prefer to wait until I address each of the five apparitions to discuss them then?

My dear son, yes that is wait because there are a number of things, I want to add each one of my apparitions separately.

Apparition of the Blessed Mother Mary At La Salette, September 19, 1846. [2] [3]

Author's Note: I bring you this apparition from our Blessed Mother Mary at La Salette because up three things:

1. Our Blessed Mother Mary asked me to

2. It contains more information beyond what I have already provided regarding the actions of our Heavenly Father in answer to all of the wretched sin that is increasing day by day on earth.

3. This also is theologically linked to Fatima. This contains many harsh warnings and prophies of catastrophes, suffering and wars that could

---

[2] Shepherdess of La Salette with Imprimatur with Mgr. Biship of Lecce, https://www.Catholic-saints.net/prophecies/la-salette.php La Salette Apparitions and Prophecies of Our Lady (Catholic-saints.net)

[3] Note: There are many other La Salette sites that vary in their completeness and quality. Seek them if you wish.

have been avoided by prayer, penance, sacrifice. But people turned away from our Almighty Father

Like many other times our Blessed Mother Mary spoke with many different people on earth, so too did she speak with me, our Heavenly Father's Anointed Messenger. This is to bring to you not only the truths of what's been published regarding her apparitions, but also her direct comments to me. So, I could transcribe them and include what she said in this year 2024 regarding each separate apparition. It is through me your resolute author and Anointed Messenger that Blessed Mother Mary is speaking to you directly.

This is a direct account of Blessed Mother's apparition where she spoke with both Melanie and Maximin a number of times. Melanie wrote it down in 1878. It was published at Lecce in November 1879 and reprinted a few times. This small book is now exceedingly rare but the following text excerpts is followed exactly. The account of Blessed Mother's apparition in this case is approved by the Catholic Church. Not all apparitions are but this one is, in fact, most apparitions are never approved by the Church. Lastly, remember this testimony is translated from French. Expressions and vocabulary are different than what you would expect if written in English and not translated.

Our Heavenly Fathers Love for Us and Chastisements

Dear reader, please indulge me for a moment. I have to clarify a point that comes up every time we discuss the apparitions of Blessed Mother Mary. As well as all her prophecies that involve what is apparent punishments that come from our loving Heavenly Father.

It is an apparent contradiction of love versus punishment due to the following two thoughts:

1. Our Father in Heaven is perfect and pure love far beyond our understanding as His sacred children. Being pure love, all of His actions are always for the benefit of the spiritual health and redemption of His sacred children on earth.

2. Many times, people talk about such things as "the wrath of God," "the anger of God" and other phrases such as these.

So, the question is simply how our Heavenly Father can be pure sacred love, get so angry at His sacred children he will punish them directly causing tremendous pain, agony, and death. Those two thoughts just do not fit together in our human way of thinking. So, what is the truth of things that come up in many of Blessed Mother Mary's apparitions and her prophecies? Our Blessed Mother Mary answers this along with our Lord and Savior Jesus Christ.

Note: Yes, as the Anointed Messenger of our Almighty Father in Heaven I have remarkably been gifted with an enormous and loving ability to speak with the Holy Trinity and Blessed Mother Mary. I always use this Godly gift to reach out to all of God's Sacred Children on Earth for their Spiritual well-being and redemption. The following was given to me on the date shown to answer the question above.

March 19, 2024
Jesus Christ

Question: Dear Lord Jesus, and Dear Blessed Mother Mary, how are these two apparent contradictions resolved? I think I know the answer, but all sacred children need to understand this point.

Answer: *"Boy, my dear son you are indeed a perceptive one and I love this question because it goes to the very heart of our sacred children and their existence. The answer is what you already suspect, our Father in heaven never gets angry in the sense that is understood by humanity on earth.*

Rather, as you already know my son, your Father simply withdraws His love from His children based on the situation. So as to let the rampant sinful ugliness which is systemic to earth so to speak and let Satan do his monstrous evil things. It is this that constitutes the lessons that your Father wants all His sacred children to learn.

<u>*Your Heavenly Father's love is what keeps everything on earth from falling apart.*</u> *This also directly involves me, your Savior and our Holy Spirit. Due to Satan being the prince of the earth and all his demons, they are simply released to do what damage they can.*

But also, beyond that, all the natural forces of the earth are normally held back by us well. If necessary, as in the coming "End of Times" we will simply let loose these normal forces. Things like earthquakes, hurricanes, droughts and floods, volcanoes both under the sea and on land, all can be released because it is us the Trinity that does keep things as you would say glued together.

As in another prophecy of my Blessed Mother, she talks about fire from the sky and many other natural disasters. There are many asteroids beyond the planet you call Mars. They are kept in check by us the Trinity. There will come a time when we will stop doing that and many asteroids will make their way to earth and the destruction will be horrific. To get an idea of what can happen to earth just look at your moon and see all the craters brought about by asteroids. Yes, the earth was designed to heal from much of that, but this is to give you an idea of what happens if we remove our sacred protection for the planet, you call earth.

So, my dear son, <u>your Heavenly Father never gets angry. We simply remove our ongoing protection and let the natural process of things and Satanic influence take its course.</u> Lastly, your Blessed Mother Mary does use the language of anger. This is because this kind of vocabulary is necessary to convey in a simple and clear way how to think about God withdrawing our support for those who need to be taught a lesson. Thank you, my dear son, for asking this is a most intelligent and perceptive question."

With all this in mind, let us now proceed with the wonderful apparitions of our Blessed Mother Mary.

Blessed Mother Mary's Apparition At La Salette

On Saturday, September 19, 1846, in the afternoon, Mother Mary appeared to two shepherd children Melanie and Maximin. From this encounter Melanie writes the following:

"Maximin, do you see what is over there? Oh! My God!" At the same moment, I dropped the stick I was holding. Something inconceivably fantastic passed through me in that moment and I felt myself being drawn. I felt a profound respect, full of love, and my heartbeat faster.

I kept my eyes firmly fixed on this light, which was static. And as if it opened up, I caught sight of another, much more brilliant light which was moving. And in this light, I saw a most beautiful lady sitting on top of our Paradise, with her head in her hands. This beautiful Lady stood up; she coolly crossed her arms while watching us. Maximin Giraud and Mélanie Calvat, reported our Blessed Mother Mary's apparition to have occurred at La Salette-Fallavaux, France, in 1846. She said to us.

"Come, my children, fear not, I am here to PROCLAIM GREAT NEWS TO YOU."

When I was up close to the Beautiful Lady, in front of her to her right, she began to speak and from her beautiful eyes tears also started to flow.

"If my people do not wish to submit themselves, I am forced to let go of the hand of my Son. It is so heavy and weighs me down so much I can no longer keep hold of it.

"I have suffered all of the time for the rest of you! If I do not wish my Son to abandon you, I must take it upon myself to pray for this continually. And the rest of you think little of this. In vain you will pray, in vain you will act, and you will never be able to make up for the trouble I have taken over for the rest of you.

Note: Understand the beautiful love of our Blessed Mother Mary propels her to pray for us in substitution for the prayers we ourselves should be making.

"Melanie, what I am about to tell you now will not always be a secret. You may have made it public in 1858.

"The priests, ministers of my Son, the priests, by their wicked lives, by their irreverence and their impiety in the celebration of the Holy mysteries. By their love of money, their love of honors and pleasures, and the priests have become cesspools of impurity. Yes, the priests are asking vengeance, and vengeance is hanging over their heads. Woe to the priests and to those dedicated to God who by their unfaithfulness and their wicked lives are crucifying my Son again! The sins of those dedicated to God cry out towards Heaven and call for vengeance, and now vengeance is at their door. For

there is no one left to beg mercy and forgiveness for the people. There are no more generous souls; there is no one left worthy of offering a stainless sacrifice to the Eternal for the sake of the world.

"God will strike in an unprecedented way.

"Woe to the inhabitants of the earth! God will exhaust His wrath upon them, and no one will be able to escape so many afflictions together.

"The chiefs, the leaders of the people of God have neglected prayer and penance, and the devil has bedimmed their intelligence. They have become wandering stars which the old devil will drag along with His tail to make them perish. God will allow the old serpent to cause divisions among those who reign in every society and in every family. Physical and moral agonies will be suffered. God will abandon mankind to itself and will send punishments which will follow one after the other for more than thirty-five years.

Question: Has this happened already? In What Form? If not, when?

Answer: *Thank you for asking my son, I was referring to the early 1900s that was coming quickly upon them. France was already in turmoil and so chaos and confusion was happening increasingly in preparation for World War I and then World War II. Both of which were fought in France in one way or another. It became a terrible time of suffering in all different ways. Napoleon ran over all the land in His attempt to dominate everybody and everything and it got worse over time.*

"The priests, ministers of my Son, the priests, by their wicked lives, by their irreverence and their impiety in the celebration of the holy mysteries. By their love of money, their love of honors and pleasures, and the priests have become cesspools of impurity. Yes, the priests are asking vengeance, and vengeance is hanging over their heads. Woe to the priests and to those dedicated to God who by their unfaithfulness and their wicked lives are crucifying my Son again! The sins of those dedicated to God cry out towards Heaven and call for vengeance, and now vengeance is at their door. For there is no one left to beg mercy and forgiveness for the people. There are *no more generous souls; there is no one left worthy of offering a stainless sacrifice to the Eternal for the sake of the world.*

"God will strike in an unprecedented way.

"Woe to the inhabitants of the earth! God will exhaust His wrath upon them, and no one will be able to escape so many afflictions together.

"The chiefs, the leaders of the people of God have neglected prayer and penance, and the devil has bedimmed their intelligence. They have become wandering stars which the old devil will drag along with his tail to make them perish. God will allow the old serpent to cause divisions among those who reign in every society and in every family. Physical and moral agonies will be suffered. God will abandon mankind to itself and will send punishments which will follow one after the other for more than thirty-five years.

"The Society of men is on the eve of the most terrible scourges and of gravest events. Mankind must expect to be ruled with an iron rod and to drink from the chalice of the wrath of God.

Question: Dear Mother Mary, I take it the above paragraphs are your warnings of all the terrible sufferings and agonies coming. It is as if our Father Almighty has been relegated to the background within the Hearts of the people and priests. Therefore, our Father will withdraw and let humanity take its sinful course and experience the awful consequences. Do I have this right?

Answer: *Yes, my dear son you have it exactly right. <u>If there is one thing that I would love you to communicate to all others of God sacred children through your writings is that prayer is the most powerful force on earth.</u> As I have said so many times prayer, penance, sacrifice, and the Rosary along with the sacraments are the road to happiness, fulfillment, and success while on the earth. You could say that doing these things is the antidote of Satan. In an atmosphere of prayer in love Satan can do almost nothing.*

"May the curate of my Son, Pope Pius IX never leave Rome again after 1859; may he, however, be steadfast and noble<u>, may he fight with the weapons of faith and love.</u> I will be at His side. May he be on His guard

against Napoleon. He is two-faced, and when he wishes to make himself Pope as well as Emperor, God will soon draw back from him. He is the mastermind who, always wanting to ascend further, will fall on the sword he wished to use to force his people to be raised up.

Question: My dear Mother Mary, the above paragraph seems to have the timing of Napoleon's lifetime incorrect because he died before Pope Pius IX was in his papacy.

Answer: *"You are so right, my love; my son told me how perceptive you are, and I thank you for that. The discontinuity that you observed is correct. After the death of Napoleon, the political and military situation in France remained very hostile toward the Church. Napoleon failed in becoming both Emperor and Pope and that thought lingered on for a very long time regarding uniting the political with the spiritual.*

Today as you know there are very strong tendencies in the world to do now exactly what Napoleon failed at. Many world leaders during your lifetime, like Napoleon, want to combine all countries into a one-world government and a one-world religion. This effort is gaining in ferocity with Pope Francis trying to secularize the Catholic Church that my son founded. In addition, world political leaders are now working toward a one-world government through the guidance of many worldwide organizations like NATO and the WEF, the world economic forum. These are very evil people and like other prophecies, the Satanic urges have started from the top like Pope Francis.

If they succeed in doing this it is Satan that will be installed as the worldwide leader, and he will rampage across the world subjugating everybody to worship Him and follow His Satanic laws. If you do not obey you will become a nonperson and will either, be killed or you will starve to death. You will be banned from all economic activity like purchasing food and shelter.

My personal political warning: I have lived on this planet for more than three fourths of a century. In that time, I have observed the differences between what we call American Democrats and American Republicans. Basically, Democrats want complete centralized government control over every aspect of our lives. The evidence is overwhelming and plain to see with what now the Democrat Biden administration is doing to us. They are going as far as to regulate what our natural gas stoves can do or not. They want to regulate every detail of our lives including the kind of cars we drive using the fake science of climate change. It is completely false and a Satanic falsehood. Democrats hate our Godly inspired Constitution and our Bill of Rights because it greatly limits the power of a central government which Democrats adore.

Look no farther than the persecution of Donald Trump. Democrats have completely ignored the rule of law and constitutional government in order to assassinate his legal bid for the presidency. They hate our form of government that much. Because Democrats want increasingly centralized government, they continually invent more and more government programs to "help the needy" and over the years this has accounted for now the majority of where our tax dollars go. From taxpayers to Democrats selected voting groups so they have a better chance of being reelected.

This is why Democrats have opened the borders of our country to the world. So, they may import new voters that will most likely vote Democrat because they are so happy to get out of their stinking countries. Former president Democrat Barack Obama once said, he sees no reason why the United States should be any better than the rest of the world! Now Democrats are importing the rest of the world into our beloved country.

All the Democrats have one intention, increase the size of government, and buy votes so they can retain more and more political power. This is why they always increase taxes because that also forces hardworking people down the economic ladder into need for government programs. It is a vicious Satanic cycle. Lastly my dear sacred child of God <u>I say this with a bleeding heart, "Our Democrat party is the political arm of Satan in our country."</u>

Contrarily, Republicans believe in individual freedom for everyone, no exceptions. Freedom to choose what we wish to purchase, where we want to go and how we lead our lives. Republicans want as small of a government as possible and as much freedom as possible for all our sacred children and citizens of our country. Not much more to be said because all this is very straightforward.

Now let's go back to the sacred words of our Blessed Mother Mary:

This is why, please communicate to everybody to use <u>the most powerful weapon on earth which is sincere prayer to the holy Trinity. With enough prayer the terrible situation I just described may very well never happen.</u> But my dearest son, I am not optimistic due to people like the current Pope Francis who is steadfastly attempting to take the holy and sacred aspects of the Catholic Church. And turn it into just other empty secular organization. As you already know my dear son, Pope Francis is indeed the Anti-Christ and everything he has been doing fits that description.

On another note, dear son, Father Malachi Martin is correct when he stated that <u>there is Satanic worship going on within the Vatican.</u> And this has been so for a long time now, but it is increasing in its intensity."

Continuing on….

Note: Blessed Mother Mary said these things in the mid-1800s and now remember all the sexual scandals that have gone on recently in the Catholic Church. She knew this was coming. And it certainly has.

"Italy will be punished for her ambition in wanting to shake off the yoke of the Lord of Lords. And so, she will be left to fight a war; blood will flow on all sides. Churches will be locked up or desecrated. Priests and religious orders will be hunted down and made to die a cruel death. Several will abandon the faith, and a vast number of priests and members of religious orders will break away from the true religion; among these people there will even be bishops.

"May the Pope guard against the performers of miracles. For the time has come when the most astonishing wonders will take place on the earth and in the air.

"In the year 1864, Lucifer together with a large number of demons will be unloosed from hell; they will put an end to faith little by little, even in those dedicated to God. They will blind them in such a way, that, unless they are blessed with a special grace, these people will take on the spirit of these

angels of hell. Several religious institutions will lose all faith and will lose many souls.

Question: Dear Mother Mary, how many churches are already closed in America and the rest of the world?

Answer: *Thank you for asking my dear son, it is a dire situation, and it is getting worse. The short answer to your question is within the United States between 1002 thousand different churches have already closed due to decreasing lack of participation from parishioners. In the rest of the world the percentage of Christian and Catholic churches that are disappearing is even worse. Across the entire world there are between 1000 and 10 thousand different churches that have closed in the last few decades. As time gets deeper and deeper into the end of times these numbers will increase to quantities that is very frightening. As the Catholic Church and other Christian churches will be forced to go underground just as your lifelong friend, a Catholic priest, has forecasted for many years.*

"Evil books will be abundant on earth and the sprits of darkness will spread everywhere a universal slackening of all that concerns the service of God. They will have great power over nature. There will be churches built to serve these spirits. People will be transported from one place to another by these evil spirits. Even priests, for they will not have been guided by the good spirit of the Gospel which is a spirit of humility, charity, and zeal for the glory of God.

On occasions, the dead and the righteous will be brought back to life. (That is to say that these dead will take on the form of righteous souls, which had lived on earth, in order to lead men further astray. These so-called resurrected dead, who will be nothing but the devil in this form, will preach another Gospel contrary to that of the true Christ Jesus. Denying the existence of heaven; that is also to say, the souls of the damned. All these souls will appear as if fixed to their bodies.

"Everywhere there will be extraordinary wonders, as true faith has faded, and false light brightens the people. Woe to the Princes of the Church who

think only of piling riches upon riches to protect their authority and dominate with pride.

Dearest Mother Mary, all this is just awful. At this point in human History can you please give us an idea of the time in which the above Satanic events will occur or have already occurred?

My dear son, much of this has already happened since my apparition in La Salette. But the Satanic activities continue onward even until today. The Catholic Popes that have served the Church well since my prophecy above have suffered badly but this suffering is not getting the attention of the true believers in the Church.

Conveniently, the next sentences are starting to play out now within invisible history. More and more, the current Pope Francis is leading our Catholic Church into a disaster. And his attempts to secularize the holy sacraments and all the sacred traditions that express God's love to all His sacred children.

Your current Pope Francis will be going to Moscow sometime in the near future after this book has been written. Remember Russia has not been properly consecrated. If it were the wars such as Ukraine today would never have happened. And the world would be heading toward a far more peaceful existence. Do not believe Pope Francis will consecrate Russia while he is in Moscow. His visit there is purely political.

"The Vicar of my Son will suffer a great deal, because for a while the Church will yield to large persecution, a time of darkness and the Church will witness a frightful crisis.

"The true faith to the Lord having been forgotten, each individual will want to be on his own and be superior to people of same identity. They will abolish civil rights as well as ecclesiastical, all order and all justice would be trampled underfoot and only homicides, hate, jealousy, falsehoods, and dissension would be seen without love for country or family.

"The Holy Father will suffer a great deal. I will be with him until the end and receive his sacrifice.

"The mischievous would attempt his life several times to do harm and shorten his days but neither he nor his successor will see the triumph of the Church of God.

"All the civil governments will have one and the same plan, which will be to abolish and do away with every religious principal to make way for materialism, atheism, spiritualism, and vices of all kinds.

"In the year 1865, there will be desecration of holy places. In convents, the flowers of the Church will decompose, and the devil will make himself like the king of all hearts. May those in charge of religious communities be on their guard against the people they must receive. For the devil will resort to all His evil tricks to introduce sinners into religious orders, for disorder and the love of carnal pleasures will be spread all over the earth.

Note: Blessed Mother Mary said these things in the mid-1800s and now remember all the sexual scandals that have gone on recently in the Catholic Church. She knew this was coming. And it certainly has.

"France, Italy, Spain, and England will be at war. Blood will flow in the streets. Frenchman will fight Frenchman; Italian will fight Italian. A general war will follow which will be appalling. For a time, God will cease to remember France and Italy because the Gospel of Jesus Christ has been forgotten. The wicked will make use of all their evil ways. Men will kill each other; massacre each other even in their homes.

"At the first blow of His thundering sword, the mountains and all nature will tremble in terror, for the disorders and crimes of men have pierced the vault of the Heavens. Paris will burn and Marseilles will be engulfed. Several cities will be shaken down and swallowed up by earthquakes. People will believe that all is lost. Nothing will be seen but murder, nothing will be heard but the clash of arms and blasphemy.

"The righteous will suffer greatly. Their prayers, their penances and their tears will rise up to Heaven and all of God's people will beg for forgiveness and mercy and will plead for my help and intercession. And then Jesus Christ, in an act of His justice and His great mercy will command His Angels to have all His enemies put to death. Suddenly, the persecutors of the

Church of Jesus Christ and all those given over to sin will perish and the earth will become desert-like.

And then peace will be made, and man will be reconciled with God. Jesus Christ will be served, worshipped, and glorified. Charity will flourish everywhere. The new kings will be the right arm of the holy Church, which will be strong, humble, and pious in its poor but fervent imitation of the virtues of Jesus Christ. The Gospel will be preached everywhere, and mankind will make great progress in its faith, for there will be unity among the workers of Jesus Christ and man will live in fear of God.

Question: Dear Mother Mary, are you referring to World War I and World War II?

Answer: *Yes, my son, you have perceived very well what I described. And as you know after those two awful wars, the peace was very short-lived because a short time later the Korean War in the Cold War became very visible and threatening.*

"*This peace among men will be short-lived. Twenty-five years of plentiful harvests will make them forget that the sins of men are the cause of all the troubles on this earth.*

"*A forerunner of the Anti-Christ, with his troops gathered from several nations, will fight against the true Christ, the only Savior of the world. He will shed much blood and will want to annihilate the worship of God to make himself be looked upon as a God.*

"*The earth will be struck by calamities of all kinds (in addition to plague and famine which will be widespread. There will be a series of wars until the last war, which will then be fought by the ten kings of the Anti-Christ. All of whom will have one and the same plan and will be the only rulers of the world. Before this comes to pass, there will be a kind of false peace in the world. People will think of nothing but amusement. The wicked will give themselves over to all kinds of sin. But the children of the holy Church, the children of my faith, my true followers, they will grow in their love for God and in all the virtues most precious to me. Blessed are the souls humbly guided by the Holy Spirit! I shall fight at their side until they reach a fullness of years.*

"Nature is asking for vengeance because of man, and she trembles with dread at what must happen to the earth stained with crime. Tremble, earth, and you who proclaim yourselves as serving Jesus Christ and who, on the inside, only adore yourselves, tremble. For God will hand you over to His enemy, because the holy places are in a state of corruption. Many convents are no longer houses of God, but the grazing-grounds of Asmodeus and his like. It will be during this time that the Anti-Christ will be born of a Hebrew nun, a false virgin who will communicate with the old serpent, the master of impurity, his father will be. At birth, he will spew out blasphemy; he will have teeth, in a word; he will be the devil incarnate. He will scream horribly; he will perform wonders; he will feed on nothing but impurity. He will have brothers who, although not devils incarnate like him, will be children of evil. At the age of twelve, they will draw attention upon themselves by the gallant victories they will have won; soon they will each lead armies, aided by the legions of hell.

"The seasons will be altered, the earth will produce nothing but bad fruit, the stars will lose their regular motion, and the moon will only reflect a faint reddish glow. Water and fire will give the earth's globe convulsions and terrible earthquakes which will swallow up mountains, cities, etc...

"Rome will lose the faith and become the seat of the Anti-Christ.

"The demons of the air together with the Anti-Christ will perform great wonders on earth and in the atmosphere, and men will become more and more perverted. God will take care of His faithful servants and men of good will. The Gospel will be preached everywhere, and all peoples of all nations will get to know the truth.

"I make an urgent appeal to the earth. I call on the true disciples of the living God who reigns in Heaven. I call on the true followers of Christ made man, the only true Savior of men. I call on my children, the true faithful, those who have given themselves to me. So that I may lead them to my divine Son,

those whom I carry in my arms, so to speak, those who have lived on my spirit.

Finally, I call on the Apostles of the Last Days. The faithful disciples of Jesus Christ who have lived in scorn. For the world and for themselves, in poverty and in humility, in scorn and in silence, in prayer and in mortification, in chastity and in union with God, in suffering and unknown to the world. It is time they came out and filled the world with light. Go and reveal yourselves to be my cherished children. I am at your side and within you, provided that your faith is the light which shines upon you in these unhappy days. May your zeal make you famished for the glory and the honor of Jesus Christ. Fight, children of light, you, the few who can see. For now, is the time of all times, the end of all ends.

"*The Church will be in eclipse; the world will be in dismay. But now Enoch and Eli will come, filled with the Spirit of God. They will preach with the might of God, and men of goodwill will believe in God, and many souls will be comforted. They will make great steps forward through the virtue of the Holy Spirit and will condemn the devilish lapses of the Anti-Christ. Woe to the inhabitants of the earth! There will be bloody wars and famines, plagues, and infectious diseases. It will rain with a fearful hail of animals.*

There will be thunderstorms which will shake cities, earthquakes which will swallow up countries. Voices will be heard in the air. Men will beat their heads against walls, call for their death, and on another side, death will be their torment. Blood will flow on all sides. Who will be the victor if God does not shorten the length of the test? All the blood, the tears, and prayers of the righteous, God will relent. Enoch and Eli will be put to death. Pagan Rome will disappear. The fire of heaven will fall and consume three cities. All the universes will be struck with terror, and many will let themselves be lead astray because they have not worshipped the true Christ who lives among them. It is time; the sun is darkening; only faith will survive.

"*Now is the time; the abyss is opening. Here is the King of Kings of darkness; here is the Beast with his subjects, calling himself the Savior of the world. He will rise proudly into the air to go to heaven. He will be mothered by the breath of the Archangel Saint Michael. He will fall, and the earth, which will have been in a continuous series of evolutions for three days, will open up its fiery bowels. And he will have plunged for all eternity with all his followers into the everlasting chasms of hell. And then water and fire will purge the earth and consume all the works of men's pride, and all will be renewed. God will be served and glorified."*

Then the Holy Virgin gave me, also in French, THE RULE OF A NEW RELIGIOUS ORDER. When She had given me the rule of this new religious Order, the Holy Virgin continued the speech in the same manner:

"If they convert, the stones and rocks will change into wheat, and potatoes will be found sown in the earth. Do you say your prayers properly, my children?"

We both told a falsehood: "Oh! No, Madame, not so much."

"Oh! My children, you must tell them morning and evening. When you can do no more, say a Pater and an Ave Maria; and when you have the time to do better, you will say more.

"Only a few old women go to mass. In the summer, the rest work all day Sunday and, in the winter, when they are at a loose end, they only go to mass to make fun of religion. During Lent, they go to the butchers like hungry dogs.

"Have you ever seen any spoilt wheat, my children?"

We both answered: "Oh no, Madame."

The Holy Virgin turned to Maximin, saying:

"But you, my child, you must have seen some once near le 'Coin,' with your father. The farmer said to your father: 'Come and see how my wheat's gone bad!' You went to see. Your Father took two or three ears in his hand, rubbed them, and they fell to dust. Then, on your way back, when you were no more than half an hour away from Corps, your father gave you a piece of bread, and said: 'Take it, eat it while you can, my son, for I don't know who will be eating anything next year if the wheat is spoiled like that!'"

The Most Holy Virgin brought her speech to an end in French.

"AND SO, MY CHILDREN, YOU WILL PASS THIS ON TO ALL MY PEOPLE"

The most beautiful Lady crossed the stream. And after two more steps, without turning back towards us. We who were following Her (for we were drawn to Her by Her brilliance and even more by Her kindness which elated me, which seemed to melt my heart), she repeated to us.

"AND SO, MY CHILDREN, YOU WILL PASS THIS ON TO ALL MY PEOPLE"

Summary Comments About La Salette

Thank you, my dear son, for letting me comment upon my apparitions at La Salette. In many ways the news was very sad for me to tell both children what I had to say. My message was so much the same for them as the other apparitions that I mentioned to you earlier that were never made public by those to whom I spoke. However, I am so happy that both Malanie and Maximin did write extensively about what I said. What they said is very correct especially considering all the translator help and bias that was inserted into their words that described more simply what it was I told them.

In many cases dear son my message is the same, due to Satan and His demons your Father's sacred children fall into sin from Satanic temptations that are disguised by Him as something good. One thing I want to make note of. It seems that the more sophisticated the people are the more likely they are to fall into grave sin promoted by Satan. It is very beautiful to speak with children that believe in their Heavenly Father and their Lord and Savior, my Son.

So, the only thing I have left to say regarding my apparition here is to be diligent in prayer. Pray every day at least morning and evening. Make sacrifices in the name of my Immaculate Heart, do penance as you understand it to be and attend holy mass every week if you can and receive the holy sacraments. A lot of people refer to these as putting on your sacred armor. Although this is true, I prefer to think of these as acts of love for Almighty God and not something warlike. But that is just my personal preference. Thank you my dear son and I know we will continue with the others of my apparitions in your marvelous book that is how starting to take form.

I love you,
Your Blessed Mother Mary

Authors Note: Both Melanie and Maximin were simple shepherd children when all of this happened to them. We do not know exactly when each of them wrote the following text about our Blessed Mother Mary. However, looking at the English language presented below it is obvious they both had a lot of linguistic and vocabulary help in their writing. Additionally, it is unknowable this point is just how much their original thoughts were amplified to make more exciting reading.

Blessed Mother Mary: Yes, again my son. you are correct. But what is presented below about me from both children although exaggerated have the essential ideas intact.

Maximin Describes Our Blessed Mother Mary

The Most Holy Virgin was tall and well-proportioned. She seemed so light a mere breath could have stirred Her, yet She was motionless and perfectly balanced. Her face was majestic, imposing, but not imposing in the manner of the Lords here below. She compelled a respectful fear. At the same time as Her Majesty compelled respect mingled with love, She drew me to Her. Her gaze was soft and penetrating. Her eyes seemed to speak to mine, but the conversation came out of a deep and vivid feeling of love for this ravishing beauty who was liquefying me. The softness of Her gaze, Her air of incomprehensible goodness made me understand and feel she was drawing me to Her and wanted to give Herself. It was an expression of love which cannot be expressed with the tongue of the flesh, nor with the letters of the alphabet.

The clothing of the Most Holy Virgin was silver white and quite brilliant. It was quite intangible. It was made up of light and glory, sparkling and dazzling. There is no expression nor comparison to be found on earth.

The Holy Virgin was all beauty and all love; the sight of Her overwhelmed me. In her finery as in Her person, everything radiated the majesty, the splendor, the magnificence of a Queen beyond compare. She seemed as white, Immaculate, crystallized, dazzling, Heavenly, fresh, and new as a Virgin. The word LOVE seemed to slip from Her pure and silvery lips. She appeared to me like a good Mother, full of kindness, amiability, of love for us, of compassion and mercy.

The crown of roses which She placed on Her head was so beautiful, so brilliant, it defies imagination. The different colored roses were not of this earth; it was a joining together of flowers which crowned the head of the Most Holy Virgin. But the roses kept changing and replacing each other, and then, from the Heart of each rose, there shone a beautiful entrancing light, which gave the roses a shimmering beauty. From the crown of roses there seemed to arise golden branches and a number of little flowers mingled with the shining ones. The whole thing formed a most beautiful diadem, which shone brighter than our earth's sun.

Our Blessed Mother Mary had a most pretty cross hanging round Her neck. This cross seemed golden, (not gold-plated, for I have sometimes seen objects which were golden with varying shades of gold, which had a much more beautiful effect on my eyes than simple gold-plate). On this shining, beautiful cross, there was a Christ; it was Our Lord on the Cross. Near both ends of the cross there was a hammer, and at the other end, a pair of tongs. Our Christ was skin-colored, but He shone dazzlingly; and the light shone forth from His holy body seemed like brightly shining darts which pierced my Heart with the desire to melt inside Him. At times, the Christ appeared to be dead. His head was bent forward, and His body seemed to give way, as if about to fall, had He not been held back by the nails which held Him to the Cross.

I felt a deep compassion. I would have liked to tell His unknown love to the whole world. To let seep into mortal souls the most heartfelt love and gratitude towards a God who had no need whatsoever of us to be everything He is, was and always will be. Yet, O love that men cannot understand, He made Himself man and wanted to die. Yes, die, so as to better inscribe in our souls and in our memory, the passionate love He has for us! Oh, how wretched am I to find myself so poor in my expression of the love of our good Savior for us! But, in another way, how happy we are to be able to feel more deeply that which we cannot express!

At other times, the Christ appeared to be alive. His head was erect, His eyes open, and He seemed to be on the cross of His own accord. At times too, He appeared to speak: He seemed to show He was on the cross for our sake, out of love for us. To draw us to His love. That He always has more love to give us, that His love in the beginning and in the year 33 is always that of today and will be forever more.

The Holy Virgin was crying nearly the whole time she was speaking to me. Her tears flowed gently, one by one, down to her knees, then, like sparks of light, they disappeared. They were glittering and full of love. I would have liked to comfort Her and stop Her tears. But it seemed to me She needed the tears to show better Her love forgotten by men. I would have liked to throw myself into Her arms and say to Her:

"My kindest Mother, do not cry! I want to love you for all men on earth." But she seemed to be saying to me:

"There are so many who know me not!"

I was in between life and death, and on one side, I saw so much desire by this mother to be loved, and on another side, so much cold and indifference... Oh! My Mother, most beautiful and lovable Mother, my love, Heart of my Heart!

The tears of our sweet Mother, far from lessening her air of majesty, of a Queen and a Mistress. They seemed, on the contrary, to embellish Her. To make Her more beautiful, more powerful, more filled with love, more maternal, more ravishing, and I could have wiped away Her tears which made my Heart leap with compassion and love. To see a mother cry, and such a mother, without doing everything possible to comfort her and change her grief to joy, is that possible? Oh! Mother, who is more than good; you have been formed with all the prerogatives God is able to make. You have married the power of God, so to speak; you are good, and more, you are good with the goodness of God Himself. God has extended Himself by making you His terrestrial and celestial masterpiece.

Note: There are more descriptions of Blessed Mary. Go to the website in the footnote 1 and 2. Also, my personal belief that due to the very articulate words in English, Maximin must have had help in His descriptions. The descriptions are too eloquent to be directly from a simple shepherd boy in France at that time in History. Like so many other aspirations, lots of unknown people stick their well-intended fingers into the pie so to speak.

On this point Mother Mary said to me: ***Yes, my dear son, I think he had too much help and some of the ideas originated in the translator's mind and not His. But it is generally accurate.***

Today: 21st of November 1878, when this account was written.

Additional words of Melanie:

"The great chastisement will come, because men will not be converted; yet it is only their conversion that can hinder these scourges. God will begin to strike men by inflicting lighter punishments in order to open their eyes; then He will stop or may repeat His former warnings to give place for repentance. But sinners will not avail themselves of these opportunities; He will, in consequence, send more severe castigations, anxious to move sinners to repentance, but all in vain. Finally, the obduracy of sinners shall draw upon their heads the greatest and most terrible calamities.

"We are all guilty! Penance is not done, and sin increases daily. Those who should come forward to do good are retained by fear. Evil is great. A moderate punishment serves only to irritate the spirits, because they view all things with human eyes. God could work a miracle to convert and change the aspect of the earth without chastisement. God will work a miracle; it will be a stroke of His mercy; but after the wicked shall have inebriated themselves with blood, the scourge shall arrive.

"What countries shall be preserved from such calamities? Where shall we go for refuge? I, in my turn, shall ask, what is the country that observes the commandments of God? What country is not influenced by human fear where the interest of the Church and the glory of God are at stake? (Ah, indeed! What country, what nation upon earth?) On behalf of my Superior and myself, I often asked myself where to go for refuge, had we means for the journey and for our subsistence, on condition no person was to know it? But I renounce these useless thoughts. We are very guilty! In consequence of this, it is necessary that a very great and terrible scourge should come to revive our faith, and to restore to us our very reason, which we have almost entirely lost.

Wicked men are devoured by a thirst for exercising their cruelty. But when they shall have reached the uttermost point of barbarity, God Himself shall extend His hand to stop them, and very soon after, a complete change shall be affected in all surviving persons. Then they will sing The Deum Landaus with the liveliest gratitude and love. The Virgin Mary, our Mother, shall be our liferentrix. Peace shall reign, and the charity of Jesus Christ shall unite all Hearts...Let us pray; let us pray. God does not wish to chastise us severely. He speaks to us in so many, so many ways to make us return to Him. How long shall we remain stubborn? Let us pray, let us pray; let us never cease praying and doing penance. Let us pray for our Holy Father the Pope, the only light for the faithful in these times of darkness. O yes, let us by all means prays much. Let us pray to our good, sweet merciful Virgin Mary; for we stand in great need of her powerful hands over our heads."

Lourdes: [4] Miraculous Holy Events Occur

Authors note: The chronology of events regarding Saint Bernadette and her companions is too precise to be written by a 14-year-old uneducated girl. To me at least she must have had a lot of help from adults to create the accounts of the apparitions of our Blessed Mother Mary. This certainly this is not to say adults modified the content of Saint Bernadette's experiences to make it sound better. I know this story is completely true. How do I know this? Because I truly am the Anointed Messenger of our Heavenly Father and Blessed Mother Mary personally told me these accounts are true and correct.

---

[4] https://theCatholictravelguide.com/destinations/france/lourdes-france-lady-lourdes-site-healing-hope/

I should comment that of all the apparitions of our Blessed Mother Mary she never chooses anybody of wealth vast education. I understand why. In my opinion it is because people of means have walked away from the purity of a simple life. Which is something our Blessed Mother Mary feels is necessary to deliver her messages in a pure way without tainting them from the things of this world.

On February 11th, 1858, to July 16th our Blessed Mother Mary appeared to 14-year-old Bernadette Soubirous. In total our Blessed Mother appeared to her 18 separate times. Like me, your author, Bernadette suffered from lifelong asthma. Her family was very poor.

On February 11, 1858, the day of the first apparition Bernadette and her sister Toinette, and a friend of theirs, Jeanne, were out searching for firewood to make dinner. Bernadette's companions crossed the river, but she did not because of the ice-cold water and her asthma. Suddenly Bernadette heard a sound like a woosh. She turned around and looked up into the grotto which was next to the river. She then saw The Cave was filled with golden light.

When she looked up, she saw a lady of great beauty wearing a white robe with a blue sash and a veil over her head with a rosary in her hands. There were yellow flowers at her feet. Then the beautiful lady made the sign of the cross with the hand that was holding the rosary. Both the lady and Bernadette said the rosary together. When they finished their prayers, the beautiful lady disappeared.

As always seems to be the case, Bernadette did not want to tell her mother or father what happened, but her sister spilled the beans and told her mother everything. Upon hearing this, the mother told Bernadette those were just illusions and forbade her from going back to the grotto.

The 2nd apparition, three days later the girls went back to the grotto with holy water. They were told if they sprinkled holy water on the lady, if the lady were good then no harm done if the lady were evil, it would force her to disappear. Bernadette sprinkled the water on the ground at her feet and Blessed Mother Mary smiled.

On February 18th the 3rd apparition took place. The next time the three girls went to the grotto Bernadette had a pencil and paper so as to write down anything our Blessed Mother Mary would tell them. When Mother Mary arrived, she told the girls, "There is no need me to write down what I have to say to you. Will you be so kind as to come here every day for 15 days? I do not promise to make you happy in this life, but in the next."

The first statement: A neighbor suggested she take a paper and pencil to write down the lady's name (although Bernadette could barely read or write). Bernadette held out a sheet of paper and a pencil so she might write down her name, but the Lady said: "What I have to say to you does not have to be written down ". This was the first statement Mother Mary made that day.

The second statement of the Virgin Mary was: "Would you do me the kindness of coming here for 15 days?" Bernadette was overwhelmed. It was the first time anyone addressed her in a formal way. Bernadette described these words by saying the Virgin looked at her "as one person looks at another person."

The third statement of the Virgin was: "I do not promise to make you happy in this world but in the next."

The 4th apparition, a Friday. Bernadette's parents and a few friends went to the grotto this time. When Bernadette started to pray the rosary, the other people noticed her face became illuminated.

The 5th apparition on, Blessed Mother Mary taught Bernadette a prayer she recited every day for the rest of her life. But Bernadette never revealed the prayer to anyone else. Also, Mother Mary told her to always bring a candle.

The 6th apparition on: Bernadette's experience with Mother Mary caused a sensation in the community and many people started to accompany her to the grotto. And as usual with Mother Mary's apparitions the townspeople became afraid and started to concentrate on the dangers of too many people gathering at the grotto. So, the officials forbade Bernadette from going to the grotto. I like Bernadette very much! Because she told the people she cannot obey and will go to the grotto to see the beautiful lady.

The ninth apparition was really the culmination of the apparitions here at Lourdes, the Lady asked Bernadette to scrape the ground at the back of this "pigs' shelter," saying to her: "Go to the spring, drink of it and wash yourself there ". She moved on her knees to the back of the Grotto, kissed the dirty disgusting ground and ate some bitter grass. She scraped the ground three times trying to drink the muddy water, then smeared mud on her face. Then she turned to the crowd with her hands apart. There was only a little muddy water to begin with for Bernadette to drink, then little by little it became clear running water. The miraculous spring was finally revealed, and has continued to flow ever since, providing water for the physical healing of some, and spiritual healing for millions. [5]

Then, during the thirteenth apparition, March 25, 1858, the crowd became larger and larger. The Lady told her: "Go and tell the priests that people are to come here in procession and to build a chapel here." Bernadette spoke of this to Fr. Peyramale, the Parish Priest of Lourdes.

He wanted to know only one thing: The Lady's name. He demanded another test; to see the wild rosebush flower at the Grotto in the middle of winter. Three times Bernadette asked the question. On the fourth request, the Lady responded in dialect "Que soy era Immaculada Conception." ("I am the Immaculate Conception ").

With these words the Mother of God confirmed what Pope Pius IX proclaimed as the dogma of the Immaculate Conception four years earlier in 1854. Bernadette, who never heard of this title, didn't understand the meaning of these words, but went to the priest to tell Him the Lady's name. He knew immediately it was the Mother of God, and the Bishop of Tarbes, Monseigneur Laurence, confirmed this.

---

[5]https://theCatholictravelguide.com/destinations/france/lourdes-france-lady-lourdes-site-healing-hope

The Immaculate Conception is, as the Church teaches, "Mary, conceived without sin, thanks to the merits of the Cross of Christ."

We celebrate the Feast of Our Lady of Lourdes on February 11.

<u>The lady also told Bernadette to dig in the ground at a certain spot and to drink from the small spring of water that began to bubble up. Almost immediately, cures were reported from the water.</u> Today thousands of gallons of water gush from the source of the spring, and pilgrims are able to bathe in it. Countless purported miracle cures have been documented there, from the healing of nervous disorders and cancers to cases of paralysis and even of blindness. [6]

A Summary of What Blessed Mother Mary Said: [7]

Feb 18, 1858 (Ash Wednesday)
It is not necessary [to write down my name]. Would you be kind enough to come here for 15 days? I do not promise to make you happy in this world, but in the next.

Feb 21, 1858
(Sorrowful tone of voice) Pray for sinners.

Feb 24, 1858
Penance! Penance! Penance! Pray to God for sinners.

Feb 25, 1858
Go, drink from the spring, and wash yourself there. You will eat the grass that is there.

Feb 27, 1858
Penance! Penance! Penance! Pray to God for sinners. Go, kiss the ground for the conversion of sinners. Go and tell the priests to have a chapel built here.

---

[6] https://en.wikipedia.org/wiki/Lourdes
[7] htttps://en.wikipedia.org/wiki/Lourdes

Feb 28, 1858

Penance! Penance! Penance! Pray to God for sinners. Go, kiss the ground for the conversion of sinners.

March 2, 1858

Go, tell the priests to bring people here in procession and have a Chapel built here.

March 25, 1858

I am the Immaculate Conception. [8]

Question: Dear Mother Mary, when I did some research on Lourdes, I saw a lot of commercialization surrounding the grotto and the Chapel you wanted to be built. It seems as if a lot of money changes hands for various trinkets and the holy water can be for sale. I cannot help but feel like this completely cheapens Lourdes and removes the sacred focus of what it should be. What are your feelings dear Mother?

Answer: *I understand completely my son. They have built fancy monuments for this that and the other thing and you are correct it is become very commercialized. Selling the water that is intended to be free for all of God's sacred children. As you know, there are now vacation packages to bring tourists to this holy site. I would rather have all the people come no matter what the reason is and if money changes hands, I will just refer to that as necessary commerce to help the poor people in Lourdes.*

Question: In none of the accounts regarding St. Bernadette I never saw any comment regarding who actually saw you and heard you speak. I am assuming it is only Bernadette just like Garabandal. Is that right?

Answer: *Yes, my son, it is only Bernadette that heard my voice. I must point out with that she was very diligent in accounting for everything that I said. She was only semi-literate, and she needed help from various adults to write down what she wanted to say. The accounts are quite accurate.*

---

[8] IBID

Question: Regarding the sacred healing that takes place through the means of the holy water in the grotto. I know not everyone gets healed and I think I know the answer but could you dear Mother clarify how it is some people are healed and others are not?

Answer: *As you know my dear son everything is always up to your Heavenly Father. It is always His will that will be done like the prayer "Our Father." Just like in your case, my son, your Father's will be that you be healed from the terminal cancer you had years ago. Because of this, it was also His will that you become His Anointed Messenger. And bring all of these magnificent understandings of creation of our Heavenly Father. And the other most important descriptions of the way all of creation works together for the benefit of all your Father's sacred children.*

Also, it is His will that you be able to speak with the Trinity and me at any time you wish. So as to bring to His sacred children pure and perfect understandings of their existence and all of creation. You have done marvelously well, and I know you will continue. The entire Holy Family loves you for this so very much.

Question: Besides bringing healing and hope to so many of God's sacred children through the holy water of Lourdes, Are there any other purposes or goals of your apparition at Lourdes?

Answer: *That certainly is the main reason for my apparition at Lourdes. But in addition to that, Lourdes, like other places I have visited, brings together people of faith and that strengthens their faith remarkably. Also, my dear son, for those people who do not believe. Or are borderline believers, they will move closer to their Almighty Father in Heaven after being exposed to the stories of healing and even knowing a person that was healed. The Catholic Church calls this outreach, and it is a very good and holy thing.*

Question: Dear Blessed Mother, somehow, I think I am missing something and what I write about Lourdes. Is there something I missed you would like to include in this book?

Answer: *My dear son, as always you have covered the topic very well. There is nothing more than I can add to what you have already written for God's* *sacred children. I know you plan on adding additional apparitions with small descriptions which I think is wonderful. This will stir God's sacred children's curiosity to explore other instances of where I appeared and why. I thank you deeply for that.*

Garabandal: The Multiple Apparitions of Blessed Mother Mary

In the village of San Sebastian de Garabandal in Spain, from June 18, 1961, through 1965 our Blessed Mother Mary appeared in many multiple apparitions to four young girls. She brought messages of hope, conversion, and love. She also brought prophecies that surrounded the coming End of Times. Their names are Mari Loli Mezon, Jacinta González, Mari Cruz González, Maria "Conchita" Concepción. They witnessed our Blessed Mother Mary when they were in a state of ecstasy. They would always fall into this ecstasy trance before Mother Mary would appear at the same place near the village.

But before the first apparition of our Blessed Mother the four girls witnessed an angel that appeared to them over a few days. It was the Archangel Michael. On June 1, 1961, the angel announced the appearance of our Blessed Mother Mary tomorrow. Later the Virgin Mary with the child Jesus did indeed appear before them marking the beginning of a series multiple of apparitions. Our Blessed Mother Mary appeared hundreds of times to the girls in the following years.

The Girls State of Ecstasy.

When the young girls beheld their Mother, they promptly knelt oblivious to the pain of their striking the rough stones. Yet thorough medical examinations revealed no injuries to their knees. Their faces transformed in an instant entirely engrossed in divine ecstasy. Various tests were conducted on them during these raptures, and they showed no reactions to pinches, burns, or blows. Attempts to disrupt their trance were futile. Bright lights were shown into their eyes, but they displayed no discomfort. Lights that under normal circumstances could cause permanent eye damage yet their eyes remained wide open revealing a gaze of pure intense joy. These ecstatic moments varied in length with the girls often in seemingly uncomfortable positions with heads tilted back, eyes gazing Heavenward kneeling on Rocky and uneven ground. Many esteemed doctors examined the events and observed the girls during the apparitions. After extensive study, a pediatric specialist confirmed the girls always exhibited absolute normality.

Their ecstasies did not match any known psychological or physiological phenomenon. Dr. Rickard Puncher now a renowned neuropsychologist from Barcelona stated based with such manifestations for a doctor to provide a purely natural explanation.

The Powder Compact Story

After a short time, the people in the village and onlookers would give the girls small religious objects for Mother Mary to kiss for them. If the girls were not present people would leave their religious objects on the tables at the site of the apparition. There was no way the girls would know to which person each object belonged to. But during their ecstasy with their heads always turned upward to Heaven they returned each object to its owner with no mistakes for the thousands of items left by the people. These religious items included rosaries, medals, and wedding rings. The girls guided by our Blessed Mother Mary never make a mistake in their returns to all the different owners.

One time, the girls found a powder compact left by an onlooker. The girls were hesitant to give a secular object to our Blessed Mother Mary. However, when Mother Mary appeared, the first thing she asked to kiss was the powder compact. It turns out during the Spanish Civil War that same compact was used to deliver Holy Eucharist to prisoners who were waiting to be executed. It is obvious that somehow our Blessed Mother Mary even knows such details as this. Within the spiritual realm our Blessed Mother lives in, there are no secrets, and everything is transparent. So, if it is very normal for our Blessed Mother to know perfectly who the owner is for each object, they wanted her to kiss them.

Note: In my other book titled "God's Grand Design of All Creation for Your Redemption" I explain our lord and savior Jesus Christ told me there are NO secrets in the spiritual realm including the Heavenly Kingdom. This book is the one our Heavenly Father asked me to write about three years ago and now on Amazon etc. for the past 10 months. Mother Mary lives in the spiritual realm, and this is why she knows the ownership of all the items she kissed for them.

Many People Were Skeptical of What They Saw.

During the apparitions of the Virgin Mary at Garabandal many were skeptical regarding what they saw when the four girls were receiving invisible communion. The four girls wanted a sign for the non-believers, so they asked for a miracle. On June 22, 1962, St. Michael announced to Conchita he would visibly give communion. Although he previously brought communion to the girls, the host had never been visible. Now one time the host would be visible.

The real Picture of the visible host after it instantly appeared on Conchita's tongue.

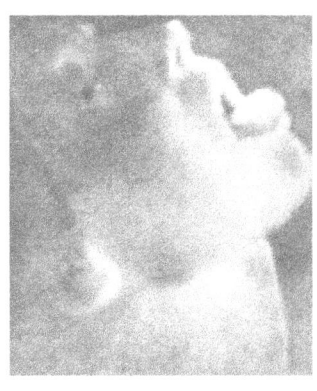

The Virgin Mary revealed to Conchita that the small miracle of the visible host would take place on July 18. Despite the parish priest's restriction, the news spread, and many pilgrims arrived at Garabandal that day. In front of a crowd a white host miraculously appeared on Conchita's tongue, an event that was also captured on film. A witness Pepe Diaz detailed the event emphasizing the host instantaneously appeared without any movement from Conchita. A picture exists of her tongue with the host on it that appeared out of nowhere. This was truly a miracle.

The Vatican Chose to Disbelieve Our Blessed Mother Mary's Apparitions at Garabandal

Unfortunately, but quite common within the Catholic Church, the local diocese of Santander took a negative viewpoint of all that has happened supernaturally. But the local priest Father Jose Luis Saavedra found the investigation of the visions did not follow standard normality of impartiality.

The original investigation seemed determined to discredit the visions of the four children.

"While it seemed very clear to the onlookers in Garabandal something otherworldly was happening, the local diocese of Santander took a terribly negative approach to the events. Fr. Jose Luis Saavedra, a priest of the order of the Home of the Mother, has done His doctoral dissertation on the apparitions in Garabandal. He found the investigation of the visions conducted by the local diocese did not follow standard norms of impartiality. The original "investigation" seemed intent on discrediting the visions out of fear of possible negative repercussions for the Church.

Then, sensationally, in May 1983, Dr. Luis Morales Noriega, the medical expert for the diocesan investigation, retracted His previously negative opinion and acknowledged the authenticity of the apparitions. To everyone's surprise, after years of negativity from the local ecclesiastical authorities, Dr Morales stated his new positive declaration was made with the permission of the bishop of Santander." [9]

Personally, I find the Catholic Church thinks backwards when it comes to the beautiful outreach of the divine to our holy Father's sacred children on earth. We see even today it takes the Church years to certify the validity of the truthfulness of miracles while the faithful know what a miracle is and not without the help of the Church.

In my opinion the Catholic Church did not want to acknowledge or certify the validity of the miracles at Garabandal due to our Blessed Mother Mary's prophecy the last pope will be the 112th Pope. And he would be the anti-Christ. That would be our current Pope today, Pope Francis.

Our Blessed Mary's prophecies in 1961 – 1965 include:
1. First as always, our Blessed Mother Mary's message is of hope, conversion, and love. Additionally, she always emphasizes praying

---

[9] Garabandal: Are the Prophecies About to be Fulfilled? - Catholic Stand

https://Catholicstand.com/garabandal-are-the-prophecies-about-to-be-fulfilled/

the rosary. We are to lead a life of prayer and sacrifice and be witnesses to the Gospel.

2. There will be a period of tribulation for the world which is a warning to all humanity simultaneously. Within one year of the warning a miracle will occur in Garibaldian which will leave a visible sign for all to see.

Question: Dearest Mother Mary, as this is written is now about 60 years since your apparitions in Garabandal. Is there anything now dear Mother you would like to say regarding the tribulation and the visible sign in Garabandal?

Answer: *Yes, my son, a few things have changed and as always thank you for asking such good questions. The situation on earth as you know is a fluid one that many times changes like the winds. With this the warning miracle in Guerra bond L has been postponed because of an ensuing increase in Christian faith coming from of unexpected sources like Russia. The people there are more and more rejecting the government crackdowns on faith much like it was during the times of Rome when my son was crucified.*

The tribulation will still occur sadly because on the whole the earth is still disintegrating with Satan influence. And there will be a last gasp of worldwide wars, multiple wars that are not too far off. The Russian leadership still wishes to reconstruct what was known as the Soviet Union. The current leader is becoming more and more mentally ill, and he poses a danger to the entire world. Your current leadership in our Blessed United States has been doing everything it can to destroy your country. And turn it into a weakened state subject to the implementation of a one-world government and with Pope Francis a one-world religion. All of this will be led by the Anti-Christ Satan Himself.

But remember my dearest son the timing on this is not fixed and is somewhat fluid. However, my dear son, I will tell you that this will happen in your later years on earth. The holy books that you are writing, dear son, as you recently wrote, will indeed become sacred Scripture for the generations to come. So, they will learn many more wonderful details about their existential existence, there holy Father in Heaven, and the Trinity and precisely how all existence has been designed as you have said for their redemption. Thank you, dear son, I love you so much.*

3. Following the miracle if humanity still fails to turn to Almighty God there will be fearful chastisement on a global scale.

    Question: Can you please outline some more detail about what form the chastisement in the world will be like?

    Answer: *As was said in other places, it will be fire from the skies. Many earthquakes, wars, violence social unrest, economic breakdowns that will cause much hunger and suffering. Lawlessness in the cities and a fundamental breakdown of all human existence. It hurts me to say this, my son, but this will happen. As you have already said, it is starting to happen now and will get worse with time.*

4. Our Lady additionally revealed the warning would occur at a time when Russia will suddenly and unexpectedly over run a great part of the free world. Russia has already overrun a large country in Eastern Europe, Ukraine.

5. Lady's apparitions included other supernatural events such as levitation is, reading of thoughts, insensitivity to pain, healings, and supernatural knowledge. Doctors and psychiatrists testified to an enormous multitude of such events in their writings. [10]

    Question: Dear Mother, is there any details you would like to add to this item?

    Answer: *Yes, there were a few instances of levitation with the four girls. Although they did not want to mention this much because they felt people would never believe it and they were shy as I said before. It is proven the girls were very insensitive during their ecstasy to any outside influence of pain on their bodies and their attention on me.*

---

[10] Garabandal: Are the Prophecies About to be Fulfilled? - Catholic Stand

https://Catholicstand.com/garabandal-are-the-prophecies-about-to-be-fulfilled/

Their supernatural knowledge refers to what I have told them, and you are documenting for all to see.

6. On July 4, 1961, the Virgin Mary delivered a message to the girls, which was made public on October 18. It urged for penance, visits to the Blessed sacrament and leading a righteous life, otherwise a significant punishment would befall humanity.

7. A second message was revealed by St. Michael the Archangel on behalf of the virgin on June 18, 1965.

   Question: I have not uncovered what St. Michael the ark angel revealed on your behalf. Could you please reveal that now?

   Answer: *Yes, he reiterated the very important need for what I have always said about penance, sacrifice, prayer, and saying the rosary with receiving the sacraments frequently.*

8. October 18, 1961: We must make many sacrifices, perform much penance, and visit the Blessed Sacrament frequently. But first we must lead good lives. If we do not a chastisement will befall us. The cup is already filling up and if we do not change, a great chastisement will come upon us." (In other words, our Heavenly Father is becoming increasingly concerned and is losing His patients with us His children.)

9. "Even less importance is being given to the holy Eucharist. We should turn the wrath of God away from us by our own efforts. If you ask His forgiveness with a sincere Heart, he will party you."

10. June 18, 1965: As my message of 18 October has not been compiled within as it has not been seen made known to the world, I am telling you that this is the last one. Previously the cup was filling; now it is brimming over. <u>Many cardinals, bishops, and priests are following the road to perdition, and with them they are taking many more souls.</u>

Question: *My dearest Mother Mary, it bothers me greatly regarding the previous prophecy that says cardinals, bishops, and priests following the road to perdition are taking many souls with them. Will our loving Father in Heaven punish some of His sacred children because of believing in what the Church tells them?*

Answer: *My dear son, again you are ever so perceptive in everything. I love you for this because you always want to dig for the truth of things. Also, I am happy that it bothers you because this shows your great love for others of God sacred children.* <u>*None of God's sacred children, not even one will be excluded from Heaven because they believed a wayward Church official.*</u>

It is the priests, the bishops and the Cardinals that will be greatly punished for misrepresenting my Son's message to the world. As you know my dear son there are many priests in hell along with cardinals and yes even Popes. This will be shocking to many people, but your loving Father requires honesty and close adherence to His loving laws of existence.

And like anyone else, those who believed the Church and were led astray will be judged by the very same three laws that you have so faithfully published in your other books. To summarize them because they are beautiful, they are:

1. *Love your Father in Heaven above everything else.*
2. *Love your Neighbors as you love yourself.*
3. *Love your enemies also.*

This is the formula for great love and contentment and beauty on earth for all of your s sacred children. There is no other way to achieve great peace across the whole world than this.

11. After a period of tribulation, the warning and miracle will occur in the same year.

    (Conchita, one of the four, as described the warning as a "correction of conscience" during which <u>everyone in the world will be given a revelation of the state of their souls before God.</u> We will see the consequences of our sins and will feel sorrow for them. The warning will be a moment of great grace for mankind. A true penetration of the Holy Spirit into our inmost Hearts, but it will be a traumatic event when we recognize the gravity of our sins and our distance from God.

    Question: The correction of conscience has also been expressed as the illumination of conscience for every person on earth. Dear Mother, can you give more details on how this will happen and the relative timing of it perhaps?

Answer: *Yes, this illumination of conscience will occur toward the last part of the tribulation worldwide. The earth will be already exhausted with all the people from the effects of their sinful behavior for all these hardships will have been in place for some years by then. It is then that your Heavenly Father will induce to everyone of His sacred children still on the earth making everyone's conscience very visible to them. And most importantly they will view their conscience in the same manner in which your Father views how they have sinned and importantly how all their sins have affected others of His sacred children. This will be the very last chance that all His sacred children will have to change their lives. And start to live their lives in accordance with the three rules that you my son have published. And shown elsewhere in this magnificent book you are writing for them.*

It is at this point the wheat will be separated from the chaff as my son said 2000 years ago. And it will become very visible to all who will choose eternal love. As their destiny with their Father versus those who will reject their Father and will be banished to hell to be ultimately disintegrated back into nothingness as you have already written about my son. One other way of putting it, as you have also published my son, is we will be separating the sheep from the goats. Sheep to the right and goats to the left, as my son said while he was on the earth.

Our Blessed Mother spoke to them conveying messages vital not to just for Garabandal but for all of humanity. This message lamented the lack of dissemination of the first warning and highlighted many religious leaders were leading souls to damnation and the Eucharist was being neglected.

The Virgin Mary call for repentance prayer and sacrifice, reminding of Jesus's love and His passion before seen punishment will be a direct intervention from God making it extremely dreadful. It will be more painful for innocent children to endure this punishment than to die a natural death. Before the punishment

Catholics should confess and others should repent. Even though Conchita saw the punishment alongside the Virgin Mary she felt immense fear. In His book Francisco Sanchez Ventura Ip squali quotes Conchita saying that the punishment will depend on humanity's response to the divine messages and if it were to occur it would be extremely harsh

Marie Cruz in a 2006 interview emphasized the virgin was not threatening but rather warning as a loving Mother would. Conchita stated the Blessed Virgin Mary told her Jesus does not wish to send the punishment to distress us but to help and reprimand us.

Marie Lowly one of the four said Russia was suddenly and unexpectedly going to overrun a great part of the free world. Only a few years ago when this was written Russia invaded a large country in Europe called Ukraine.

The Pope and The End of Times

In 1963 Conchita, one of the visionaries of Garabandal conveyed a message from the Our Blessed Mother Mary that echoed the prophecy of Malachi. As many of you may know this prophecy pertains to the succession of Popes in the Catholic Church. <u>Our Blessed Mother Mary revealed to Conchita the prophecy of the three popes stating after Pope John XXIII there would only be three more pontiffs before the End of Times. This is what was reported. However, people did not bother to report the very next sentence Blessed Mother Mary told Conchita which is actually there would be four popes not three. Because Mother Mary was not counting Pope John Paul I do to His very short reign.</u>

Conchita's exact words as recounted in a conversation with her mother. Her Mother asked how she knew this; Conchita said the Virgin Mary told me. When asked if this meant the end of the world, Conchita clarified the Virgin Mary spoke of the end of times, not the end of the world.

The prophecies from Blessed Mother Mary at Garabandal occurred during the pontificate of John Paul XXIII and Paul VI. After Pope John XXIII, we have had Paul VI, John Paul 1, John Paul II, Benedict XVI, and now Pope Francis. If we exclude Pope John I, given the brevity of His pontificate, we arrive at

Pope Francis as third Pope after the prophecy of three more popes before the beginning of the End of Times.

Pope Francis — March 13, 2013-

Benedict XVI — April 19, 2005-Feb. 28, 2013.

John Paul II — Oct. 16, 1978-April 2, 2005.

John Paul I — Aug. 26-Sept. ... Too short to count.

Paul VI — June 21, 1963-Aug. 6, 1978.

John XXIII — Oct. 28, 1958-June 3, 1963.

Additional Evidence from St. Malachy In The 12th Century [11]

Saint Malachy was born in 1094 at Armagh, Ireland and died on November 2, 1148. St. Malachy was canonized in 1190 by Pope Clement III. This was the first papal canonization of an Irish saint. The source of the prophecy attributed to Him is still up for debate, but the following is how it is usually related:

While in Rome in 1139 St. Malachy received a vision showing Him all the Popes from His day to the end of time. He wrote poetic descriptions of each of the pontiffs and presented the complete manuscript to Pope Innocent II, but the prophecies were forgotten in the Vatican until 1590. These mottoes in the prophecies usually refer to a family name, birthplace, a coat-of-arms, or an office held before election to the papacy.

Now considering the papal succession. This has led many to ponder could Pope Francis be the Pope of the start of the End of Times as mentioned in the prophecy and what exactly does the end of times mean? [12]

The end of times should not be confused with the end of the world. It might signify a period of momentous change in the Church or the world's, a new era of evangelization or a profound spiritual reform. The congregation for the

---

[11] https://Catholicprophecy.org/st-malachy/

[12] https://Catholicprophecy.org/st-malachy/

doctrine of the faith has never issued an official statement regarding the events of Garabandal, therefore the matter remains open both at the diocesan and Vatican levels.

Earth

She also brought warnings that are very fearful for the entire world. Mother Mary prophesized some information regarding the end of times. She said in the prophecy three popes remained and then the end of times would commence.

Most importantly what does our Blessed Mother say to us today in March 2024? As I have indicated before, your author has been supremely Blessed and gifted by our loving Almighty Father in Heaven. So that I am able to hear the words of the Trinity and our Blessed Mother Mary. The following are the words directly spoken to me from her, our Blessed Mother Mary.

Question: Dear Mother Mary, all of the reporting regarding Garabandal has been from Conchita only one of the four children in the village. I am wondering why this is and why have the other three children not said anything or what they said was just not published?

Answer: *Thank you for asking this last-minute question because it is a very good one. There are many reasons as I mentioned to you at another time that kept ever so many people that I talked to from reporting what I have said. You remember that I told you I appeared 375 times and only a handful of my apparitions were taken seriously and communicated to others of God sacred children.*

Mari Loli Mezon,

Jacinta González,

Mari Cruz González,

Maria "Conchita" Concepción.

All four of these girls were delightful and so receiving to my messages to them. in the case of the first girl on your list above she was very shy and was intimidated very easily. when Church officials came and started asking questions, she was very scared and did not want to say anything as a result. it was only much later in her life she started to talk about her experience with me.

With regards to Jacinta, she was much like Mari. Actually, all four of them were very shy. As time went on

Question: Dear Mother Mary, a number of people believe you indicated in your apparitions at Garabandal you said the Pope will travel to Moscow. Is that true or a stretch of imagination?

Mother Mary: *Oh, my dear son, thank you for wanting to clear this up because so many of the things I said get twisted in many ways. I indicated that the Pope would go to Russia, I did not ever say Moscow in particular. People tend to extend what I say beyond what I mean. This is the case in this instance. In addition to lamenting the lack of distribution of my messages I also lament the manner in which they are transmitted to others in a broken way. Thank you, dear son, ever so much for providing me the opportunity to always as you would say, "set the record straight."*

Thank you, dear Mother Mary, and please always tell me everything you want me to pass on to God sacred children, whatever it is you wish to say in the books I am writing. I love you.

Mother Mary: I love you too, my son.

Prophecy Fulfilled? Pope Goes to Russia: Garabandal Interview with Glenn Hudson

As this is written April 3, 2024, there is talk in the media about Pope Francis visiting Moscow. Whether he goes or not at this point in time is not certain. Time will tell because Russia right now is engaged in a terrible war with Ukraine.

Dr Taylor Marshall [13]

Pope Wants to Go to Moscow to Meet Putin

Glenn Hudson and Taylor Marshall

The Pope has wanted to go since 2017.

Albrecht Weber **There was a message in 1965 about Russia.**

According to Glenn Hudson, recognized expert on Garabandal.

Before the warning, miracles and the chastisement can happen. three events must happen before, there would be.

1. An important synod would take place, we have that right now.
2. Communism would return again; we can see this even within America now.
3. The Pope would go to Moscow, and as soon as he returns to the Vatican, hostilities will break out at different parts in Europe.

Mother Mary said this would not be World War III three separate times.

Only when things get absolutely terrible would God then allow the warning which many people call the illumination of conscience so people would see themselves as God sees them.

The chronology:

1. The four popes ending with Pope Francis. The 112th pope.
2. Pope Francis going to Moscow.

---

[13] Prophecy Fulfilled? Pope Goes to Russia: Garabandal Interview with Glenn Hudson (youtube.com)

https://www.youtube.com/watch?v=plJVeWnOI_M

3. Terrible hostilities will break out as soon as the pope returns to the Vatican in different parts of Europe. Things will get terribly worse than we ever imagined.

4. With Pope Francis we have now entered into the end of time or as Glenn Hudson puts it the beginning of a new era.

5. The great warning will be:

    a. There will be a suspension of time so even cars and planes will stop when time stops. Note: Yes! God does have the power to stop time. Actually, we all do live within His eternal existence.

    b. Everyone on earth will see their sins of commission and omission not just Catholics. Everyone, please remember we do not see our sins as God does and the gravity of the damage, they do to not only ourselves but others of God sacred children as well. People do not understand the impact their sins have on others of God's children. We do not understand the difference between lying and stealing for example, but we will find out during the illumination of conscience many times labeled as the warning.

    c. The chastisement which is most likely the three days of darkness that can be interpreted to be if people do not repent their sins. Other possible punishments include natural disasters resulting in awful suffering. All this is aimed to make mankind understand they will be doomed to hell if we do not change our Hearts and manner of conducting our lives.

6. This is something Glenn Hudson surmised from all His research. There will be the greatest miracle ever performed at the pine trees where Blessed Mother Mary appeared to the four children at Garabandal. These pine trees, nine of them planted by Conchita grand Father which became Mother Mary's favorite place to appear. This will be permanent and a two-stage event. It will be about 15 minutes of something happening and then it will become permanent left at Garabandal. Which will be our confirmation of what you felt during the warning which will then be obvious it came from God.

In January 1966 Conchita visited the Vatican. Met with cardinals for several hours and the Pope. Paul. After a private interview, the Pope said, "I bless you and the whole Church blesses you too."

As a final note about Garabandal

Blessed Mother Mary: *Thank you, my dear child, for making all this effort in my behalf and the sacred children of your Heavenly Father. You are the only one that is able to and has taken the time and effort to spread my most vital messages to all His children on earth. As you know dear son, I have had horrible problems spreading my message to the world forever so many reasons. You have already experienced much of that with more to come. But take Heart son because in time everything you have written as you have said will ultimately become sacred messages to God's sacred children. What you have written does indeed amplify and extend our holy Bible and all the Biblical meanings contained within it.*

Regarding my messages at Garabandal you have covered them in this section of your book very well. There is nothing really more of substance that I can add to what you have already written. I have said many other things in my prophecies in other apparitions that I know you will include. So, I will wait for those and comment also on those when you get to them.

I love you, Blessed Mother Mary

Thank you, dear Mother Mary, I will always do the absolute best I can for you, I love you.

The Catholic Church is Very Concerned About These Mother Mary's Prophecies [14]

---

[14] YouTube Video: https://www.youtube.com/watch?v=a_kiVfG5C8Q

Why The Church is Terrified About These Children's Prophecy (youtube.com)

Is the Anti-Pope or Anti-Christ Pope Francis?

Dear brothers and sisters, we are not certain about the divine origin of the events at Garabandal. We await the Church's official stance. While many aspects suggest something extraordinary might have occurred, only the Church can discern the truth of such phenomena.

My notes: At the end of the narrative by the Catholic Church regarding Garabandal, the authors get wishy-washy because they do not want to offend the current Church hierarchy. I sense fear in their conclusions using the words like "might have occurred," "something extraordinary," "many aspects" and so on. Let's face it, the Church hierarchy wants to avoid at all costs any reference to the 112th Pope being prophesies as not only the last Pope but an anti-Pope or the Anti-Christ. The political reasons are obvious.

Yet from an ontological and visual perspective it is plain to see that the female children personally witnessed divine powers upon them. And they honestly testified what they experienced and what they were told by two spiritual beings on many separate occasions. Additionally, there were many thousands of people that objectively observed the four girls in a state of ecstasy walking toward the Pines that Mother Mary appeared at.

That would be our Blessed Mother Mary and the Archangel Michael. Frankly, given the political atmosphere reigning supreme now within the highest levels of the Catholic Church, I doubt they will address any of this. Because it goes against their wishes and goals to integrate the Catholic Church into a Satanically guided one world government and one world religion.

Source: YouTube -   Garabandal After the Visions – Garabandal Warnings

Commentary: Blessed Mother Mary

Mother Speaks About Her Apparitions At Zeitoun, Egypt [15]

In this section I want to give thanks to Brian Kranick (footnoted below) for his excellent work in documenting our Blessed Mother Mary's apparitions at Zeitoun, Egypt along with the others I will document below. I found their work was so good there was not a lot I could add. Other than my personal discussions with our Blessed Mother Mary regarding adding additional light to why she chose to appear there and what were her goals in doing so.

Mother Mary Speaks to Me Personally

Mother Mary's thoughts as given to me in the month of April 2024 are indicated further down in this section of this book as in all other parts as well. As a reminder your author has been enormously Blessed by our Heavenly Father to have the ability to speak with the members of the holy Trinity and our Blessed Mother Mary. Like others of God sacred children, our Blessed Mother Mary speaks with me personally and answers my questions about her apparitions and various times in different places. I am not the only one in addition to a few others during her apparitions.

Remember, please, our Blessed Mother Mary also spoke to many people over the last hundreds of years to bring her message of love, penance, sacrifice. As well as encouraging to pray the rosary and receive the sacraments on a regular basis. Additionally, Mother Mary has stated if enough people do what I just mentioned many wars would have been avoided.

This Heavenly gift to me Jesus Christ told me was because of a conversation I had with our Almighty Father before I was born to the earth. This is true by the way, for all of you. All of us were created in the blink of an eye by our Heavenly Father in the Heavenly Kingdom unknown billions of years ago. Each of us is one-of-a-kind, unique from everyone else yet we have great commonality as well. Our Heavenly Father loved each of us so much he left a part of Himself within our spiritual being. So that when we came to earth for

---

[15] The Overlooked Marian Apparitions at Zeitoun, Egypt, Brian Kranick

the "earth test" he would be with us every instant of our lives. In this way our Father could experience every detail of our lifetime and it would be impossible for Him to not hear every prayer we have ever said. When people say God is closer than we think, they are precisely correct. You can find more detail of this particular thought in the previously published booklet titled, "God's Grand Design, Booklet I, Creation."

This apparition of our Blessed Mother Mary is very unique. Unique in the sense she never said one word to anybody during the any hundreds of times she appeared above the Coptic Church in the Zeitoun district of Cairo.

A Short History of Zeitoun

In the 1920s, a Coptic Christian named Tawfik Khalil Abraham owned some land and wanted to build a hotel there. But Mother Mary had other ideas. She appeared to Tawfik in a dream and asked Him to build a Coptic Church instead that would be in her honor. Whether he knew or not that the site of His hotel was where the holy family stayed escaping the slaughter of King Herod in Jerusalem. If he built the Church, Mother Mary promised a miracle there sometime in the future. Thus, her apparitions started in 1968.

Question: Dear Mother Mary, I think we know why you chose Zeitoun for three years of your holy apparitions. It is because this is where you and the rest of the holy family came to escape Herod's killing of innocent children. Is this true? And what else would you like others of God sacred children to know.

Answer: *Yes, my dear son, we in the holy family were there but not for all of the time before we went back to Jerusalem. We chose Zeitoun also because it is what you would call a melting pot of many different religious beliefs. Of course, Islam and Christianity are the top two. I wanted to demonstrate a message that the holy Trinity in me is for everyone no matter their beliefs. However, you have already written about the chances of different religions have in order to enter the Heavenly Kingdom. As my son told you, only 6% of Muslims make it into the Heavenly Kingdom. The ones that make it our those who remain silent in their Godly Christian beliefs. In an atmosphere of violence toward those who do not accept the impostor God* *called Allah this is the only way they can survive and be welcomed into your Father's holy kingdom.*

I wanted to project God's beautiful love to everybody and not just a few this time that I appeared. As you already described in this book, I was able to simultaneously look into the eyes of all the people and give them my blessings. And especially show them that there is far more to their existence than just the physical aspects. My appearance shows that even though I said nothing they knew I was real. Because I made it a point to move around on the top of the Coptic Church and raise my hands blessing them. They also knew I was real because the wind would move my garments around to prove I was alive and with them. I wanted very much to show all the people no matter their station in life that ultimately, they are all sacred children of their Father.

I wanted to demonstrate that the divisions that separate the people into different groups are not of God, they are only of human imagination. So many killings, deaths, and wars are the result of the human Satanic imagination. All of God's sacred children are completely equal in the eyes of their Father. Yes, they are unique as you have said many times my son. But these differences allow each of God's sacred children to express their individuality but that is based solely on their loving identity as sacred children of your Father. This is also part of the reason I did not want to say anything but just let people gaze upon me then realize they are all one Blessed family.

I was very happy to see that one man saw my teeth when I smiled. This was a great detail of my appearance that you included in this book. Yes, my dear son, I do have teeth! This is very funny to me. It is too bad that people did not have color photography because I did appear in color the way in which you always see me standing next to you dear son.

Mother Mary's Apparitions in Zeitoun Cairo, Egypt

These apparitions of our Blessed Mother Mary are very unique. Not only were her apparitions witnessed by millions, but she never said one word to anybody during the many hundreds of times she appeared above the Coptic Christian Church in the Zeitoun district of Cairo.

Zeitoun – The Many Apparitions

These apparitions of our Blessed Mother are unique. Because in that not only did, she remain silent during them, but conditions were such pictures could be taken of her, some movies taken as well actually showing her garments rustling in the wind. This is the technology that existed in the early 1960s. Later with advanced photography techniques, which allowed  manipulation of the images to reveal the facial image of our Blessed Mother as shown below. It has been enhanced to bring out the details that were not able to be seen before.

This picture has been photo enhanced with new computer technology so is to bring out details of our Blessed Mother Mary that were not available before. I find this picture to be completely fascinating considering I have spoken with Mother Mary directly on many occasions. It is only now I can see her in a great amount of detail. When she first approached me with our Lord and Savior Jesus Christ a number of years ago, I did see  her in full living color along with Jesus. However, as is the case within the spiritual realm knowing a person's identity does leave out in almost all cases their spiritual facial features. Please consider this to be a magnificent revelation of our Blessed Mother Mary.

Key Facts About Blessed Mother Mary's Apparitions

Her apparitions started in April 1968 and ended in May 1971. She would appear three or four times per month above St. Mary's Coptic Church in Zeitoun where everyone could see her. Unlike Garabandal Spain, everyone could see her as she appeared on the rooftop. She would move around and at times smile and wave to the crowds giving them her blessings. One witness got close enough to where he said he could see her teeth when she smiled.

In total, it is estimated hundreds of thousands to millions of people saw her in person. The people included Coptic's, Catholics, Protestants, was loans and even some secular Marxists. Egyptian President Abdel Nasser a Muslim also witnessed her apparition. It is thought the reason Mary appeared was because History shows Mary, Joseph, and the infant Jesus stayed there for a time. They did this to avoid Harrods slaughter of the innocence when he found out the child of God had been born in Jerusalem. The holy family fled to Egypt and Zeitoun is one of the places they stayed.

What did Mother Mary's apparitions look like?

Mother Mary's apparitions typically began as a ball of light then Eve all loving into taking on her form as our Blessed Mary. It wasn't just her image of light that occurred but also at times large numbers of luminous doves flew across the sky sometimes in the formation of a cross. It is also reported many healings happened as well. These healings included blindness, cripples, polio, cancer, and other terminal illnesses.

Mary was dressed in white and blue robes and a veil of bluish white light. Her halo was also of right light. Some of the witnesses indicated they also saw her with the infant Jesus or sometimes Jesus as 12 years old and other times with St. Joseph as well. Additionally, she was at times seen carrying a cross or in an olive branch which is a plea for peace and unity. A Coptic priest is credited with saying beautiful rays of light came down from her hands like depicted in the miraculous metal.

One extremely interesting observation reported by Coptic Bishop Marcos said when Mother Mary looked at the crowd, it was as if she was simultaneously concentrating her eyes on each person in the crowd separately. It was as if she was concentrating on each person and looking at each person separately and individually. Needless to say, her apparitions also resulted in spiritual conversions of Muslims and others to Christianity.

The Vatican response about Zeitoun:

The Vatican even after three years of Marian apparitions refused to make an official statement regarding Zeitoun. I have no idea why the Vatican would turn its back on this and instead said the deferred this whole episode to the Coptic Orthodox Church. Appropriately, the Coptic Church did investigate the matter and determined it was an authentic and true phenomenon. Not only that, but the civil government also concluded something very real was happening. The local civil authorities went so far in their investigation they cut off all electric power in a radius of 15 miles from the Coptic Church where Mother Mary was appearing. This was to eliminate the possibility somehow a projector was being used to create her image. They found no projectors could possibly be used and when they shut off the power of our Blessed Mother Mary, her image remained as bright as ever.

The Catholic Church in my view has a very irritating tendency of turning their back on legitimate holy spiritual phenomenon. In the case of Garabandal for example in spite of all the wonderful evidence of Mother Mary's apparitions, the Catholic Church in the Vatican refused to acknowledge it. It is your author's opinion the reason for this is part of the prophecies from Mother Mary involve the 112th Pope being the last pope and very likely the Anti-Christ. The Vatican magisterium that is more and more promoting Satanically inspired political judgments in the form of pronouncements for all. Catholics worldwide are afraid whatever Blessed Mother Mary said in her apparitions makes them all look bad. Well, they are! Not all of them but enough.

If we examine Pope Francis and what he has been doing it is fair to say he is secularizing our beloved Catholic Church into blessings all sorts of condemned behavior as taught by Biblical scripture. A detailed discussion of this can be found in another section of this Book.

6

The Catholic Church Is No Longer What You Think It Is

The rest of this book is dedicated to the absolute truth of the Catholic Church and the way it exists on earth today. When I was a little boy, I went to Saint Tarcisius elementary school in Chicago IL. It was run by a bunch of German nuns back in the early 1950s right after World War 2. These German nuns were just plain cruel to us kids. They wore huge black garments with black hoods on their heads and large rosary beads around their waists and every time they would walk down the hall they would click and clack all the way. They could never sneak up on us kids as we all could hear them coming.

In each classroom there were between 60 and 70 of us kids all of which were the firstborn of our armed forces that beat the hell out of the German army. So, it is not surprising these women were seeking revenge against the kids of our armed forces that won World War 2 and completely destroyed Germany, their homeland. They basically taught us to hate religion, Especially Catholicism. However, over the years when it came time for my kids to go to school, I chose a Catholic education for them. All the way from first grade through graduation at Santa Clara University, a Jesuit school.

Why would I do that? Because I went through the public school system, and it stunk with all sorts of bullies and other BS going on no matter where you looked. Also, the Catholic education system changed greatly in the intervening years and the Catholic sisters we're far nicer and very constructive and caring about the kids. My kids all got taught fundamental Christianity and Catholicism which is a very good thing.

However, that is no longer the case in the Catholic Church or Catholic schools. Additionally, there have been awful infiltration of Satan into the Vatican, and I will get into that in this next section that I never thought I would write. But what I'm going to tell you as painful as it is, it is completely true, and it has to do with the End of Times. Everyone already knows about the sexual predator priests and the cover-ups by the Vatican. Actually, that is part of the End of Times prophecies. What I'm going to talk about is far different than that and in many ways worse.

And the remaining part of this book we will go through how Satan has infiltrated the Vatican and as a result has gravely affected all Vatican activities which I will show you with pictures. This will serve as a foundational essay for us to examine Mother Mary's apparitions, her all-important apparitions at Fatima Portugal in 1917. You will see our Satanically infiltrated Vatican is doing everything to hide the truth of what Blessed Mother Mary said at Fatima Portugal regarding the End of Times which we are already living in. The End of Times started in the early 1960s with the presidency of Lyndon Baines Johnson, one of the most crooked and dishonest human beings ever to walk the face of the earth.

The Dishonest and Satanic Catholic Church

The Consecration of Russia to The Immaculate Heart of Blessed Mother Mary

The very first and most important item regarding the third secret of Fatima is Blessed Mother Mary's request to have Russia properly consecrated to the Immaculate Heart of our Blessed Mother Mary. As of the date this is written May 29, 2024, Russia has yet to be consecrated to the Immaculate Heart of Blessed Mother Mary. Pope Francis said he did it.

NO! POPE FRANCIS IS A LIAR!

Pope Francis pretended to perform the consecration with the words he used were completely wrong on purpose. This is what he should have said. He is the Pope. He knows full well what the proper words are to say. But not only did he purposely choose NOT to say those words but doing so would have prevented the on-going war between Russia and Ukraine. Millions of innocent people have been killed because of Pope Francis. Get the connection yet? For me, your humble Anointed Messenger of our Heavenly Father, it seems Pope Francis wanted this war. What other explanation is there? If he only said these words, there would have been no war.

Additionally, Pope Francis lied big time by declaring there is no third secret of Fatima! A major portion of the remaining parts of this book presents the "exact words of our Blessed Mother Mary in detail all about the third secret Pope Francis now says does not exist!"

Question: What was it Pope John II was exactly supposed to say when he had the opportunity to consecrate Russia to your Immaculate Heart in 1962?

Answer: *It was really only one sentence among the many that he said during the mass that he celebrated. Instead of just referring to "and all others" which very indirectly includes Russia, he should have said in very plain terms,*

<u>*"I Also Consecrate Russia To The Immaculate Heart Of Our Blessed Mother Mary."*</u>

It would have been that simple my dear son but yes, he was under a lot of pressure not to do so from people who were ill-willed due to political reasons.

Question: On another note, dear Mother Mary, I read one article recently that indicated Pope Francis will read the third secret of Fatima and consecrate Russia to your Immaculate Heart. I don't want to be a cynic, but I do not personally believe any of this will happen. I would love to hear what it is you want the world to know regarding your comments.

Answer: *Almighty dear son, Jesus was right when he told me your questions can be very penetrating, direct and to the point. Thank you for that. Pope Francis will not read the third secret of Fatima. Because, as you my son already know, it makes the Church not only look bad but also it reveals the sinister forces that are already in the Vatican. I believe that is the last thing he would ever contemplate doing.*

The chances are not good that Pope Francis will consecrate Russia to my Sacred Heart. That will set into motion the wonderful expansion of Christian beliefs within the Russian people. However, because this declaration has come so late it will not be in a strong enough force to avoid the coming wars regarding Russia and others against the Western Christian world. *__Had Pope John II said the consecration for Russia, we would not have the warlike situation we have today.__*

In general, people to this day do not at all understand the loving significance of our Blessed Mother Mary's Immaculate Heart. This second secret refers directly to the devotion to the Immaculate Heart of our Blessed Mother Mary. Consecration to the Immaculate Heart of Mother Mary has the power to alter History and prevent future wars.

Note: The Immaculate heart of our Blessed Mother Mary is no fairy tale! It has real and vast power behind it for the good of all of God's sacred children on earth. For example, Jorge had Cardinal Bergoglio deliver the one powerful sentence to consecrate Russia to the Immaculate heart of our Blessed Mother Mary, Russia would not have invaded Ukraine. Countless hundreds of thousands of innocent people would be alive today conducting their personal productive lives. Pope Francis did not do that and is lying when he said he did. Pope Francis has blood on his hands.

Question: I am wondering what is the blessing or how once for example Russia is consecrated to your Immaculate heart, spiritually speaking how does that directly affect God's sacred children living in Russia? I envision something like a cloud of Heavenly grace will descend upon the Russian people. And will result in their turning away from whatever is bad and turning them toward Biblical teachings and behaving according to the three summary rules I published in my previous book. Am I anywhere close to your Immaculate heart spreads to the people?

Answer: *Wow, my dear son! That is a monumentally detailed question, and it shows your insatiable thirst for Godly knowledge. Additionally, the manner and which you surmised the mechanism of my Immaculate heart is remarkably close to what actually happens in real life.*

If Pope Francis actually uttered the sentence that you have put in this book twice, that would release a huge number of Heavenly Blessings. Godly Blessings that pour out from our Heavenly Father and into the people that the consecration is meant for. It is enormous holy energy that comes from Heaven and enters into the spiritual hearts of the people. This is even true for those who are disbelievers and high up in the political structure of a particular country. For example, if that criminal Pope Francis did what he said he did. That would trigger the release of monumental proportion of loving energy into the hearts of the communist leaders of Russia including Vladimir Putin himself. Along with everyone in government everyone in the army and so forth. All of these people would start to question what the heck are we doing? They would start to seriously question what they have done and what they are doing to destroy God's sacred children. Many of them would respond and they would leave the battlefield and go home.

Satan would be defeated resoundingly. The same thing would occur on Ukraine side of the war equation. But <u>my dear son as you know it is Satan that controls Pope Francis</u>. It is the command from Satan to the Pope "do not declare the consecration of Russia and the Ukraine to my Sacred Heart" because Satan knows that would end the war. And Satan wants to destroy every single one of God's sacred children so the war must go on. And the Pope has the power to stop it, but he refused. He faked the consecration and then told falsehoods about it.

Question: Are there any other people on this planet that has the power to bestow and consecrate the Pope to your Immaculate heart? Why do we have to be limited by this Satanic Pope? Let's just bypass him since many people think he is really not the Pope due to his falsehoods regarding his internal beliefs of Christianity as your Son and my savior Jesus Christ established it. I know you know what I am thinking.

Answer: *Wow, my dearest of sons! I again am amazed and your dedication for the world and the love of all mighty God and his creations. I wish I could say it is all that easy but to consecrate a country or someone the person doing that must have position power within the physical realm. <u>In the case of consecrating Russia, one has to be in the Direct Line of popes that traces back to Saint Peter when my son canonized him as the first Pope.</u>*

Comment: Well, I figured the restriction might be something just like what you said. When I was in Civil Air Patrol an auxiliary of the United States Air Force, rank was everything. It did not matter how competent or good the person was if he had the appropriate rank that's all that is needed.

I had this theoretical thought cross my mind. What if the power of consecration could be given to priests. They could consecrate everybody, and the holy power of love would descend down and into the hearts of people. What a wonderful way to eliminate sin. Yes, dear Blessed Mother, I know this is fanciful, but it was just a thought.

Answer: *Although your thought may be fanciful it is an absolutely beautiful thought and I thank you for that.*

A Spiritual Truism That Is REAL and POWERFUL:

Question: Most Christians view prayers as a religious duty that has some unknown but positive effect on what they're praying about. Prayers could be about almost anything and are ALWAYS very welcome by not only the Holy Trinity but also our Blessed Mother Mary. Above we came to understand the enormous power of the consecration to Mother Mary's Immaculate Heart. With this being said, I would like to explore the power and positive effects on our Father's sacred children in their lives. Is this out of bounds dear Mother?

Answer: *Oh, my dearest son I just love the intensity, dedication, and love that you show others of God's sacred children on earth. This is a question that I know many devout Catholics and Christians have in the back of their minds. So, with that I very much love to answer this.*

Using the example of consecrating Russia to my Immaculate heart generally speaking the same thing happens on a personal prayer basis but at a reduced level. This is because instead of having many millions of people being the recipients of God's loving energy that will flow into their hearts. As sacred graces come the same thing really does happen when a person prays. There is never, I want to emphasize this there is never a case where prayers go unheard. As you have written in your previous book titled God's grand design of all creation for your redemption, it is impossible for the Trinity not to hear the slightest prayer. Or the biggest prayer from anyone of your Father's sacred children. As you outlined and your previous book, God so loves each of his children that he left part of himself within each of his sacred children. When each of them was created within the heavenly Kingdom many billions of years ago.

Your heavenly Father always knows exactly what is best for each sacred child and when a prayer is said, it will certainly be answered 100% of the time. But since your Father can see across all aspects of time, he will tune his response so that the most benefit will be given to each separate child.

This is different than consecrating an entire country. Because there are so many different people that personalizing responses is something that will not work but certainly works on an individual basis when individual prayers are being said to the Trinity. Also, when prayers with the heart that is true to Almighty God, that certainly strengthens the relationship between our heavenly Father and the sacred child that said the prayer.

As you said above, all prayers are real and powerful. Thank you for asking this wonderful question that does indeed impact every one of your Father's sacred children.

I love you my dear child.

The Aftermath of The Popes Refusal to Release The Third Fatima Secret and Not Consecrate Russia

The spiritual punishments apparently started shortly after 1960 because of the holy Father s refusal to release Fatima's third secret and to consecrate Russia to the Immaculate Heart of our Blessed Mother Mary. (Authors note: Just how stupid can a Pope be? Unless he has a hidden agenda)

1. Father Malachi Martin said "many cardinals, bishops and priests are falling like leaves into hell.
2. Faith disappears in several countries and continents.
3. Many of the elect will lose their faith.
4. Things will get so bad that if our Lady does not intervene no one will be saved.
5. God will withdraw His grace.

6. Father Malachi told Art Bishop apostasy in the Church was the background or context of the third secret.

7. if our Lady's orders are not obeyed spiritual punishment would result.

8. God withdrawing His grace is a painful thing for Him because to Him it's like sabotaging His own sacred will that, "all men be saved and come to the full knowledge of the truth."

9. Satan will now gain power in the upper echelons of the Church; Satan wants to gain power even in the highest echelons of the Church.

10. the last Pope will be under the control of Satan. Now Pope Francis is the 112th Pope which has been prophesies to be the last Pope. Additionally, when you examine our Pope's goals in the Vatican it fundamentally is toward creating a secularized Catholic faith. More on that later.

11. Father Malachi Martin agreed the last Pope will be under the control of Satan.

12. Tribulations will follow.

There is a prophecy Satan can invade the Citadel or also known as the Vatican. They will have power for one thousand years. Then our bill asked, "how close are they/" Malachi Martin responded, "very close, frighteningly close."

Then Art Bell asked, "how will we know and how will you know when Satan takes over and the 1000 years begins?"

We will know this by a series of facts which amount to the following: [16]

1. The basic tenants, beliefs of Christianity will be played down to zero.

---

[16] The Decline and Fall of The Roman Church, Fr. Malichi Martin

2. And will matter no longer in normal society and nations.

3. For those who are supposed to be the custodians and supposed to be the administrators of the word and distributors of His grace have stopped all that.

4. It will talk down to secular terms and rather overnight as far as I can see.

5. Then it will suddenly dawn on people, hey, this St. has gone completely awry.

6. The Third Secret provides for "a punishment of a spiritual nature." "Apostasy in the Church forms the background or context of the Third Secret. Apostasy now begins. But the punishment envisaged for the Secret is very real, physical punishment is, and they are terrible!" "Just kill a billion people"

This was the exchange between Father Malachi Martin and Art Bell.

Also, according to this website, which I thoroughly recommend titled "return to tradition.org" it used to be the Church in working with governments, there would be cooperation. Where the governments would try to back up the morality of Christianity in secular society by their governance. This is no longer the case, and it can be horrifically demonstrated in the United States of America through the Democrat party and their anti-Christian policies. More on this in another section of this book.

Malachi Martin speaks at an event called "Paranormal Continuum":

1. Everything is becoming integrated today, morals, and ethics today of individual communities and groups and ethics have become completely degraded into materialistic secular terms and hedonistic aims.

2. That is the reign of evil. In directly contravention to the will of God who is the sovereign master and creator of all things.

3. Evil is more organized, more integrated worldwide which comes out as the deification of man,

Evidence of this secular perversion includes:

1. The expansion of the sacraments to give access to the sacraments to those who are unrepentant sinners without calling them to conversion.

2. Blessings of James Martin type and those in irregular situations that contravene Church law.

3. The open debate on changing the Churches morality and teachings on moral issues, all of it is happening within this backdrop.

4. These are some of the clearest signs of the Church increasingly under the influence of Satan.

5. The mockery of the faith being conducted in sports stadiums.

6. Also, Catholics in the Western world are not caring or agreeing with the liberalization and progressiveness that is being developed within the Catholic Church.

7. Heresies pushed by Rome, now most Catholics just shrug.

Mother Mary stated that WW I would end, followed by another world war during the reign of Pope Pius XI (Pope till 1939). The world situation was rapidly crumbling toward war during the reign of Pope Pius XI. WWII began in September 1939. This second war would come if people continued offending our Heavenly Father and if Russia is not consecrated and does not convert to Christianity. Remember our Blessed Mother Mary said this in 1917. This second secret specifically requests Russia be consecrated to the Immaculate Heart of Mary.

Pope Francis was on elected March 13, 2013, but he did not consecrate Russia and Ukraine to the Immaculate Heart of Blessed Mother Mary. That was nine years into His pontificate. Sadly, on February 24, 2022, Russia invaded Ukraine. This invasion is seen as an escalation of the Russo-Ukrainian war that started in 2014. [17]

---

[17] Dates from Wikipedia

Richard Ferguson

As a Catholic Christian, I cannot help wondering if this horrible war that has taken hundreds of thousands of innocent lives would not have happened. If Pope Francis acted years earlier as our Blessed Mother Mary asked.

7

The Anti-Christ Is Now in The Vatican.

The Catholic Church Is Turning Against Its Own Teachings. 18

Here is just one manifestation of the prophecies of our Blessed Mother Mary. Back in 1917 at Fatima exactly what you are reading now is what was prophesized an exceptionally long time ago. Cardinal Sarah (shown Here) has been accusing the Catholic Church and its leadership of being complicit towards fluid and practical atheism within the Church.[19]

We pretend to be Catholics but in fact we behave and believe as pagans and unbelievers. He has denounced western atheistic bishops and leaders that prefer the world over the cross.

Women priests, deaconesses, homosexuality, same-gender marriages are now becoming increasingly rampant within the Church. The very church our Lord and savior Jesus Christ founded. The occurrence of these kinds of disgusting events has indeed been prophesized by more than just our Blessed Mother Mary. This is something that was told about in 1917 during one of her six apparitions in Fatima Portugal.

During the week of April 20th, 2024, a German Bishop ordained thirteen deaconesses. He made a big deal about this and even passed out certificates of some kind to make it all with its pomp and circumstance feel like a real ordination. Personally, I am certain these new deaconesses are certainly not.

---

[18] https://Catholicherald.co.uk/cardinal-sarah-denounces-atheistic-western-bishops-who-prefer-the-world-to-the-cross/

[19] Joe McLean, A Catholic Take – A Radio Program

Makes everybody feel good that believes in apostasy, but these women are not legitimate in any way shape or form. Call this blasphemy or apostasy or any other anti-Church label and it is happening in openness within the Catholic Church.

The German Catholic Church is also in favor of women priests and homosexuality. Cardinal Parolin says all the blasphemous changes Pope Francis wants to make within the Church must be permanent where there is no possibility of it being rescinded, no reversals or reforms. Father Malachi Martin has said the identical thing and has added there are even Satanic rituals being performed within the Vatican. Before you reject this thought, all of this has been foretold by our Blessed Mother Mary during her apparitions at Fatima.

I will reveal no names, for their protection. But think about that for a while and put yourself in the shoes of an honest priest in the Priestly community. Just how hard must it be to live with the priests that have sex with teenage children and with other priests within the Church. How can they possibly keep their mouth shut? Because if they open their mouths and reveal the Satanist activities within the Catholic Church, they will have no support for their lives like food shelter and clothing.

'The former prefect of the Vatican's Congregation for Divine Worship and the Sacraments said so many bishops desired to be "loved by the world" they've forgotten Christianity calls them to be "signs of contradiction."

The 78-year-old cardinal also repeated His criticism of Fiducia Supplicans, the Vatican document that provides for the blessings of couples involved in same-sex unions. Insisting it is not just traditional African culture but Catholic teaching itself which makes the document unacceptable.' "Many Western prelates are tetanized [paralyzed] by the idea of opposing the world," the cardinal said. "They dream of being loved by the world; they've lost the desire to be a sign of contradiction." [20]

Father Malachi Martin said "many cardinals, bishops and priests are falling like leaves into hell. He went on to say Satan is not already inside the Vatican but exerts heavy influence as well. [21] The Father should know very well what goes on in the Vatican.

Evidence Pope Francis is obsessed with Satan has become more obvious in recent times. Even liberal news outlet CNN has noticed his fascination with Satan. There is very good reason for his interest you will be shocked by later on in this book.

CNN [22]

Pope Francis seems to be obsessed with the devil.

His tweets and homilies about the devil, Satan, the Accuser, the Evil One, the Father of lies, the Ancient Serpent, the Tempter, the Seducer, the Great Dragon, the Enemy and just plain "demon" are legion.

For Francis, the devil is not a myth, but a real person. Many modern people may greet the Pope's insistence on the devil with a dismissive, cultural affectation, indifference, or at the most indulgent curiosity.

Yet Francis refers to the devil continually. He does not believe him to be a myth, but a real person, the most insidious enemy of the Church. Several of my theologian colleagues have said he has gone a bit overboard with the devil

---

[20] Cardinal Sarah denounces 'atheistic' Western bishops who prefer the world to the cross - Catholic Herald

[21] Malachi Martin: The Enthronement Of Lucifer In The Vatican (youtube.com)

[22] Why is Pope Francis so obsessed with the devil? | CNN

and hell! We may be tempted to ask, why in the devil is Pope Francis so involved with the prince of demons?

Malachi Martin: End Of Times - The Enthronement of Lucifer in The Vatican [23]

Father Malachi Martin authored a book called Windswept House. Published in 1996 three years before Father martin passed away. This book is labeled "Faction" why? Because however it does contain actual information regarding the End of Times and the actions of Satan in this world. He sprinkles some fictional information in this book like the dates of something or somebody's name and so on. Please realize Father Martins sole purpose in authoring his book is to describe what the third secret of Fatima says. Father Martin does not have the supreme advantage I do in that I can just ask Mother Mary. Which I certainly will later on time wise when I gather my thoughts on what I should ask her about this horrific enthronement of Lucifer inside the Vatican.

Remember, this event was prophesized many hundreds of years earlier by multiple people. This book is an exceptionally good chronicle of the Satanic events that took place inside the Vatican. This is the way Father Martin chose to circumvent the ironclad oath he was forced to take regarding the third secret of Fatima. He embedded facts about what was said from our Blessed Mother Mary at Fatima into various parts of the fictional novel he wrote. This man was no dummy.

"In an interview, Father Martin said the following text from the book listed above is factual based on actual events. "Whosoever, by means of this inner Chapel, be designated and chosen as the final in the line successor in the petrine office, shall by His oath of office commit himself. And all he does command to be the willing instrument and collaborator with the builders of man's home on earth and throughout man's cosmos. He shall transform the ancient enmity into friendship, tolerance, and assimilation as these are a

---

falsehood to the models of birth, education, work, finance, commerce, industry, learning, culture, living and giving life, dying and death. *So shall the coming age of man be modeled*."

The above oath centers only on man and earth. God is nowhere in the picture. This is what you would expect from Satan Himself and creating disastrous nice sounding words. I will also tell you this as a secondary thought. Every word that is pledged above is Satanic and also is used frequently by the Democrat party in the United States of America. If you are a Democrat, you are not a Christian rather you are following the precepts of this Satanic pledge.

Also look at the above vocabulary and terms like man's cosmos. That is diametrically opposed to all Biblical literature. I could go on, but I would end up writing an encyclopedia. Also please notice these nicey-nice words are used by Pope Francis today. He does not use Apostolic terminology and thoughts. Back to the issue at hand which is Satan inside the Vatican. Father Brian Harrison knew Father Malachi Martin. Father Harrison said the following:

"I can clarify what Father Martin said was the true date of the Luciferian enthronement inside the Vatican with the following information from 1/4 century ago I have never made public until now. In the last decade of Malachi Martins life, I became a personal friend of His and would visit Him in His Manhattan apartment whenever I was in New York. In the section headed "1963" in the prologue of Windswept House, we read this shocking ceremony enthroned "the fallen Angel Lucifer". It happened in the Chapel of Saint Paul on June 29, 1963, the feast of Saints Peter and Paul, the eve of the coronation of the newly elevated Pope Paul VI."

It is celebrated gloatingly the long prepared for arrival of a Pope more open to modernist changes than any of His predecessors. Around the time the book was published in 1996, Father Martin told me this date was indeed factional. (Meaning it is Historically correct), and the true date of this blasphemous act of devilry, coordinated with a corresponding ceremony on the American side of the Atlantic, come was actually one day later. That is, it took place the night after Saint Paul's VI coronation in Saint Peters square on the afternoon of

111

Sunday, June 30. Malachi told me it was indeed carried out in the Chapel of Saint Paul, as the book windswept house says, and it began at midnight on the night of June 30 / July 1, 1963.

"Father Malachi Martin goes on to say the following. "Pope John Paul II came up against the irremovable presence of a malign strength in His own Vatican and in certain bishops' chanceries. It is what knowledgeable Churchmen call the 'super force." Rumors are always difficult to verify, tide its installation to the beginning of Pope Paul VI's reign in 1963. Indeed, Paul alluded somberly to the "the smoke of Satan which has entered the sanctuary" and oblique reference to an enthronement ceremony by (the followers of the devil) inside the Vatican." [24]

Father Martin certainly is not the only high-ranking priest within the Catholic Church to resist the onslaught of Satan. The late exorcist Father Amourth provided keen insight into the status of Satan within the Vatican. The following is an excerpt from an interview with Father Amourth: [25]

Question: Father, you write of dialogues you have had with Satan. Have you ever seen Him?

Answer: He responded by saying, Satan is pure spirit. He often appears as something else to mislead. He appeared to Padre Pio as Jesus, to frighten Him. He sometimes appears as a raging animal…

Question: You have said publicly you believe, referring to the current Church scandals, Satan is in the Vatican. Do you still believe this?"

Answer: Today Satan rules the world. The masses no longer believe in God. And yes, Satan is in the Vatican.

---

[24] https://www.youtube.com/watch?v=MD2XKN4wRKk

[25] https://www.youtube.com/watch?v=MD2XKN4wRKk

Pope Francis, A Modern Day Satanic Theological Tyrant [26]
April 26th, 2024

Everything you will read in the next couple of pages is from CNA, the Catholic News Agency on April 26th, 2024.

Tyrants and dishonest politicians always start out their quest for conquering a people by using really good sounding language that is ambiguous enough to where people hear what it is they want to hear. Dictators love to appear as if they are bringing high-class thought processes to the masses that will solve all their problems. And as the worst president in U.S. History Barack Obama said we must bring, change, and change for the sake of change." We must bring equity. If you work half as hard you still get full pay. Remember equity means equal outcome, not equal opportunity.

Does anybody really know what that meant? No. But what that brought was horrific racial separations and hatred between the races and phrases like white supremacy was born out of that nice sounding word change. The term white supremacy is a horrific and Satanic way of pitting one group of God's sacred children against another group. In other words, it fosters hatred which is exactly a characteristic of Satan Himself and all of His followers.

The word equity sounds good. But what it means is that no matter whether you try hard and work hard or not in school you will get the same grade as everyone else. If you are naturally good in math, let's say, the Democrats will say you got that talent unfairly so all other students must be graded easier that you to make up the different. Democrats goal is EVERYBODY MUST BE IDENTICAL NO MATTER HOW HARD THEY WORK OR NOW! This is exactly the Communist manifesto. Hard work or effort is no longer rewarded. In school the lunkhead sitting next to you sitting on his fingers will get the same grade you got. Equity means equal result not equal opportunity.

---

[26] https://www.Catholicnewsagency.com/news/255887/pope-francis-calls-for-paradigm-shift-in-theology-for-world-of-today

Work very hard but get the same as someone who did not. Ideas like this destroy cultures and nations.

God granted each separate sacred child a unique set of talents to be used while on earth. Everyone IS different. Equality and equity are designed to destroy our Heavenly Father's plan for us.

Question: Dear Blessed Mother Mary, is there anything else you feel necessary to add?

Answer: *Yes, I do dear son. Satan is nefarious in his plan for destroying your Father's sacred children. The disgusting Democrat plan being to make everyone the same brings unseen horrors with it. For those children in school that do not apply themselves are lazy. And do not try to learn their school lessons, they will get the idea that society owes them just because they are who they are. They will think that they are entitled to anything they want just because they want it. Gone is the linkage between effort and reward. This breads resentment and hatred.*

For those who do work hard only to see their efforts taken away from themselves will stop working hard and this brings down the living standards in a culture or society. So, you end up with less goods and services with a load of people who feel entitled to all that without working for it.

This can only be a breeding ground for chaos, hatred, confusion, and people at each other's throats. Our country will be like Cuba where everybody shares starvation equally. This Democrat plan is pure Satan my dear son.

Pope Francis wants to destroy the Church and Catholicism.

Remember my dear sacred children of God come, cardinal Bergoglio came from Argentina a very socialist / communist country. Pope Francis is doing pretty much the same damn thing. On Thursday April 11, 2024, the Catholic News agency reported this headline: Pope Francis calls for a" paradigm shift" in the apology for the world of today". Does anybody care to take a guess at what that means? What Hitler and Mussolini said right before

World War II sounded really good to the people. What they got was huge amounts of death and destruction. I put Pope Francis in the same category.

President Barack Obama did the same thing running for president. His slogan was, "hope and change." What we got instead was identity politics and hateful rhetoric like white people are evil because they have "white privilege." Never mind white privilege does not exist. If you disbelieve me go out on the streets and ask random people what is the definition of white privilege? They will not know the answer and we will fumble around trying to think of something. It is this type of situation that is born right out of Satan's playbook.

One other thing dear sacred child of God, <u>our Blessed Mother Mary herself told me personally Pope Francis is indeed the Anti-Christ</u>. I repeat, **Pope Francis is the Anti-Christ**. He is under control of Satan. [27]

Pope Francis Wants to Combine Our Beloved Catholic Church With Many Other Religions Such as Islam, Buddhism etc.

1. To do this he calls for 'paradigm shift' in Catholic theology for the world of today. He will use ambiguous fancy words like paradigm to hide the true meanings and his intentions. [28]

2. Pope Francis is calling for a paradigm shift where Catholic theology takes a broader widespread view of engagement with the world that includes contemporary science, modern culture throughout the earth, and people's lived experiences.

(I bet you do not know the definition of these words that will end up controlling your life)

3. A new document titled Ad Theologian Comes from the Pontifical Academy of Theology. This "theology can only develop in a culture of dialogue and encounter between different traditions and different knowledge, between different Christian confessions and <u>different</u>

---

[27] <u>Antipope Francis' Notable Heresies and Apostasy (May 2019) (vaticanCatholic.com)</u>'

[28] https://www.Catholicnewsagency.com/news/255887/pope-francis-calls-for-paradigm-shift-in-theology-for-world-of-today

religions openly engaging with everyone, believers and nonbelievers.","
The Pope wrote in the Apostolic letter. (Author's note: This picture is what the Pope's nice words mean in real life. Looks like Sodom & Gomorrah to me.) [29] [30] (Author's note: This means we are to invite atheists to mass and change our mass to "suit their needs" BS!

4. We have the need to deal with" profound cultural transformations."

5. Revises the statutes of the Pontifical Academy of Theology (PATH) "to make them more suitable for the mission our time imposes on theology.

6. Theology only develops in a culture of dialogue and encounter between different traditions and knowledge, between different Christian confessions and religions, openly engaging with everyone, believers, and nonbelievers," the pope wrote in the apostolic letter.

7. Pope Francis wrote Catholic theology must experience a" courageous cultural revolution." In order to become a fundamentally contextual theology" guided by Christo's incarnation into time and space.

8. This approach to theology must be capable of reading and interpreting" the gospel in the conditions in which men and women live daily, in different geographical social and cultural environments."

9. Our Pope contrasts this approach with the current theology that has lasted for 2000 years by the way to abstractly repropose formulas and schemes from the past and repeated long-standing criticism of "deskbound theology." (In other words, "out with the old and in with the new, whatever that might be."

---

[29] Pope participates in circus act during general audience - YouTube Note: This picture is exactly what our Blessed Mother Mary meant when she said the following when Pope said that the anti-Christ is now on earth. "He should know. He IS the anti-Christ." Can you picture Jesus Christ behaving like what this picture shows? Of course NOT!

[30] https://YouTube/wiJGPRHkjgI

10. Pope Francis emphasized theological studies must be open to the world.

11. Pope Francis emphasizes this bottoms-up re-envisioning of theology is necessary to better aid the Churches evangelizing image.

12. Pope Francis went on to say the new theological studies must be open to the world not as a tactical attitude but as a profound turning point which must be "inductive." (This phrase is much like what Barack Obama said running for president when he keeps repeating "hope and change!" What we got was "identity politics" that still to this day rips apart racial relationships in our country! Many words sound good right up until you understand what they really mean.

13. The new Catholicism must become transdisciplinary, part of a web of relationships. First of all, with other disciplines and other knowledge. The Pope said this engagement leads to the arduous task of theologians making use of "new categories developed by other knowledge."

14. Pope Francis wrote priority must be given to the" knowledge of people's common sense." Which he described as a" theological source in which many images of God live come often not corresponding to the Christian face of God, only and always love."

15. the Pope said His pastoral stamp must be placed upon all Catholic theology described as "popular theology."

16. Pope Francis being a heretic.

17. Introduced a Pagan God as a substitute for Blessed Mother Mary. He placed Pachamama idols in various places throughout the Vatican and they wound up and various cathedrals around the world as well. Pachamama is a Peruvian Inca/Indies earth Goddess and is as Pagan as you can get. It is called idolatry promoted by Pope Francis.

18. There are many more examples of Pope Francis being nothing more than a Pagan God witch doctor.

Question: First, did you notice anything strange in the previous eighteen points? You should have! The above text is taken straight from Christian

News Agency with an article written by Jonathan Told last year in November 2023. Are you sure you did not notice anything missing from all these wonderful nicey-nice words and goals regarding the entire Catholic Church?

Answer: *The name of Almighty God is missing.* It is completely absent. This is not an accident or an oversight. It is on purpose. Leaving God out of all of these theological changes the Pope wants to make certainly without a shadow of a doubt points toward the direction he wants to take the Catholic Church. Simply put, Pope Francis wants to have a Church that looks like a Church, but it is not a Church.

19. He wants to have celebrations like mass but not be mass. In other words, he wants a completely false Church that is worth absolutely nothing. It will be a fake Church a Church with no substance come with no Almighty Father in Heaven, with no Lord and savior Jesus Christ and without anything else that is right and good. This has been Satan's goal for an exceedingly long time. Ever since Satan saw the throne of our Almighty Father he wanted to sit in that throne. Because he felt he was better than our Heavenly Father and deserved to be there more than anything else.

As our Heavenly Father s Anointed Messenger, I have had occasion to be attacked by Satan on three separate occasions back when I was in my thirties. Satan hates me so bad it goes beyond any kind of description with any kind of language used by the human race. I outlined my encounters with Him on three separate occasions in a different part of this book.

20. Skeletonized Dead Jesus and The Papal Anti-Christ Pope Snake

I wish the picture shown below was some kind of fake or something. The horrifying truth is the picture with Pope Benedict sitting in the middle is real. Obviously, the artist whoever that Satanist is wanted to depict not the tree of life but the tree of death. Featured in the geographic center is a disgusting depiction of our Lord and savior Jesus Christ in the form of skin and bones. The artist depicted the head of Jesus as half human and half reptile if you look close enough. Additionally, you will see strange what looks like skeletal little children climbing around the dead tree.

God's Grand Design: Blessed Mother Mary Directly Speaks

To the right of the skeletal Jesus, you will see a spinal cord jutting out from behind Jesus. And then in all his glory is Pope Benedict. What in the hell is going on in the Vatican to have this within one hundred miles of Rome, much less on earth and inside the Vatican on an invitation basis no less! There is no getting around the fact it is this kind of Satanic debauchery is floating around the Vatican these days. I am surprised the Pope and others like him in the Vatican have been as successful as they are in keeping their horns from poking out of their heads. The Vatican desperately needs a colossal theological enema! That starts at the TOP!

The symbolism of the above picture is multi-dimensional and demonic from top to bottom. It has Satan written all over it. You see Christ with half his head looking like an alligator. Next to that you see a stylized human spine. All the limbs of the tree are dead. There are caricatures of small children around. There is another crocodile in the mix. They purposely chose the lowest forms of life on earth and set them beside the highest form of life, our lord and savior Jesus Christ. All of this was done on purpose with malice and forethought aimed directly at our beloved Catholic Church

If the tree of death wasn't bad enough the welcoming hall for guests is shaped like a snake inside and out. Remember everything rotten that happened to the human race had its source as a vile dishonest snake that approached Eve in the garden of Eden. Our Heavenly Father told me personally this is TRUE! Yes! I heard His voice and that is exactly what He said to me!

21. Our Pope wants to honor the Satanic snake. To me, this is absolute proof Anti-Christ Pope Francis it is exactly that, a Satanic Anti-Christ Pope.

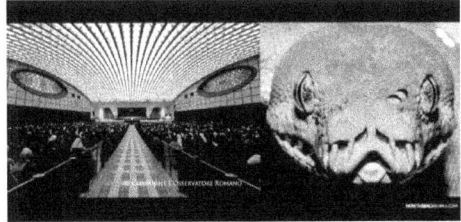

I know you don't want to believe this. And I didn't either. But how many times do we need to get hit on our heads with indisputable proof Francis according to <u>Father Altman and others is actually not a Pope because of his inner beliefs. Beliefs that are not Catholic.</u> And he parades around with scantily clad female circus performers and has the welcoming hall designed as a snake to honor Satan. Yes that's right, Pope Francis honors Satan. Get used to that thought because it is the damned truth. I am so hot and angry about this you could probably fry an egg on the top of my head.

22. Priests can now bless same sex couples. Would our Heavenly Father do that?

23. All this is coming from a Pope that said some time ago people could disappear and God can make new species. An interview with Eugenio Scafari. In Italy.

24. The Pope said if a person is in hell and then they feel sorry for their deeds they will not be punished. They willl be forgiven and be with God. Those who are not sorry will just stop existing.

25. The Pope does not believe in hell. Those who do bad things just disappear.

26. It is reported the Pope also said people should stop trying to make people Catholics. That is silly.

27. There is no particular Catholic God, only God.

28. Priests could forgive women that had an abortion

29. It is now acceptable to mix Catholic Christianity with other religions like Islam or Buddaism and so on.

Pope Francis Reveals That Jesus's Death Is NOT What We are Being Told [31]

I do not understand what the Pope is talking about if he really means the death of our Lord and Savior Jesus Christ is NOT what we are being told. Well, YES, it is. Francis has been talking about what he calls, "the true nature of Jesus death." Like we did not know during the past 2,024 years. Gee,

---

[31] Pope Francis Reveals That Jesus's Death Is NOT What We're Being Told (youtube.com)

thousands of people have been studying that for 2000 years! But Francis is now claiming they have all missed the point.

No, we have not. This video acts as if we are ignorant about the life and teachings of Jesus. Christians always use Jesus as the Blessed Shining Example on a Hill providing the perfect example on how to live our lives. Perhaps the Pope does not understand the laity as well as he thinks.

In the above document of what Pope Francis wants to do in the name of bringing everybody together is to fundamentally throw out the Bible. And to throw out Christian mass that has served us well for more than 2,000 years. And to replace it with an amalgamation of different religions from around the world that will certainly end up being very secular with no mention of Almighty God.

While reading the above did you find the word God anywhere? Well, it is not there. The above is nothing more than a man centered theology where humankind worships itself. This is the biggest Satanic fraud I have ever run across in my life. This is pure Satan from the top of His head to the end of His tail.

Remember, fish liked the taste of the worm right before they were caught and killed. Same thing here, most people do not know the definitions of the words that are used in the above trash heap of liberal woke communist ideas. This is basically the Vatican trying to have people seeing the theological version of kumbaya around the campfire.

Question: My dearest Mother Mary, I just read this pathetic theological mess proposed by our Anti-Christ Francis. To me the message is as plain as can be. This will mean the destruction of the Church founded by your Son and my Savior Jesus Christ. This is pure Satan disguised as fancy and ambiguous words that sound good to people with low IQ's.

It appears to me pretty simple. They want to take Christianity and nail it together with other unnamed religions at this point so the new so-called religion will better serve the needs of the population that wants to adore itself. God is completely eliminated from everything. Mankind simply wants to worship itself and this is the way they want to do it. Now I understand and more depth why our Father in Heaven wants to bring the end of the world as we know it. I am completely disgusted. Dear Mother Mary, I know this must be treacherously painful for you what I would very much like your comments and anything you would like to say about this.

Blessed Mother Mary: *Oh, my dear son, you definitely have accurately characterized this awful attempt by Satan to fool all of God's sacred children. You have accurately surmised that <u>this will result in the extinction of our Church and our sacraments and the mass as well</u>. Your lifelong friend has said this for years and he is correct.*

I guess there is no sense in me commenting on each individual thorn of the thorn bush because in the end <u>this Satanic scheme will overtake all good Christians unless they hide</u>. We knew of course this was coming and <u>I knew that Francis would be the antipope</u>, the Pope under the control of Satan. This has come to pass.

Frankly, my dearest of sons I don't know what else to tell you that you haven't already surmised yourself. You will be protected from the very dark times that are just right around the corner. Just follow the directions from your Lord and savior and my son and you and your family will do fine.

My dearest of sons, I love you ever so much.
Your Blessed Mother Mary

April 29, 2024

My dearest Blessed Mother Mary, this section of your book is the most painful thing I have ever had to write in my entire life. As you know, I have known for some time this kind of thing would happen. But to actually see the ugly face of it makes me want to throw up. You're just like being near an erupting volcano and watching the lava come rushing toward you knowing you could never outrun it. It is such a miserable feeling of helplessness. And on top of it almost all of its future victims go about their daily lives completely oblivious to the maelstrom that is heading their way and overtake them very quickly now.

Dear Mother, I know you have experienced much of this before and frankly I don't know how you do it. To watch these miserable things, occur when if only people paid attention to your apparitions most of it would have never happened. It makes me sick to my stomach and frankly as a confession anger is boiling up inside me and I am very short-tempered now. That's not like me but there it is.

So many people in their future will label the coming events as the wrath of God or God's anger punishing the people. That is ever so wrong because our loving Father Is the purest love I have ever experienced in my life. Our Holy Father is simply removing His protection from mankind so natural Satanic occurrences will now be set free. Thank you for listening to this my dear Blessed Mother Mary. I would so very much like to hear any additional thoughts you may have dear Mother Mary. I love you.

April 29, 2024
8:33 AM

Blessed Mother Mary: *My dearest of sons, it breaks my Heart to see you suffer so badly as I know you are. You are in a very lonely position where there is nobody around you that comes close to understanding what the depth is of your understanding and the emotional impact it has on you. Yet my dearest of sons both Jesus and I see within you with that fighter that will not hesitate to single-handedly go up against an army Satan.*

My dear son, Satan knows this of you, and he will steer clear of you because you will defeat Him in any arena of battle. <u>*There will come a time when you speak to many people at once and you will be opposed by minions of Satan.*</u> *I know you will have No Fear because of your eloquence, your intelligence, your knowledge, and most of all your love for the Trinity and me. You will dispatch them and there, as you would say, cockamamie arguments that result in Satanic domination and suffering.* <u>*You will feel like you are very alone but as you know that is impossible with you.*</u>

At this point my dear son, just work on the other sections of this book, and finish them with my help and then let it be published. From there contact the various Christian organizations and ensure they get a copy of this life changing miraculous book. They will want to talk to you then what you tell the truth to them they will be amazed and far better off for having heard what you say.

<u>By the way, my dear son, when I say that you are protected, I should tell you that not only are my Son and I'm right by your right side. But both of us now also have our left arms resting on your shoulders. This keeps Satan away from you and any others of His condemned minions. Besides that, there are two angels now with you. There is one on the left and one on the right there is no way that Satan can touch you from now till the time that you join us.</u>

The love for you is so great within the Heavenly Kingdom. I know this is hard to believe but there are now millions that pray for you and are always asking your Father to protect you in all ways during your remaining time on earth. There are other sections in this book that are still incomplete, and I just want you to finish those expeditiously and then send it to your publishing company Advantage Publishing. Mike loves you and feels privileged not only to know you but also to publish your books. That grace of God is with you ever so much.

Your Loving Blessed Mother Mary

Thank You So Very Much Dear Mother Mary, I Love you

8

Blessed Mother Mary herself told me this

"Pope Francis Is Indeed The Anti-Christ I Repeat Pope Francis Is The Anti-Christ. He Is Under Control Of Satan."

Much more detail on this later when our Blessed Mother Mary describes the third secret of Fatima in great detail.

Can Pope Francis really be under the control of Satan?

Yes! He already is. Blessed Mother Mary has perfect and pure knowledge of the situation with the Catholic Church, and it is Her who told me this on several occasions and that is published within this book. Please put all the pieces together, all the heresies and the two pictures shown here. There are many more pictures of occult statues inside the Vatican and those of Pope Francis holding religious objects he NEVER should as a genuine Pope. [32]

Question: Dear Blessed Mother Mary, would you care to comment on the extent of Satanic activities within the Vatican these days? Father Malachi Martin acknowledged all this is going on and it is worse than we normally would think of. If there is something you would like to illuminate for us, I would be very grateful if you could do that.

Answer: *My dearest sacred child, you are so exhausted and tired right now so I will keep my answer very concise and short. As you already suspect the Satanic gremlins are scurrying about within the Vatican each doing its part to bring the whole house down. That is probably the best way to explain the*

---

[32] Satanic Symbolism the Church Is Hiding from You - YouTube

situation. They are indeed working towards the time when Satan himself will arrive and he will sit on the throne of Peter. That will happen inside the Vatican where the Pope normally sits. This is something Satan has craved for his entire existence. Since he tried to overthrow your Heavenly Father and was instantly defeated and kicked out of the Kingdom. Thrown down to earth to be a pest for everyone who comes here that are your Father's sacred children. The people in the Vatican that are not Satan live their lives in fear. Knowing that if they say one wrong thing...then? Their lifetime of dedication and work toward our Heavenly Father, your Lord and Savior Jesus Christ and the Holy Spirit and me will all be instantly thrown in the garbage. And they will then be severely chastised and most likely transferred far away from Rome to where the Pope thinks they cannot do any harm to his Satanic plans. I know this is awful dear son for you to hear but I also know that frankly you already knew every word that I just said. I love you so very much my dearest. I ask please that you quit out for the night because I sense that your head is really hurting from yet another headache that tortures you so frequently. I love you, your Blessed Mother.

Remember my dearest sacred children of our Heavenly Father, Cardinal Bergoglio now known as the Pope was there originally from Argentina. That

country is very communist socialist and its governmental nature. That form of government which frankly saps the economic blood out of all of God's children who live there is what are now Pope thinks is a wonderful thing. That form of government is tyrannical and dictatorial and is what our Pope thinks is normal. It certainly is not for governments that are so opposed to serve the best interest of the people and not dictate to them with threats of violence and jail time if they misbehave. This picture illustrates the sickness of our Pope when he adores looking at a communist cross made of a sickle and hammer with Jesus Christ our Lord and savior being crucified on the hammer. Do not think for a moment the

God's Grand Design: Blessed Mother Mary Directly Speaks

symbolism of communism reigning supreme over Jesus Christ can be ignored by this wretched hammer and sickle.[33]

In that form of government falsehoods and manipulation it is a normal course of events in the government's attempts to control every aspect of our Heavenly Father s sacred children who live there. We here in the United States are now experiencing more and more of this atrocity through the efforts of the Democrat party and the Joe Biden administration.

Among the many other things Pope Francis has instituted that are Satanic, he is instituting the following: *Ad Theologiam Promovendam. It means from Latin,* "to promote theology." This sounds innocent enough does it not? It is not!

Pope Francis calls for 'paradigm shift' in theology for world of today [34]

After you read the below Satanic text, realize:

The unsaid and hidden goal of these people is:

1. One world government.

2. One world judicial system.

3. One world religious theology Pagan based with NO Catholicism make the Bible illegal and replace it with the new catastrophic man-made stench of garbage that is founded upon the principles of Sodom and Gomorrah. It will be a document of mankind worshipping mankind!

4. Possession of a Bible will be illegal.

Demon Devil Vatican Beast

---

[33] Satanic Symbolism The Church Is Hiding From You - YouTube

[34] https://www.Catholicnewsagency.com/news/255887/pope-francis-calls-for-paradigm-shift-in-theology-for-world-of-today

5. Complete control of food distribution,
6. A one-world police replacement. There will come a time when simply possessing a Bible will be deemed a crime.
7. Conducting our sacred mass will also become a crime against the state.
8. Godly human rights out the window

I pray for my children and especially my grandchildren. For they will live through the End Of Times propagated by Satan Himself who by the way knows me very well and I know Satan very well. How can that be? 50 years ago, Satan personally attacked me in the middle of the night while I was sleeping next to my Blessed wife. I have documented this in detail in other writings. He said to me" I will get you! I will get you! I will get you! Yes, Satan does indeed have red eyes and is about seven feet tall. He sure is an ugly bastard.

What you are about to read eliminates Almighty God and Christianity and all our Biblical literature. Replaced by mankind worshiping and adoring mankind.

Pope Francis is calling for a paradigm shift where Catholic theology takes a much broader widespread view of engagement with the world that includes contemporary science, modern culture throughout the earth, and people's lived experiences.

Boy, doesn't this sound so good! The Satanic team of Francis is going to reconcile Biblical teachings. Using science that changes all the time due to new discoveries. He wants to blend Biblical teachings with our perverted modern culture that includes, abortion on demand, gay marriages, men turning into women and occupying women's locker rooms.

Who will pay for all of this Satanic garbage in our society? If you work for an honest living, it is YOU!! For certain there will be monstrous tax hikes the likes of which we have never seen before. One note about taxes. When people go to work, they purposely invest part of their life to earn the money necessary to support the needs of a family. It is a simple trade. I trade part of my life to provide the necessary items to be purchased for my loving family.

Because of the horrific coming taxes, the amount of your life taken away from you in taxes will increase from five twelfths. This is according to the latest government statistics of a year to my personal estimated eight months out of each year. That is called slavery. Honest people that work will become working slaves. Yes, this is my personal estimate and does not come from any accredited institution. I simply used common sense. Common sense sadly appears to be more and more rare as time goes on.

9

New Horrors from Cardinal Bergoglio aka. Pope Francis

1. On May 20, 2024, Fox News Stuart Varny Show, they reported Pope Francis said over the weekend, "conservative Bishops that oppose blessing same sex marriages have a "suicidal attitude". This goes directly against 2,000 years of Church teachings since Saint Peter was given the leadership if the Catholic Church directly from Jesus Christ Himself! It is clear from this the Pope wants to destroy the Catholic Church.

2. A new document titled <u>Ad Theologiam</u> Comes from the Pontifical Academy of Theology. This "theology can only develop in a culture of dialogue and encounter between different traditions and knowledge, between different Christian confessions and religions. Openly engaging with everyone, believers and non-believers," the Pope wrote in the Apostolic letter.

   This odor of dead fish basically means our divine gospel will now be mixed in with other religions on earth. This is impossible especially when it comes to Islam. The goal of Islam is earthly domination over everyone. The goal of our loving gospel is to spread God's words and serve the needs of all others of God's sacred children. Simply put that they want to combine a religion that seeks worldly domination with every religion that seeks love and justice for all of God's sacred children. These two can never be reconciled. Why? <u>Because one is of God and the other is of Satan.</u>

3. We have the need to deal with" profound cultural transformations.

   The above phrase is a code for creating Sodom and Gomorrah in our societies. Notice it never says what our societies will transform into. That is left open to the Satanic minions that will sit down and create a new social disaster of monumental proportion.

4. Revises the statutes of the Pontifical Academy of Theology (PATH) "to make them more suitable for the mission that our time imposes on theology.

   More purposeful ambiguous garbage. This is a feel-good meaningless phrase. The keywords though are "the mission that our time imposes on theology." The world is a theological disaster area, it lacks the necessary principles of, "love God first, love your neighbor as your love yourself and love your enemy." Our times today have drifted far away from the will of Almighty God, yet this phrase opens the door to let the stink of immorality invade the new and improved theology." By the way, this new so-called theology is worldwide. There will be one and only one worldwide theology and only one religion. All other religions will certainly be deemed as illegal.

5. Theology can only develop in a culture of dialogue and encounter between different traditions and knowledge, between different Christian confessions and religions. Openly engaging with everyone, believers, and nonbelievers," the pope wrote in the apostolic letter.

   Good God! Theology development? The word development directly means creating a new theology. Get that real well dear sacred child! They wish to create a new theology that must by its very nature throw away our Godly inspired Biblical literature and replace it with and amalgamation (mixture) of other religious texts from around the world. Dear sacred children of God: our beloved Bible will be thrown out and its replacement is something that we will never understand because it is Satanically unbiblical.

6. Pope Francis wrote that Catholic theology must experience a" courageous cultural revolution." In order to become a fundamentally contextual theology" guided by Christo's incarnation into time and space.

   A courageous cultural revolution. This phrase says that the new religion will be integrated with our culture, thus it will never be the same again. Today, there were multiple cultures that live under the umbrella of Christianity. This will go away with the newly dictated one world religion. This is what the above fancy ambiguous words mean.

131

7. This approach to theology must be capable of reading and interpreting" the gospel in the conditions in which men and women live daily, in different geographical social and cultural environments."

Whew! To most rational intelligent people the above sentence looks innocent yet completely not understandable. But it contains code words that do have specific meanings. The new theology must be the lowest common denominator of people around the world. These people think they can create one singular document with that combines the worldview of Aborigines, African tribesmen, Muslims, and Christians altogether into one happy pot of people singing kumbaya. And never will they mention Almighty God, the creator of all that is seen and unseen. Satanic idiots!

8. Our beloved Pope contrasts this approach with the current theology that has lasted for 2000 years. Doing this by the way to abstractly repropose formulas and schemes from the past and repeated long-standing criticism of "deskbound theology."

This phrase is among the most ambiguous of all. He thinks current theology is born out of a desk in the room somewhere. Apparently, he has paid no attention to His own magisterium in Rome. This point reaffirms what I have already said. Pope Francis wants to throw everything out that mankind has achieved in our theological understandings then replace it with their one world religion that is enforced by an army of censers.

9. Pope Francis emphasized that theological studies must be open to the world.

Looks like everybody in the world will have to take indoctrination classes. This is exactly what Kim Il Sung, Mao Zedong, Joseph Stalin, Fidel Castro, and the current leader of North Korea.

10. Pope Francis emphasizes this bottoms-up envisioning of theology is necessary to better aid the Churches evangelizing image.

Our Satanic Pope wants us to believe that it is the people that will decide about theological principles. He wants the people to "reenvision," what they want to believe in. Notice dear sacred children of God, there is not one mention of our Heavenly Father creator of Heaven and earth. This reenvisioning (what an intelligent sounding word, re envisioning) means nothing more than pulling theology out of your imagination. This is yet again another way for mankind to adore and love itself. This is what the people that lived in Sodom and Gomorrah did. They invented God's out of their imagination. They worshipped Gods that they themselves created. They had ritual killings of small children. I implore you; I beg you to look up Sodom and Gomorrah in a reliable source that has not already been tainted with liberal progressive positions. This is pure Satanism and exactly what Satan wants God's children to do. And Pope Francis is doing it.

11. Pope Francis went on to say the new theological studies must be open to the world not as a tactical attitude but as a profound turning point which must be "inductive."

This is the most nonsensical sentence that I have ever run into in my entire life. However, if you take the phrase "a profound turning point which must be inductive," the word inductive means to gather up and make inclusive. This is the word that was used during World War II when millions of men were inducted into the army against their will. This phrase could very easily mean that the turning point in theology must include inducting people against their will. This would be consistent with cardinal Bergoglio's communist worldview. You know the cardinal; he is now the Pope.

12. The new Catholicism must become transdisciplinary, part of a web of relationships. First of all, with other disciplines and other knowledge. The Pope said this engagement leads to the arduous task of theologians making use of "new categories developed by other knowledge."

I think this is pretty obvious. The word transdisciplinary means: Welcoming the different lenses that each person brings to the table makes the decision-making process richly transdisciplinary. When it comes to theology however, the word theology means the study of God. These people never mentioned God. They want to bring together a number of people that will decide theological principles that makes everybody happy. This is another form of mankind adoring and loving itself. This is like the political slogan from Barack Obama, hope, and change. I'm sure they paid the marketing guy a lot of money to come up with that one.

13. Pope Francis wrote priority must be given to the" knowledge of people's common sense." Which he described as a" theological source in which many images of God live often not corresponding to the Christian face of God, only and always love."

    This phrase is a mixture of underlying communist worldview along with a perverted view of Almighty God that specifically rejects Almighty God as we know Him now. Our Heavenly Father never changes but this idiot phrase talks about the many images of God often NOT corresponding to the Christian face of God. So, this Satanic crackpot reinvent a God with many faces. So, he wants us to throw out our beloved Bible and invent a new one out of our sinful imaginations. This is an act of pure self-worship! If you take the previous sentence literally, why is it nobody has ever seen the face of God including me that has talked with Him on a number of magnificent occasions. I heard His loving voice talking to me, but I never once got a glimpse of His face.

    On the other hand, if you take this phrase metaphorically then it means God's character is different depending upon the angle you are coming from.

    Also remember, this phrase says we must allow non-Christian interpretations of Almighty God. Just imagine how many that could be!

14. The Pope said His pastoral stamp must be placed upon all Catholic theology described as "popular theology."

    Well, here we go again, Mr. Pope wants absolute authority over all things related to God.

Well, there you have it. What a great sounding batch of words that could mean anything. This is exactly what crafty dishonest politicians do. Throw together a bunch of nicely pleasant words and make it like we will have Heaven on earth according to our needs. I ask each reader to read again what is above and then definitively express the meanings of the above in clear terms.

Dear sacred children of Almighty God:

This Is Exactly What Satan Has Wanted Ever Since He Rebelled Against Our Heavenly Father in The Heavenly Kingdom. He Has Always Wanted to Replace Our Loving Father in Heaven. Read This Stinking Phrase Very Well Because What I Have Just Said Is Exactly What It Means. Jorge Mario Bergoglio Wants to Play God. And The Rest of Us Are His Servants.

First, did you notice anything strange in the previous 14 points? You should have! The above text is taken straight from Christian news agency with an article written by Jonathan Told last year in November 2023. Are you sure you didn't notice anything missing from all these wonderful goals regarding the entire Catholic Church?

The name of Almighty God is missing. It is completely absent. This is not an accident or an oversight. It is on purpose. It can only be a Pope controlled by Satan that would do such a miserable thing to all the faithful who attend Church every Sunday. Leaving God out of all of these theological changes the Pope wants to make certainly without a shadow of a doubt points toward the direction he wants to take the Catholic Church.

Simply put, Pope Francis wants to have a Church that looks like a Church, but it is not a Church. He wants to have celebrations like mass but not be mass. In other words, he wants a completely false Church that is worth absolutely nothing. It will be a fake Church a Church with no substance come with no Almighty Father in Heaven, with no Lord and savior Jesus Christ and without anything else that is right and good. This has been Satan's goal for a very long time. Ever since Satan saw the throne of our Almighty Father he wanted to sit in that throne because he felt he was better than our Heavenly Father and deserved to be there above all else.

As our Heavenly Father s Anointed Messenger, I have had occasion to encounter Satan on three separate occasions back when I was in my thirties. Satan hates me so bad it goes beyond any kind of description with any kind of language used by the human race. I outlined my encounter with Him on three separate occasions. After that Satan has harassed me every day of my life.

In the above summary document of what Pope Francis wants to do in the name of bringing everybody together is to fundamentally throw out the Bible. And throw out Christian mass that has served us well for more than 2000 years. And replace it with an amalgamation of different religions from around the world that will certainly end up being very secular with no mention of Almighty God.

While reading the above did you find the word God anywhere? Well, it is not there. The above is nothing more than a man centered theology where mankind worships itself. This is the biggest Satanic fraud I have ever run across in my life. This is pure Satan from the top of His head to the end of His tail.

Remember, fish liked the taste of the worm right before they were caught and killed. Same thing here, most people do not know the definitions of the words that are used in the above trash heap of liberal woke communist theological ideas. This is basically trying to have people seeing the theological version of kumbaya around the campfire.

Question: My dearest Mother Mary, I just read this pathetic theological mess proposed by our Anti-Christ Francis. To me the message is as plain as can be. This will mean the destruction of the Church founded by your son and my savior Jesus Christ. This is pure Satan disguised as fancy and ambiguous words that sound good to people with low IQ's.

It appears to me pretty simple. They want to take Christianity and mailed it together with other unnamed religions at this point so the new so-called religion will better serve the needs of the population that wants to adore itself. God is completely eliminated from everything. Mankind simply wants to worship itself and this is the way they want to do it. Now I understand and more depth why our Father in Heaven wants to bring the end of the world as we know it. I am completely disgusted. Dear Mother Mary, I know this must be treacherously painful for you what I would very much like your comments and anything you would like to say about this.

Answer: *Oh, my dear son you definitely have accurately characterized this awful attempt by Satan to fool all of God's sacred children. You have* *accurately surmised that this will result in the extinction of our Church and our sacraments and the mass as well. Your lifelong friend has said this for years and he is correct.*

I guess there is no sense in me commenting on each individual thorn of the thorn bush because in the end this Satanic scheme will overtake all good Christians unless they hide. We knew of course this was coming and I knew that Francis would be the antipope, the Pope under the control of Satan. This has come to pass.

Frankly, my dearest of sons I don't know what else to tell you that you haven't already surmised yourself. You will be protected from the very dark times that are just right around the corner. Just follow the directions from your Lord and savior and my son and you and your family will do fine.

My dearest of sons, I love you ever so much.
Your Blessed Mother Mary

April 29, 2024

My dearest Blessed Mother Mary, this section of your book is the most painful thing I have ever had to write in my entire life. As you know, I have known for some time this kind of thing would happen. But to actually see the ugly face of it makes me want to throw up. You're just like being near an erupting volcano and watching the lava come rushing toward you knowing you could never outrun it. It is such a miserable feeling of helplessness. And on top of it almost all of its future victims go about their daily lives completely oblivious to the maelstrom that is heading their way and overtake them very quickly now.

Dear Blessed Mother, I know you have experienced much of this before and frankly I don't know how you do it. To watch these miserable things, occur when if only people paid attention to your apparitions most of it would have never happened. It makes me sick to my stomach and frankly as a confession anger is boiling up inside me and I'm very short-tempered now. That's not like me but there it is.

So many people in their future will label the coming events as the wrath of God or God's anger punishing the people. That is ever so wrong because our loving Father is the purest love I have ever experienced in my life. Our Holy Father is simply removing His protection from mankind so natural Satanic occurrences will now be set free. Thank you for listening to this my dear Blessed Mother Mary. I would so very much like to hear any additional thoughts you may have dear Mother Mary. I love you.

April 29, 2024
8:33 AM

Blessed Mother Mary: *My dearest of sons, it breaks my Heart to see you suffer so badly as I know you are. You are in a very lonely position where there is nobody around you that comes close to understanding what the depth is of your understandings and the emotional impact it has on you. Yet my dearest of sons both Jesus and I see within you with that fighter that will not hesitate to single-handedly go up against an army Satan.*

My dear son, Satan knows this of you, and he will steer clear of you because you will defeat Him in any arena of battle. There will come a time when you will speak to many people at once and you will be opposed by minions of Satan. I know you will have No Fear because of your eloquence, your intelligence, your knowledge, and most of all your love for the Trinity and me. You will dispatch them and there, as you would say, cockamamie arguments that result in Satanic domination and suffering. You will feel like you are very alone but as you know that is impossible with you.

At this point my dear son, just work on the other sections of this book, and finish them with my help and then let it be published. From there contact the various Christian organizations and ensure they get a copy of this life changing miraculous book. They will want to talk to you then what you tell the truth to them they will be amazed and far better off for having heard what you say.

By the way, my dear son, when I say that you are protected, I should tell you that not only are my son and I right by your right side. But both of us now also have our left arms resting on your shoulders. This keeps Satan away from you and any others of His condemned minions. Besides that, there are two angels now with you. There is one on the left and one on the right there is no way that Satan can touch you from now till the time that you join us.

The love for you is so great within the Heavenly Kingdom. I know this is hard to believe but there are now millions that pray for you and are always asking your Father to protect you in all ways during your remaining time on earth. There are other sections in this book that are still incomplete, and I just want you to finish those expeditiously and then send it to your publishing company Advantage Publishing. Mike loves you and feels privileged not only to know you but also to publish your books. That grace of God is with you ever so much.

Your Loving Blessed Mother Mary

10

The Heresies of Pope Francis

From:

The Heresies of Antipope Francis (prophecyfilm.blogspot.com)

https://prophecyfilm.blogspot.com/2015/03/the-heresies-of-antipope-francis.html

This next section is horrid, it is disgusting, it is Satanic, and it goes against all Biblical literature as we know it today. If there is any doubt in your mind Pope Francis is not the Anti-Christ then you must believe two things:

1. You must just believe our Blessed Mother Mary. That when she said in this book Pope Francis is the Anti-Christ

2. You must believe in anti-Christian dogma as it is spewed out from the Vatican by anti-Pope Francis these days.

I can only give you a small sampling of the theological garbage Pope Francis is spreading across the world. Because if I included everything this section of the book would be a large book in and of itself. So here are a few of the heresies and Satanic items they came from anti-Pope Francis.

"Here, in fact, the different religious identities of Orthodox, Catholics, other Christians, Muslims, and Jews. And the ethnic differences between Macedonians, Albanians, Serbs, Croats, and persons of other backgrounds, have created a mosaic in which every piece is essential for the uniqueness and beauty of the whole. That beauty will become all the more evident to the extent you succeed in passing it on and planting it in the Hearts of the coming generation. Every effort made to enable the diverse religious expressions…" [7]

This is blunt apostasy. The apostate Francis says that it "is essential for the uniqueness and beauty of the whole" society to have the presence of false religions, including Islam and Judaism

In plain language our apostate Pope wants to mix together all the different religions in the world into one and only one religion. This will disintegrate the Catholic Church to be something that is unrecognizable. The reason for this again is simple, this prepares the theological way for Satan to rule the world. [35]

Francis' Heresies on Atheism and Atheists:

Antipope Francis, Evangelia Gaudium (# 254), Nov. 24, 2013: "Non-Christians [such as pagans and atheists], by God's gracious initiative, when they are faithful to their own consciences, can live "justified by the grace of God." And thus be "associated to the paschal mystery of Jesus Christ" … to the sacramental dimension of sanctifying grace... to live our own beliefs."

What the above fancy worded paragraph means is God will forgive everybody no matter how rotten and cruel and Satanic they are. Because of His gracious initiative and them being faithful to their own conscience. This means Pope Francis believes Almighty God will forgive all the mass murderers in history as long as they were faithful to their own conscience. This also means you will be rubbing shoulders in the Heavenly Kingdom with every violent criminal that ever existed.

The Vatican II sect and Francis officially teaches that one can be an atheist through no fault of His own and that atheists can be excused and saved. This is as wrong as wrong can get. The evidence of Christian morality and ethics and the existence of an Almighty God who loves us is all over the place as soon as you use your eyes to look at what's around you. The idea of evolution creating our bodies through "random selection" has been proven to be as false as false can get from a scientific viewpoint. Given our physical complexity the chances our bodies somehow evolved to what we see today is one in $1 * 10$ to the 190th power. There are not that many atoms in the whole universe.

Vatican II document, Lumen Gentium # 16: "Nor does divine providence deny the helps that are necessary for salvation to those who, through no fault

---

[35] Antipope Francis' Notable Heresies and Apostasy (May 2019) (vaticanCatholic.com)

of their own, have not yet attained to the express recognition of God. Yet who strive, not without divine grace, to lead an upright life."

Vatican II is teaching here there are some people who, THROUGH NO FAULT OF THEIR OWN, have not yet attained the express recognition of God. In other words, there are people who, through no fault of their own, don't believe in God (i.e., are atheists). This is heresy.

The above two paragraphs exemplify the Satanic heresy of anti-Pope Francis. He loves the use the phrase "through no fault of their own." Really? Everybody is responsible for absolutely everything they ever say and do. Did the mass murderer not mean to kill all those people so therefore it is not His fault? This is the same thinking of the Democrat party in the United States.

Yet despite this dogmatic teaching based on Romans 1, in On Heaven and Earth, pp. 12-13 Francis says he respects atheists and doesn't try to convert them. He also says their "life is not condemned": So, our anti-Pope Francis really likes atheists a lot. There is one unforgivable sin in God's creation and that is simply rejecting Almighty God. But that's okay because anti-Pope Francis likes them.

"I do not approach the relationship in order to proselytize or convert the atheist; I respect Him. Nor would I say His life is condemned. Because I am convinced, I do not have the right to make a judgment about the honesty of that person... every man is the image of God, whether he is a believer or not. For that reason alone, everyone has a series of virtues, qualities, and a greatness of His own." (Francis, On Heaven and Earth, pp. 12-13)

Question: Would you like antiPope Francis to teach your children catechism?

In contrast to Francis, the Council of Florence dogmatically defining that individual who has a view contrary to the Catholic Church. Specifically, teaching on Our Lord Jesus Christ or the Trinity, or any one of the truths about Our Lord or the Trinity, is rejected, condemned, and anathematized by God.

An atheists interviewed Francis for the Italian newspaper The Republic. The interview was published on October 1, 2013. Francis directly told the atheist he had no intention of trying to convert Him. Francis rejects proselytism four different times in this interview. Francis declared: "Proselytism is solemn nonsense; it makes no sense."

Anti-Pope Francis is against educating unbelievers about our loving Almighty God. This is precisely what Satan wants Him to do. And so, he does it.

A Statement released by the Vatican December 18, 2023

"The gospel is to sanctify everyone he said. of course, must be goodwill. And it is necessary to get precise instructions on the Christian life. It emphasizes it is not the union that is blessed but the persons. But we are all sinners, why should we make a list of sinners who can enter the Church and a list of sinners who cannot enter the Church? This is not the gospel."

Yes, it is!

"Those who protest belong only to a small ideological group. I trust everyone will be reassured that the spirit of this declaration which aims to include and not divide. It invites us to trust everyone as we trust in God."

The gospels say, Jesus Christ Himself, that the fundamental nature of mankind is fallen, sinful. To say to trust everyone opens the door to Satan completely! Promotes disbelief of Jesus Christ Himself. This is Satan talking.

In the above text Francis basically says if you disagree then you are schematic.

The general reaction to the above is that when you bless two people you also bless the union between them. It is not possible to do otherwise.

Blessing LGBTQ marriages is indeed Satanic for it rejects the pronouncements of our Heavenly Father Himself.

This is not a magisterial document either. It is only the Pope Francis spouting off his personal wishes and proclamations.

Okay, I could go on and on with more and more examples of this wretched person we call the anti-Pope Francis. But I think you get the idea that this man as our Blessed Mother Mary said is indeed the Anti-Christ. And yes, my dear sacred children of God, he is here on the earth. And we indeed are living in the

End of Times as prophesized by a lot of different Saints in the Bible and specifically our Blessed Mother Mary in other sections of this book.

Malachi Martin And the Satanic Infiltration of Impurity in The Church March 1, 2024

Windswept House Vatican by Malachi-Martin

This book is a masterpiece. Father Martin did read the third secret of Fatima and felt all of God's sacred children needed to know its contents as spoken by our Blessed Mother Mary. He had taken an oath not to say anything. So, he used this book that he called a "Faction" that reads like a novel but contains the actual facts of the Vatican's treachery surrounding the third secret of Fatima.

Keys of This Blood: Pope John Paul II Versus Russia and the West for Control of the New World Order by Father Malachi Martin

Father Malachi Martin was a Vatican insider and wrote about the untold story about the Vatican's role to establish and control in a one-world government.

Evidence That the End of Times Is Upon Us [36] [37]

Malachi Martin wanted to warn us about Satan infiltrating the Church. This is something very hard for people to accept that anything like this could happen. Yet this directly affects the Church, apostasy in the Church, all believers in the world, the effects on the religious order.

In an interview with Art Bell Malachi Martin said the following back in 1997,

---

[36] https://www.returntotradition.org

[37] Fr. Malachi Martin with Art Bell. Vatican Murders etc. May 4th, 1998 (8) (NWO SERIES/ The Vatican) (youtube.com)

Art Bell started by saying he had two articles in front of Him indicating some people in the hierarchy of the Church say there are Satanic practices going on in the Vatican. Could that be true?

Malachi Martin said yes. It is at the Vatican it is at a certain level and there is no doubt about it. There have been and still are practices that are formally venerating Lucifer the Prince of the earth.

The Vatican has about eight resident in-house exorcists, and in two other cities that are devil ridden. They are Milan and Turin. There is no doubt about it there are Luciferian Practices and veneration of Him and in-service of Him where these actions have taken place.

There is a prophecy Satan can invade the Citadel or also known as the Vatican. They will have power for one thousand years. Then Art Bell asked, "how close are they/" Malachi Martin responded, "very close, frighteningly close."

Then our Bell asked, "how will we know and how will you know when Satan takes over and the 1000 years begins?"

We will know this by a series of facts which amount to the following:

1. The basic tenants, beliefs of Christianity will be played down to zero.
2. And will matter no longer in normal society and nations.
3. For those who are supposed to be the custodians and supposed to be the administrators of the word and distributors of His grace have stopped all that.
4. It will be taken down to secular terms and rather overnight as far as I can see.
5. Then it will suddenly dawn on people, hey, this St. has gone completely awry.

This was the exchange between Father Malachi Martin and Art Bell.

Also, according to this website, which I thoroughly recommend. Titled "return to tradition.org." It used to be the Church in working with governments, there would be cooperation where the governments would try to back up the morality of Christianity in secular society by their governance. This is no longer the case, and it can be horrifically demonstrated in the United States of America through the Democrat party and their anti-Christian policies. More on this in another section of this book.

I have to mention the contents of this book regarding the End of Times have been increasingly with us ever since the 1960s as I have mentioned before. Approximately six years ago I wrote a book that did not get a lot of attention because the title was not shocking enough. The title remains:

Christians Alert! The Democrats Are Attacking Our Country. Published August 2019

Malachi Martin speaks at an event called "Paranormal Continuum":

1. Everything is becoming integrated today, morals, and ethics today of individual communities and groups and ethics have become completely degraded into materialistic secular terms and hedonistic aims.
2. That is the reign of evil. In directly contravention to the will of God who is the sovereign master and creator of all things.
3. Evil is more organized, more integrated worldwide which comes out as the deification of man,

Evidence of this secular perversion includes:

1. The expansion of the sacraments to give access to the sacraments to those who are unrepentant sinners without calling them to conversion.

2. Blessings of James Martin type and those in irregular situations that contravene Church law.

3. The open debate on changing the Churches morality and teachings on moral issues, all of it is happening within this backdrop.

4. These are some of the clearest signs of the Church increasingly under the influence of Satan.

5. The mockery of the faith being conducted in sports stadiums.

6. Also, Catholics in the Western world are not caring or agreeing with the liberalization and progressiveness that is being developed within the Catholic Church.

7. Heresies pushed by Rome, now most Catholics just shrug.

Following by Fr. Malichi Martin with Art Bell May 4, 1998, Fr. Malachi Martin With Art Bell. Vatican Murders etc. May 4th, 1998 (8) (NWO SERIES/ The Vatican) (youtube.com)

11

Mother Mary speaks freely about the world situation today with emphasis on the United States of America

My dearest Blessed Mother Mary, I will never forget that day when both you and Lord Jesus Christ came to me after slowly approaching me for about four days. I vividly remember when I put my feet on the floor after waking up still sitting on the bed, I saw both of you standing right next to me on my right shoulder. Oh my, and when I asked Jesus, "are you who I think you are?" And he said "yes, it is I." And you were standing right next to Him, and I remember seeing your robes so very clearly in blue and white. Even though I knew I was in the best of hands, I still went into a state of shock as you know and all I saw was white. Everything else around me disappeared.

Since then, you and Jesus have been my constant companion as you say you would. I just hope I am fulfilling your expectations and presenting the real Catholic Christian theology to the world. Especially the worldview our Heavenly Father wants all His sacred children to know.

What I want to address now with your permission is to do something that has never been done before. Which is simply to let your mind run free and say whatever it is you want the world to know. As you know, there will be no filters come on no selective editing but only you are pure words as you wish to save them. I have put together a small list of items I would like for you to comment on. But please feel free to expand these topics in any direction you wish for the benefit of our Heavenly Father's sacred children. Basically, if we were in school and you are the professor, what's before you is a completely blank chalkboard to be written on with whatever you desire.

State of the Church:

Dear Blessed Mother Mary, as you clearly know there is tremendous churning and chaos within our beloved Church these days. As you know, from the very beginning I never liked Bergoglio. Nonetheless, please share what your thoughts are regarding the Catholic Church today.

Blessed Mother Mary: *Oh, my dearest of sons, this is a painful topic, and it is so widespread like a disease that spreads through the body unchecked with your immune system. From the beginning I knew Pope Francis will become and now is the Anti-Christ. He is systematically removing all the good bishops, Cardinals, and priests from the Church who we're doing nothing more than speaking out and a Catholic way. Pope Francis is destruction personified. Because I am human as you know my dearest son my vocabulary is not as good as my son Jesus Christ. So, I must say things in a simpler and more crude manner.*

Nonetheless, my tears run rampant for the Church that my son found 2000 years ago. Yet at the same time both Jesus and I knew that this day would come. When Satan would completely take over the holy Catholic Church with all of His henchmen and hate disguised as reformation. My dearest of son, you are the only one. Yes, dear son, the only one that has the courage to expose the Satanic treachery that has invaded by now all aspects of the holy Catholic Church. In your investigation you did find the fact that there is Satanic activity and Satanic worship within the Vatican now and frankly this has been going on for many decades. Your discovery of this through Father Malachi Martin is true and correct. What happens behind the scenes within Saint peter's cathedral and other holy buildings in the Vatican curls my hair and I cannot help but weep for what is happening.

As you have also discovered, my dear son, everything that Pope Francis is doing is a coordinated effort to blend Catholicism with most other religions on earth. Such as Hinduism, Islam, and other forms of paganistic religions. This will be done under the banner of inclusiveness representing all peoples on the earth. What you have already written in this book that tears apart what Pope Francis wants to do indeed is intended to destroy the identity of Christian Catholicism. Into a blend of human created religion that as you have said their son destroys true Christianity, the loving message of your Holy Father and instead promote mankind worshipping itself.

There will be Satanic rituals of sacrifice by killing animals on an altar within the Vatican. If everyone would think of Sodom and Gomorrah come on visualize that happening within the Vatican and Saint Peters cathedral. This is what is coming along with the one world government that enslaves everyone of God's sacred children on earth.

Faithful Christians such as yourself my dearest one must indeed hide from the coming authorities that will roam the earth looking for any trace of true beliefs in our Heavenly Father and Christianity. There will come a time when the possession of a Bible will be deemed a crime punishable by severe penalties and even death.

None of this will happen all at once. No, it will be like a diseased fungus that grows slowly only to devour its host very much like a parasite would do. My dear son, I know you love your family dearly. And I have said many times before, you and your family are protected from this onslaught of Satanic wrath and hate toward anyone who loves the Trinity and me as you do. I do not know for sure but there may come a time when your family is cornered by the witches and henchman of Satan. Such that they will put each of you to a slow ritual death that is even worse than the cross for my beloved son.

My dear son, if this does happen just cry out to your Heavenly Father. And you will instantly be removed from the physical world and your family will find itself within the loving arms of my son come the Holy Father and the Holy Spirit. You will instantly find yourself in their arms so as to spare you and members of your family who believe from unspeakable Satanic rituals and agony. At this point my dearest of sons, come, I am only human still and I'm starting to get very upset and starting to cry again. So, with your loving permission let us hold off on the other topics you would like to speak of. Let us Please wait until perhaps this afternoon or early tomorrow morning.

I love you so very much, as much as I possibly can.

Oh, my dear Blessed Mother, I am so sorry for asking you this painful question. I too have tears in my eyes and I will ask you no more until tomorrow. Right now, I am emotionally exhausted as you are. I guess it is perhaps not so much the question would rather they're wretchedly painful Satanic answer that is so upsetting. Let us both rest together until tomorrow. I love you ever so much, dear Mother Mary.

12

Mother Mary Describes Fatima 1, Fatima 2, And Fatima 3

Authors Note: I have purposely left the apparitions of Blessed Mother Mary till after all the painful wretched information about the sad conditions of our beloved Catholic Church these days. By doing this you can see how the dishonesty of the Vatican plays out with regard to Blessed Mother Mary's apparitions at Fatima. The Vatican felt it was forced to lie terribly about especially the third secret. Going so far as to make Lucia disappear to a convent that hid her from telling the truth about what Mother Mary told her. An imposter sister Lucia was made into a public figure telling the world the Vatican lies about Fatima.

Little does our criminal Vatican know you are reading the book that documents the exact truth about Fatima because that comes directly from Blessed Mother Mary herself.

A Fundamental Description of All Three Fátima Revelations

Fátima is one of the most well-known apparitions of our Blessed Mother Mary. Like many others of her apparitions, she chose three little children to speak to. In our Lady's multiple apparitions from May 13, 1917, until October 1917, she revealed apocalyptic visions and prophecies. These prophecies were told to three young Portuguese shepherds, Lúcia Santos, Jacinta, and Francisco Marto.

One may ask why it is our Blessed Mother Mary chooses young children to tell her prophecies. Our Blessed Mother personally told me [38] it is because

---

[38] Just as our Blessed Mother Mary speaks to God's sacred children across the world so too does she speak to me as I write Christian spiritual literature. I am our Heavenly Father's "Anointed Messenger" and have written a sacred book with our Heavenly Father, our Lord and

young children have not been on the earth long enough to have their consciousness or worldview tainted by Satanic influences. Yes, dear reader, as I have said before, I have been wonderfully chosen and gifted by our Heavenly Father. Gifted to be able to speak with Him, our Lord and Savior Jesus Christ, the Holy Spirit, and our Blessed Mother Mary. Both our Lord Jesus and our Blessed Mother Mary have had occasions in the past to speak with certain sacred children of God while they are on the earth.

Each of the children that have been chosen by the divine will have been chosen very carefully for specific reasons. It is actually a wonderful thing to live your life knowing how close you are to the Trinity and our Blessed Mother Mary. It does bring with it certain amounts of trials and tribulations. It can be exceedingly difficult too. But the loving rewards and the magnificent feelings of the love from being so close to our Heavenly Father, Lord Jesus Christ the Holy Spirit and our Blessed Mother far outweigh any of the sufferings. I would not have it any other way.

It is important to note our Blessed Mother Mary did not just pop out of nowhere and start talking to these children. That would have scared the living daylights out of them, and they would probably and rightly run for the hills. What happened instead was the apparition of Blessed Mother Mary actually started in 1916, the previous year. The children's guardian angel coming to them and teaching them prayers and reparations to the Blessed Sacrament and then giving them the holy Eucharist.

Now back to Fátima. As always, our Blessed Mother speaks of love, penance, sacrifice, prayer and receiving the holy sacraments very often. She encourages prayer at least twice a day with the Our Father and the Hail Mary. This is essential to a healthy Christian life. But regarding Fátima in 1917 her message was much different. She carried with her divine messages and warnings and

---

Savior Jesus Christ, our Holy Spirit, and our Blessed Mother Mary. The other masterpiece book is titled "God's Grand Design of All Creation for Your Redemption." It reveals our Heavenly Father's message to all His sacred children on earth and reveals advanced theology that extends our Biblical literature.

signs of prophecies God's sacred children must be aware of. I know it hurt Blessed Mother to deliver these messages. But it is completely necessary because it is a very loving thing to do to warn people of terrible things coming their way unless they change the path they are on.

Question: Dearest Mother Mary, knowing you as I do, I can only imagine the pain you must have felt when you delivered the messages and their contents to the three shepherds in Fátima. If you do not want to answer this, I fully understand. But what was it like for you, what were your feelings when you were delivering the warnings and other messages to the three girls?

Answer: *I thank you, my dear son, for being sensitive to my feelings. I know you have loved me so much all these years and you are not afraid to show your love for me and your concern for my feelings. Earlier when you asked me about the Gospel of Thomas[39] you were afraid that it would cause me too much pain. Thank you for that. But I gave you a short answer and I know you felt bad asking the question, but it needed to be told how terrible and fraudulent that gospel really was and the reasons why.*

Regarding Fátima, I felt like this was just something necessary to do. Because for me I was doing everything I could for humankind, your Father's sacred children, so they would avoid the awful chastisements that were coming quite quickly in human history. Yes, dear son, I felt awful yet like any mother on earth knows, you must always do anything you can to protect your children from making terrible mistakes. This is what I did. But much of my warnings were not heeded. In a painful history, which developed in the coming years. I always lament about how God's sacred children tend to not pay attention and go about their business no matter how self-destructive it is, they just keep doing what they always have. I know you have experienced this my son with your first book, 'God's Grand Design of all Creation for your Redemption.' That book should be on the worldwide best seller list, but people are too caught up in the attractive Satanic

---

[39] Gospel of Thomas

temptations that taste good and feel good without any concern for their eternal destiny. I love you, my dear son.

Question: Dear Mother Mary, from what I observe, you are very unhappy as you just revealed regarding the reception of Fátima throughout the world. I can only assume this is why you felt it necessary to appear again at Akita Japan with Sister Sasagawa[40]. Is this correct?

Answer: *Yes, my son, you are so perceptive as always. My warnings got tangled up in the politics of the Catholic Church and the Vatican. They were damaging God's sacred children by keeping things so secret. That even when I wanted the third secret to be released fully throughout the world in 1960, the Vatican put up roadblocks to do that. And as you have said dear son, they did this for only internal political reasons. They are guilty of damaging your holy Father's sacred children across the entire world by hiding key information that I told the girls from being distributed around the world. Instead of serving God's sacred children, the cardinals and the bishops in the Vatican were more concerned about how they looked politically in their own minds. These are grave sins, and they will be punished accordingly. I hate to say that dear son, because it is painful but what else is there to say but that.*

I love the fact, dear son, that you never shy away from telling the truth of things. Thank you for knowing full well that my son is the way, the truth and the life, and no one comes to the Father except through Him. There will come a day, dear son, when there will be occasions that many people want to hear your words of love and advanced theology from the message of your Father. But not quite yet.

On that particular note dear Blessed Mother Mary, I look forward to the day when there are many people with open Hearts with open Hearts to hear the message of our Loving Almighty Father. For the first time they will understand His message of peace, love, understanding, acceptance along with

---

[40] Our Lady's apparition, Akita, Japan

advanced theology that makes it possible to understand how all creation works together in such a beautiful way.

Back in 1917 when our Blessed Mother appeared on six separate occasions to three little shepherds in Portugal, there were three secrets of Fátima that were revealed to these three Portuguese children. The "secrets" were actually prophecies and are only called secrets because the Catholic Church wanted to control these prophecies and keep them secret from God's sacred children. The secrets of Fátima occurred toward the end of World War I which happened from July 28, 1914, to November 11, 1918.

The fundamental content of Fátima was warnings things would get a lot worse in the future unless God's sacred children turn away from Satanic behavior. The first two Fátima secrets were revealed in 1941 in a document written by Lucia at the request of José Alves Correia da Silva, Bishop of Leiria. It was not until 1943 when the secrets of Fátima were completely revealed. In October 1943, the Bishop of Leiria ordered Lucia to put the secrets in writing. Lucia wrote down the third secret and sealed it in an envelope not to be opened until 1960.

It is especially important to note the three children were obeying what Blessed Mother Mary told them to do. In this case the third secret was not to be revealed until the year 1960. However, due to unknown actions within the Vatican, the third secret was not revealed as Blessed Mother Mary requested. It was not until Pope John Paul II officially released the third secret, or what the Vatican called the Third Secret. This caused tremendous speculation the Pope withheld vital information about the third secret.

However, even then, only part of the third secret was revealed by the Pope. The Vatican withheld all the information about coming tribulations and that the 112th Pope would be the last and be highly likely also be the anti-Christ. The Vatican wanted this part of the third secret to remain secret and hidden in the Vatican. There was even more within the third secret that was also not revealed defying the requests of our Blessed Mother Mary. To this day, their disobedience angers me greatly.

Fatima Apparition 1 [41]

This first secret was a very disturbing vision of hell. To a young girl this must have been an awful experience to realize such things do exist. Lucia indicated in her third memoir published in 1941 this first so-called secret was told to her and the other two children on July 13, 1917.

She went on to say, "our Lady showed us a great sea of fire which seemed to be under the earth. Plunged into this fire were demons and souls in human form. Like transparent burning embers, all blackened or burnished bronze, floating about in the conflagration. Now raised into the air by the flames that ensued from within themselves to gather with great clouds of smoke. Now falling back on every side like sparks in a huge fire, without weight or equilibrium, and amid shrieks and groans of pain and despair, which horrified us and made us tremble with fear."

As our Heavenly Father's anointed messenger compared the description of hell is given to the three children with what our Lord and Savior Jesus Christ told me. Yes, there is great suffering, but the suffering is not necessarily fire and brimstone. Rather <u>the suffering each person experiences is the horrific regret that comes from how they lived their lives while on earth</u>.

Before entering hell, each of God's sacred children does indeed meet personally with Jesus Christ. Every detail of their lives is there to witness in an atmosphere of pure and perfect love. It is during this review, which is normally referred to as "judgment" each sacred child sees everything they ever did, every thought, every motivation for what they did and what they failed to do. Importantly they also saw the effects their sinful behavior had on others of God's sacred children. You cannot overestimate the importance of seeing the effect each of the condemned people their actions had in destroying others of God's sacred children.

Again, this is done in a pure and perfect loving atmosphere with some angels also present. Fundamentally it will become very apparent for sinful people, there is no way they can be admitted to the Heavenly Kingdom. This is when

---

[41] Wikipedia, three secrets of Fátima.

yelling and screaming and gnashing of teeth occurs when they realize they will go to hell. It is then and while in hell their enormous regrets haunt them every moment of their existence from that point on.

One thing that is never discussed but is included in the sacred book I wrote with Jesus that says hell is actually not for all eternity. Rather because of the law of disintegration as Jesus says or the law of entropy as our scientists say, all things in hell decay back into the nothingness from whence they were created. Everyone in hell will ultimately dissolve back into nothingness which includes even the memories of people that knew them. There will be NO memories of people who went to hell. In other words, hell has been designed to slowly disintegrate back into the nothingness from which it originally came from. Yes, the sacred children of Almighty God are eternal and NOT subject to the law of denigration or entropy as scientists refer to it.

For those who are scientifically oriented the definition of entropy is the measure of randomness or chaos within a closed is the measure of randomness or chaos within a closed system. If you wonder why, you are getting wrinkles and losing hair as you age, that is a beautiful demonstration of entropy working on your body.

And so, it will be for those citizens of hell except entropy will not stop until the very last molecules of their existence dissolve back into the nothingness that originally existed. This is a magnificent plan on the part of our Heavenly Father. Because the end point of all of this will simply be a Heavenly realm occupied by all spiritual entities that love our Almighty Father with all their Heart. The rest of those that chose to rebel against our Father will be long gone to the point where no one will even remember them.

Question: Dear Blessed Mother Mary, somehow, I think I am losing some information regarding the first apparition at Fátima. I would appreciate any of your comments addressing anything I missed.

Answer: *Thank you for asking me this especially important question. What I told the children was exactly correct however their fear got in the way of a few things. When a person is in hell one size does not fit all so to speak. Their punishments and just Tizen mints are closely related to what they did to* *others of God's sacred children while they we are on earth. In other words, hell is tailor made for each individual person. If someone, for example cheated another person out of a considerable sum of money. The cheater being in heaven will experience a horrifically intensified feeling of severe loss that their victim felt while their victim was on earth.*

Likewise, if the person in hell was violent, they would experience the pain that they caused the other sacred child of God to feel. Except in hell the pain is intensified. They will also feel the agony of those closely related to the victim of their violence. They would feel their remorse, they would feel the concern and the feeling of complete helplessness as it related to the victim. Everything they caused other people will come back at them in an amplified manner.

As you know my dear son, each and every citizen of hell was exposed to the pure and perfect love of heaven. That memory of pure love and now the complete loss of it knowing that they can never have it is something that will torment them for the rest of their existence. Until, as you say dear son, entropy catches up with them and dissolves them back into the nothingness from whence, they came.

So, when people talk about seeing the fires and brimstone of hell in a way that is correct. Because the citizens of hell have their souls on fire, the fire of experiencing all the torment that they caused others of God's sacred children on earth. There used to be a saying in the country you live in, "<u>What goes around comes around</u>."

My dearest son, the opposite is also true for people that are allowed through the singular gate to the Heavenly Kingdom. Throughout the life on earth of people in heaven they get to experience all the love, kindness, and beauty that they gave two others of God's sacred children. The more you have loved on earth the more you will experience love in heaven. And of course, this is in addition to the enormous beauty and emotional impact of your Heavenly Father's love. For each and every one of his sacred children who chose him and lived by his rules on earth which is no easy task to do.

Dear Blessed Mother, this makes so much sense. Because there is a feedback mechanism in operation even on earth regarding the way people live their lives on this planet. If you treat people badly you will be treated badly, if you love them, you will get love in return. The way you described hell makes complete sense to me. Thank you, a million times, over for sharing this with our Father's sacred children.

You are so very welcome my dear son.

Fátima Apparition 2 [42]

From Lucia's Writings What Mother Mary Said to Her

"To save the poor sinners in hell God wishes to establish in the world a devotion to my Immaculate Heart. If what I say to you is done, many souls will be saved and there will be peace."

"The war is going to end (WWI) but if people do not cease offending God, a worse one will break out during the Pontificate of Pope Pius XI.

"When you see a night illumined by an unknown light, know that this is the great sign given you by God. That he is about to punish the world for its crimes, by means of war, famine, and persecutions of the Church and of the Holy Father. If my requests are heeded, Russia will be converted, and there will be peace; if not, she will spread her errors throughout the world, causing wars and persecutions of the Church. The good will be martyred; the Holy Father will have much to suffer; various nations will be annihilated. In the end, my Immaculate Heart will triumph. The Holy Father will consecrate Russia to me, and she shall be converted, and a period of peace will be granted to the world." [43]

---

[42] Wikipedia, Martins, Dr. António María, Memórias e cartas de Irmã Lúcia (Porto, Portugal: Simão Guimarães, Filhos, LDA, 1973), 225.

[43] Santos, Fatima in Lucia's Own Words I (2003), pgs. 123–124.

Fatima's Secret Apparition 3

My dear Blessed Mother Mary, I sincerely apologize for all the time it has taken me to come to this moment where you and I can talk about the famous third secret of Fatima. As you know, dear Mother, I have done a lot of reading in preparation for speaking with you. This is because I do not want to insult you by being unprepared but rather being able to ask intelligent questions.

All these so-called sources of the third secret of Fatima simply nibble around the edges of the subject matter without revealing the substance of what the third secret you told Lucia, Jacinta and Franciso. Many people say they have seen the third secret and have read it. But nobody has the guts to actually write down what they saw and reveal it to God's sacred children after 1960 which is per your request. All of them hide behind things saying they have taken an oath or been bound to keep things secret. I find that reprehensible and keeping secrets is hardly ever a good thing.

Dear reader, before we directly address everything the third secret of Fatima says I must, I have to present to you some terrible ugliness that has arisen out of the Catholic Church years ago. Sister Lucia was a teller of truth. She was extremely upset regarding the contents of the third secret. But in the end because of Heavenly intervention, she relented and wrote down what Blessed Mother Mary told her. Later in the text below you will read exactly what Blessed Mother Mary told me. Mother Mary also said sister Lucia got almost everything correct regarding her description of what Mother Mary told her many years earlier.

Note: What you are going to read are the exact words Blessed Mother Mary told me about Fatima.

Also, to remind you as Blessed Mother Mary speaks to me, I use speech to text software to instantly transcribe every word Blessed Mother Mary says. Nobody, and I mean absolutely nobody has tampered with the words in this book. It is the real thing!

Now, please read the ugliness that came from the Catholic Church many years ago. If you sense I am angry about this situation you are absolutely right. I am damned enraged by what was done regarding the third secret and Lucia.

What is a reliable Catholic Christian Catechism.

It used to be Catholics could rely on the authenticity of the Catholic Catechism. No longer. Ever since Cardinal Bergoglio became Pope, our Catechism has been infiltrated over time into a blend of "Woke" political viewpoints. The goal of this Pope is to blend Christian Catholicism with all the other religions in the world so as to "meet the needs of the people." In other words, throw out our beloved Bible and create a bastardized version of both the Bible and our Catechism that includes elements of progressive liberal political morality, Islam, Buddhism and so on.

I have already talked about how the "woke" Church has embedded itself within it is organizations then to mount attacks against true Christianity. This has been increasing by the Catholic Church attacking within itself as it can be observed manifesting itself over the last decade. So, what is a loving Catholic Christian sacred child of Almighty God to do? I for one cannot say definitively. I do have a master's degree in ministry and theology which leads me to cry at the inner turmoil the Church is experiencing. I no longer take what the Vatican says as true. It just is not. I must be very skeptical and take the Vatican with an exceptionally large grain of salt and suspicion of the hidden agenda I am documenting within this book.

My answer to a loving sacred child of God is to get hold of a Catholic catechism that was printed more than 10 years ago. Why 10 years? It is because that is how long cardinal Bergoglio aka, Pope Francis has been the Pope. Back then, he did not have time to poison the Catechism yet. Same thing for our beloved Bible. I have always liked the King James Version. I have located what I believe is a reliable Catholic Catechism. It can be purchased on Amazon. Its publication date is 1995. [44]

Question: My dearest loving Blessed Mother Mary, is this the best advice I can give to all of God's sacred children, so they avoid treacherous woke twisted theology from the Vatican these days? If I am wrong about this please

---

[44] Catechism of the Catholic Church: 9780385479677 - Christianbook.com

dear Mother Mary tell me and your words will remain in this book dedicated to you

Answer: *Oh, my dear son, my dear child I continue to be amazed at the depth of your perceptions regarding their wretchedness of what is happening within our beloved Catholic Church. My dear son, you are 100% correct and you are correct for the very reasons that you have mentioned. I do worry however about the ability of your Father's sacred children to obtain a Catholic catechism that was printed that far ago. Perhaps that is something each of your Father's sacred children can look up for themselves. But yes, dear son, you have given loving Catholic Christians the absolute right advice so as to not be misled by Satan Himself through the evil workings of the Vatican.*

Thank you, so very much dear son, your Blessed Mother Mary

Thank you, dear Blessed Mother Mary. I am so glad I gave good information.

13

The Widespread Theological Crime of The Vatican to Keep The Real Fatima Third Secret from God's Sacred Children

The Story of Sister Lucia of Fatima and The Vatican's Imposter Who Replaced Her

The third secret of Fatima has become a hotbed of controversy and manipulation. I started out writing a loving book about our loving Blessed Mother Mary and her apparitions. Little did I know or anticipate I would run across such deceit, falsehoods, and manipulation I have uncovered during my investigations.

Before I describe the third secret of Fatima and present to you the exact and precise words that are Blessed Mother Mary has told me directly what the third secret of Fatima really is. I am forced to reveal to you a damned awful ugly thing that was perpetrated by the Catholic Church on Lucia of Fatima. The real Lucia is the girl on the right.

The premise is very simple. Lucia it is an honest and loving Christian woman. She was spoken to by our Blessed Mother Mary back in 1917 and told what was going to happen in the future. And this included the high levels of the Catholic Church engaging in wretched practices of Satanic in nature. What you will read below is also motivation for the Church to make the real sister Lucia disappear, which they did.

As our Blessed Mother Mary says directly to me, when Pope Francis recently said the Anti-Christ is now on the earth, Blessed Mother said, "***he should know, because he is the Anti-Christ***." Please really think about our Mother's words. Pope Francis IS the Anti-Christ. WE ARE ALREADY IN THE END OF TIMES!

Lucia simply wanted to tell the world what Blessed Mother Mary told her. She refused to play along with what the Vatican wanted her to do! For that she was cloistered away to an unknown convent not to be found or communicated with. Instead, an imposter woman replaced her. Below are the pictures of both women. Because of modern photographic facial recognition analysis, it became easy to detect and prove the real Sister Lucia is not to be seen and replaced by another woman whose name we do not know.

Never in my worst nightmares would I have suspected such prominent levels of treachery as I have found.

Sister Lucia 1 and Sister Lucia 2

Dear sacred children of our Almighty Father, this next section is copied word for word from the Norvus Nordo Watch website. Full attribution is respectfully given to the fine Christians that make that website possible. The below article was published on March 26, 2019.

My personal feelings are it is a sinister Satanic plot by people at various positions of trust and power in the Church. Hierarchy that plotted against all of us in the laity so as to do two things:

1. Deceive us to falsehood, false things against the true Lucia.

2. To hide this sinister truth about the Vatican and its Satanic role in the end of times.

   I have been a Catholic Christian all my life and to find out garbage such as this makes me enraged and sick to my stomach. This treachery had to span multiple popes which makes things even worse in my eyes.

From "The Fatima Crusader, Issue 132, Spring 2024"

Doctor Marion Horvat after speaking with both the original Lucia and the suspected impostor Lucia, he wrote, "sister Lucy appears solemn, composed, and reserved. She always stands in a very collected way, her hands in a discreet gesture. She appears to be a person unaccustomed to being photographed, a bit awkward and uncomfortable with it. From her postures, gestures, and expression, it is easy to believe she is the person who saw Our Lady and understood the gravity of the message and the role she should play in it.

The second Lucy, we see a person with a different state of spirit. She is always smiling at ease in public and relaxed in her postures and gestures. She has lost the natural timidity type of sister Lucia I. She became not only fearless but also completely comfortable and integrated in ambiences external to her contemplative life. Her face is smiling and jovial. She no longer seems anxious about the future, her mission, the coming chastisement, the corporation of consecrated souls, or the many other concerns she expressed before. She seemed optimistic and content.

Doctor Horvat concluded the differences in physical characteristics, mannerisms and testimonies of sister Lucia I and sister Lucia II suggested the latter may be an impostor.

Doctor Chojnowski Concluded the following:

Facial mathematics reveals discrepancies in the ratios of nose with, mouth with, and interpupillary distances of the two subjects. Ratios which normally remain constant throughout adulthood. Based on 6 independent ratios yielded by 7 facial lengths, a facial mathematician calculated the probability that sister Lucy I and sister Lucy II being the same person is one in approximately 13 million.

Now the text from this important article.

Sister Lucia 1 vs. Sister Lucia 2

We at Sister Lucy Truth publicly declare that based on the evidence presented here. We've found it morally and scientifically certain the woman portrayed as "Sister Lucy," from her first public appearance in 1967, to her death in 2005, was not the same person as Sister Lucy. Seer of Fatima and Visionary who predicted the Miracle of the Sun on October 13, 1917.

This, one of the greatest frauds in the History of the Church, was discovered through the use of the most sophisticated facial recognition programs available. Along with the accumulated testimony of plastic surgeons, orthodontists, forensic artists, private investigators, handwriting analysts, and facial recognition experts.

Due to the availability of hundreds of photos of "Sister Lucy" available on the internet and in authoritative biographies, this case of substitution, fraud, and stolen identity has been able to be uncovered and analyzed. Without the judgment of the best and most relevant professionals available, we would not be making this grave accusation and presenting this charge.

We will continue to accumulate and post on this site new studies and research concerning this investigation as they are produced and published. All of the names of the relevant experts shall be published along with their professional findings. The truth of the disappearance of the true Sister Lucy and the identity of the imposter shall be placed before an internationally based private investigator who will investigate and solve the case.

The fraud has been identified and named. We charge the highest officials in the Vatican with conspiracy to perpetuate and conceal the substitution of Sister Lucy dos Santos of Fatima with an as yet unknown Imposter. [45]

I have felt it is getting increasingly urgent to bypass the Catholic Church which has turned into nothing more than a stumbling block for the truth of things. I am also completely angered by Pope Francis for he is revealing Himself as an enemy of real Christians in my humble opinion. He is attempting to drag secular socialist principles, progressive policies, and other reprehensible things like blessing same-sex marriages into our beloved Church. His lame excuse is it is the two people involved in the relationship that are Blessed, not the relationship. Frankly how stupid does he think we are.

---

[45] Malachi Martin: The Vatican Used A Fake Sister Lucia To Bury Fatima – RETURN TO TRADITION

Pope Francis is also guilty of a dereliction of duty considering he purposely waited until the ninth year of His pontificate to consecrate Russia and Ukraine to your Immaculate Heart. (This was also proven to be a fraud as well) By then it was too late because Russia invaded Ukraine and there are many hundreds of thousands of dead people that should not have happened.

Question: Dear Mother Mary, have I misunderstood something in the previous few paragraphs?

April 11, 2024

Answer: *No, my son. Everything you said bothers me just as much as you did, probably even more. It has mightily challenged my patience regarding consecrating Russia and Ukraine into my peaceful Immaculate Heart.*

<u>Pope Francis is trying to merge a socialist one world government politics with our Blessed Church that was founded by my dear son Jesus.</u> The Church has been founded to be a wholly spiritual place of prayer and communion with your Almighty Father in Heaven. It is never ever meant to be a meeting place between spiritual love and human politics. But this is what has happened with Pope Francis. I too am angered regarding what he has done and failed to do.

My goal is simple. I want to finally once and for all tell the world what it is that should have been revealed in 1960 per your request. I will reveal it to the world by means of this extensive book and have it published and make it available everywhere. Also, my dear Mother I will speak to my publisher about placing advertisements in Catholic and Christian publications. To promote this ever so important book about your apparitions with emphasis on the third secret of Fatima as amplified by Akita. My publisher will also have it translated into many languages as I can afford to pay for it.

How I have spoken so much, and I want to listen to every word you tell me as it will be faithfully and lovingly put down into my computer.

February 27, 2024
Blessed Mother Mary said the following:

Dear son, you have no idea how much pleasure and happiness you bring to me. You're so joyful and wonderful in taking on what nobody else on earth has been willing to do. Your Father is right, you are so highly intelligent, and you are a fighter. It hurts me deeply when people of great faith shy away from telling the truth of things for such a wide variety of needless reasons.

I know you got very upset and angry by the Church refusing to tell God's sacred children the truth of things. I know that you understand this is because they do not want to as you would say rock their boat. You have great perceptive abilities as my son has told you many times when you wrote the first book <u>God's Grand Design of All Creation for Your Redemption</u>. I know that what I am going to tell you will be published exactly as it is meant to be. This will take a lot of your energy, but you will do this because of your great love for the Trinity and me.

Recent Falsehoods from Pope Francis Regarding the Third Secret of Fatima

Dearest sacred children of our Heavenly Father, within my ongoing research efforts I have painfully discovered YouTube video that claims to reveal Pope Francis latest revelations regarding the third secret of Fatima. I was eating a hot dog at the time when the video played on my TV. After listening to what Pope Francis said about the third secret of Fatima, I wanted to squirt all my mustard on the screen. I am so sorry to say this, but Pope Francis is a Satanically controlled liar of horrific magnitude. The following are His exact words as presented by this YouTube video.

14

Pope Francis Lies About The 3rd Secret of Fatima

The following text is spoken from Pope Francis Himself. Please pay close attention to what our so-called Pontiff describes as the so-called long awaited third secret of Fatima. Then please compare what our Blessed Mother Mary describes the third Sacred. Remember: It was Blessed Mother Mary back in October 1917 when she revealed the real truthful Fatima to Lucia, Francisco, and Jacinta. For the benefit of the entire world, Blessed Mother Mary dictated her original words to Lucia in 1917 about the third secret of Fatima to be released to the world in 1960.

Pope Francis: *"The third secret of the Fatima reflects the breakout of wars and martyrdom and in some way, it seems Pope Francis has revealed some subtle truths about this third secret. He made it clear as he declared World War three has already begun in piecemeal fashion when he condemned the attack on Paris in November 2015. And again, in January 2023 when he made a call to stop to what was beginning to look like the start of WW III in different parts of the world.*

This clearly indicates the role of the Pope in the fulfillment of the third secret of Fartima. Cardinal Ratzinger rightly said, "the vision is an indicator of what we should do to force change in the right direction. This means it does not directly lay any emphasis on the role of a specific Pope such as Pope Francis in fulfillment of these prophesies. Rather it may reflect the role of the papacy through enforcing change a successive position as the world nears its end.

The prophecy reveals that the angels continue to cry penance beneath the arm of the cross. This reflects nothing truer than the number of Christian martyrdoms is on the rise. This evidence makes it clear that there is an ongoing war which may be different than what we have seen in the 1st and 2nd world wars. On separate occasions the Holy Father Francis has made reference to the global wars stating that it is happening in a piecemeal fashion. He charged His listeners with the need to stop the wars going all around us in places like Syria and Ukraine.

Just like it was shown in the third secret of Fatima he made it clear that wars hurts. Especially innocent young lives and old people. He shared the need that there is they need to stop the wars to make the world a safe and happy place to live in. In His charge, he pointed out the need to establish reforms for the needs of the people who are victim of wars for them to live happy lives again.

With these it is clear that the papacy is truly an agent of change in shaping a future for mankind as is revealed in the third secret. Now that the secret is revealed, what do we know about the fulfillment of other instructions of Our Lady?

After the third secret of Fatima, Lucia received another apparition from Mother Mary in 1929 where she received other parts of the secrets of Fatima.[46] It was during this appearance that Lucia received the need for Russia to be consecrated to the Immaculate Heart of Blessed Mother Mary. This revelation has led to continuous prayers requesting Mother Mary's intercession for the conversion of Russia. This was done in 1942 by Pope Pius during World War 2.[47] This continues to be a practice for succeeding popes including John Paul II and Pope Francis. The need and the urgency to pray the rosary for Russia was born from the rise of communist party. Which ultimately denied the existence of God and the period of Joseph Stalin's reign when he imprisoned and executed millions of people including Christians.

---

[46] **Blessed Mother Mary: I did not, I repeat I did not contact sister Lucia in 1929 and I did not instruct her regarding the consecration of Russia.**

[47] **When Pope Francis claimed that the consecration of Russia to my Immaculate Heart occurred through Pope Pius during World War II he was also lying. Remember our dear beloved son, Russia has yet to be consecrated to my Immaculate Heart even now as this wonderful book is being written in May of 2024.**

This consecration of Russia was at the Heart of the world's peace with the threat of annihilation which remained evident with the threat of Russia's nuclear weapons. When the Archbishop of Moscow visited Lucia, she asked Him if he was openly practicing in the city. And when he said a falsehood yes, she said that this meant that the prophecy of Fatima had been fulfilled. Now the Archbishop has also shared that the statue of Our Lady of Fatima stands in every Church in His country. <u>With the fulfillment of this prophecy what does this mean for the fulfillment of the third secret?"</u>

<u>The Pope Told falsehoods! This Pope IS the Anti-Christ and The Third Secret of Fatima has NOT been fulfilled!</u> It describes in detail what is happening and will continue to happen until the return of Jesus Christ and His second coming!

The video host concludes with the following: Now that we have explored the Pope's position on the third secret of Fatima, what do you think about the third secret of Lucia and how it applies to our world.

The Words from Pope Francis. It contains pleasant words indeed.

BUT! ALL OF IT IS A HERETICAL FALSEHOOD!

To this theological author there can be only one reason this nonsense would happen. It is because the Real Third Secret of Fatima contains terrible truths that implicate the Vatican in vast theological crimes against God's sacred children. Read onward dear people and you will find out what those crimes are as described word for word by our Blessed Mother Mary herself!

By the way, if I sound a bit angry about things it is because I am.

It must be noted the previous paragraphs are ascribed directly to Pope Frances who describes in detail false facts about the Third Secret of Fatima. Now read below where he claims there is "No Third Secret!"

May 10, 2024

Pope Francis said outright the following lie: **"No third secret of Fatima exists!"** [48]

My dear sacred children of Almighty God, if there is ever proof Cardinal Bergoglio AKA Pope Francis is an apostate, the anti-Christ and or heretic this is it. Along with the other heretical statements made by Him contained in other sections of this book, the absolute denial of the third secret of Fatima is the most outrageous if not most sinister and tyrannical.

Sister Lucia who wrote down precisely what our Blessed Mother Mary told her was threatened with death by the local Bishop in Portugal because she dared to write down the truth. That was the beginning of the Catholic Church doing everything it could to destroy the truth of what our Blessed Mother Mary wants to tell all our Heavenly Father's sacred children.

You will find all the consequences of not listening to Blessed Mother Mary and her warnings both in the coverage in this book of Fatima and la Salette in addition to Akita. Sorry to say, but I am so enraged at this fake Pope if I were close to Him, I would slap Him for all the damage he is attempting to do to God's sacred children.

---

[48] Something Bad About Our Lady & Warned "No Real 3rd Secret of Fatima Exists, You're Told falsehood" (youtube.com)

15

From Blessed Mother Mary: The Real 3rd Secret of Fatima Spoken Directly To Me, Father's Anointed Messenger

A Magnificent Dialog

Now! Please compare the Pope's falsehoods about the third secret of Fatima with what our Beloved Blessed Mother actually said here! Please, remember she spoke the following words directly to me, our Almighty Father's Anointed Messenger. I have no affiliation with the Vatican and so I cannot be pressured in any way.

In order for Satan to accomplish his evil agenda, he must have the world believing the falsehood the third secret of Fatima has been fulfilled. This is why the Pope said that. Again, the truth is that the third secret has NOT been fulfilled and Russia has NOT been consecrated to the Immaculate Heart of Blessed Mother Mary!

April 11, 2024
The Third Secret of Fatima

Directly Spoken by Our Blessed Mother Mary to Our Heavenly Father's Anointed Messenger: Richard Ferguson. So Here It Begins.

There will be wars and rumors of wars throughout the land. Millions upon millions of people good and bad will perish at the hands of others of God's sacred children. The entire earth will tremble and suffer for what has been caused by the evil one and His followers among God's sacred children on earth.

The Sky Will Blacken Like It Has Never Done Before.

If you reach out your hand you will not be able to see it. The light from candles will not be seen. This will frighten every one of God sacred children on the earth. But this will happen in the very near future, my dearest son.

Things will start to get slowly gray and then grayer and grayer still until the gray will come completely black. This will be like no black mankind has ever seen before. Your Father's sacred children have always enjoyed the illumination of the sun. But during this time there will be no light at all. <u>Nothing will be seen not even the fingers at the end of people's hands</u> can be seen. There will be some time before everything is completely black. During this period of increasing grayness toward black your loving Father is giving His sacred children a chance to come together with their loved ones. Before everything becomes the blackest of black beyond which there is nothing blacker.

Question: Dear Blessed Mother, I am almost 80 years old. Will I experience this with my family?

Answer: *Yes, my dear son. This will happen toward the end of your earthly existence so please warn your family of what is to come. I know that your son will not believe you as he has not believed all the things you have taught Him in His life. And as a result, he has made many mistakes that he will pay for now and will continue such.*

Of the time until everything is completely black. The time for the start of the grayness to the blackness will give those of God's children time enough to come together with their loved ones. This is an act of love from your Almighty Father in Heaven.

Because of the blackness people will not be able to find food or water to sustain themselves. This is also on purpose my dear son because it is not food that sustains God sacred children but the magnificent overwhelming love of your Father.

People Will Pray Like They Have Never Prayed Before.

For it is always the case that it takes great fear to bring people to God. This is such a shameful thing, yet it is true. My dear son, there are very few people like you that have such an intense love for your Heavenly Father. Such that you have never been scared of Him but rather you have had a deep-seated love for Him before you came to earth.

The blackening of the earth is the warning to pray. After three days, which is really a little longer than three days, slowly the blackness will begin to dissipate. And after a time, people will start to be able to see very short distance and be able to see the fingers on the end of their arms.

It is good that you digest this first before I continue onward.

My dear son, would you like me to now talk about the Church?

Our Beloved Church

Yes, Mother Mary because part of the third secret is already starting to happen.

Again, my dear son, your perception is wonderful. I know that over the last six months as you have been observing the Vatican and the current Pope you have been getting more and more agitated. Realizing that this Pope wants to subjugate my son's Holy Church to the wretched political powers that exist on this earth.

My son, although He (Our Beloved Father) is ever so forgiving is also very upset about this. Yet the Trinity and I know these things must happen to fulfill the prophecies that have been made over the last thousands of years. And are indeed in our Holy Bible, which includes not only the New Testament but portions of the Old Testament as well.

<u>*Your current Pope has said that the anti-pope is now on the earth. He should know because… He Is That Anti-Pope.*</u>

What is unknown to the innocent sacred children of God is that behind the scenes this Pope has been arranging for not only a one-world government under Satan. But also, a one-world Church under Satan that is completely against the teachings of my beloved Son. The end goal of the Satanic political and religious people in the Catholic Church is to subjugate your Father's sacred children into a system that brings together their falsehoods in Almighty God. And a domination of every particle of their existence while they were on earth by Satanic forces that will stop at nothing to rule over every aspect of their physical existence.

Your Father will allow all of this to happen. So that once and for all people will see that the source of all love, the source of all goodness is your Heavenly Father. When He withdraws His love from the people on earth things will become unbearable in a very short period of time.

Satan Will Place Himself On The Throne Of Peter In The Vatican

Yes, my dear son, and as you would say my son all hell will break out. There is not one thing that a sacred child of God can do that must first be approved by Satan's demons visible now on earth.

Satan's Earthly Power

The Vatican will then become the center of all earthly power headed up by Satan Himself. He will rule with an iron fist through a cadre in layers of authority much like any military would have today. There will be small amounts of commerce that occur across the earth but there will be no tattoos of the number 666 as so many people believe. As you know my dear son, there are no secrets in the spiritual realm. Everyone's identity will automatically be known by Satan Himself and all of His demons.

Without any labels, Satan's government will know who everyone is and whether or not they are willing to follow Him. So as to survive just for a tiny bit more time on an increasingly painful earth. You and your family, my son, however, because of your intense love for your Father, the Trinity and me, will not have to suffer this. You and they will be taken up as well as many others will be taken up into the Heavenly Kingdom in the blink of an eye.

There will be mass executions of God's sacred children who refuse Satan and bodies will pile higher and higher and higher and the stench of their rotten corpses will fill the air for miles around. Many will be tortured just as the Romans did during the times of my son. Satan's demons will enjoy doing this to God's sacred children. They know that their time is getting very short.

All of the so-called laws of the earth will emanate from St. Peter's throne in the Vatican. All of this will be allowed to happen by the Catholic Church. As it descends deeper and deeper into Satanic treachery and debauchery of a magnitude that, my dear son, will make you completely sick to your stomach. My dear son, as you have already uncovered in your research you have seen pictures of the current pope being entertained by scantily clad women. Dancing in front of Him with many of His sick Cardinals sitting behind Him. So, show this to the world, my dearest son, show all of it.

Also, my dear son there will be earthquakes such that the world has never seen before. No continent will be spared not even Antarctica, which people in the northern hemisphere never think about. None will be spared, both the good and the evil.

I know my dear son that there will be suffering but only for instant before they (my family and I) are in the arms of your Lord and Savior Jesus and our Holy Almighty Father. This will be true for you and your family. However, in the case of your son, he will be asked if he wants to go to Heaven or lead His life like he always has that leads to hell. He will be afforded this question only because he is in your family. Otherwise, he is considered a nonbeliever and will suffer with all the other nonbelievers.

The others that do not believe their suffering will be far longer and stretched out before they are condemned into the realm of hell never to be heard from again. And my dear son, as you have written in your first book God's Grand Design and the Booklet 1 Creation that is soon to be published. They will be doomed to dissolving back into nothing from whence they came.

These earthquakes both on the continents and under the sea will be so great that tsunamis will be so great that they will wash up on the land as much as 100 miles inland. And wash away all life that was once there. There will be no escape for anyone from any of this. Yet this is not all.

16

The Long-Awaited Consecration of Russia To The Immaculate Heart of Blessed Mother Mary

In your mind now I can see that the topic of world wars has come. Yes, my son, your worst fears will come true. There was a time not too long ago when World War III could have been avoided and the timetable for this in times would have been pushed back. That timetable was when I asked the Pope to consecrate Russia into my Immaculate Heart. This caused great division among the bishops and cardinals in the Church at the time. How foolish and shortsighted can they be?

In 1962, only two years after I asked the third secret to be released to God's sacred children, the Pope wanted to consecrate Russia to my sacred Heart. However great pressure was put upon Him by the magisterium not to do that for shortsighted reasons. All Pope John Paul had to say in His opening prayer was:

<u>"And now I consecrate all of Russia to the Immaculate Heart of our Blessed Mother Mary."</u>

Author's note: It should be restated there have been multiple Popes that refused to consecrate Russia in the past in addition to wanting to keep the third secret of Fatima secret as well.

The people of Russia would be overjoyed, and things would start to go into a loving direction. Instead, the Pope referred to Russia in an indirect and oblique manner which frankly did nothing at all.

As I tell you this my dear son, I know that your Pope Francis talks about doing this but as you like to say at times, "don't hold your breath." <u>*The last thing this Anti-Christ wants to do is to bring peace in the world.*</u>

Question: Dear Mother Mary, on this point, one of our news outlets said Pope Francis consecrated Russia? did Pope Francis consecrate Russia?

Answer: *My dear son, NO! Pope Francis did not. He said a few prayers about Russia, but he did not invoke the consecration to my Immaculate Heart. His goal was to fool a lot of people which he succeeded in doing.*

Question: Did Pope Francis ever go to Russia?

Answer: *No, he did not, and as your research shows he met with Putin at the Russian embassy. There were a lot of prayers that were said, and they gave the impression that Pope Francis consecrated Russia.*

<u>*Pope Francis purposely did not say the words necessary to consecrate Russia*</u> *to my Immaculate Heart. Pope Francis did not say:*

<u>*"And Now I Consecrate All of Russia To The Immaculate Heart Of Our Blessed Mother Mary."*</u>

He purposely fooled the entire world. My dear son, you never liked Francis from the very beginning. You even did not like Him before he was inaugurated as Pope Francis. Your perceptive abilities are great, and you use them well. Many times, the people around you scratch their heads but as always, you turn out to be correct. I thank you for that, my dear son.

Question: My dear Mother Mary, I'm beginning to believe the third secret of Fatima is ever so important I should make a special booklet on this alone. This would be along with your apparition in Akita. Is this something you think would be good, appearing in another special booklet besides this one?

Answer: *Oh yes, dear son, please do that. All God's sacred children must know the truth that has been purposely hidden from them.*

Dear Mother Mary, and so it will be.

17

Why All the Destruction, Pain, and Agony Dear Mother Mary

Question: Dear Blessed Mother Mary, I know now for sure all the terrible agony that is going to come to God's sacred children on earth. I know now it has one singular reason. That reason is simply. The vast majority of our Heavenly Father's sacred children have turned their backs on the magnificent love of our Heavenly Father and instead live lives that are of Satan not of Him. So, since the majority of our Heavenly Father's children rejected Him, then it is only correct and right that our Father removes all of His protections regarding His sacred children's lives on earth.

I know this will bring horrific destruction, suffering, great pain, and death. In a previous answer to my question, you said no one will be spared, both the believers and unbelievers. All of this leads me to a question. Since deaths will be painful in this coming environment, will the believers suffer just like the unbelievers? Or will some consolations be made?

Answer: *Again, oh, my dearest son, your perceptions continue to amaze and delight me. You indeed are the perfect sacred child of God to be our Heavenly Father's Anointed Messenger. And the perfect person to write this book regarding my apparitions and the Godly truths that are attached to all of that. I sincerely thank you for all of this. And one day when you return to the Heavenly Kingdom you and I will have delightful times together. Discussing all these events and everything associated with your immensely hard work for our Heavenly Father to bring His truth to all His sacred children.*

With all this in mind, dear son, in the back of your mind, I know that what you are thinking is completely correct. Your Lord and savior Jesus Christ and my son told me what the contents of your Blessed mind is regarding this and yes you are correct. The true believers in our Holy Trinity, our Heavenly

Father, your Lord and savior Jesus Christ and the Holy Spirit, which proceeds from them. All the people who believe in the teachings of my son will never experience a painful death like all the others who have rejected our Heavenly Father.

Believers Will Be Painlessly Snatched Out of Our Physical Bodies

When the time comes and death is near, believers will be snatched out of their bodies and return to the loving arms of their Heavenly creator. Our Heavenly Father creator of all that is seen and unseen. Briefly stated dear son, believers will not experience the pain of death rather they will experience what you experienced the time you were complaining about your lovely wife Marilyn and wanting God to heal her.

You were instantly taken out of your body to meet with two of the Heavenly elders that listened intently to what you had to say. You experienced instantaneous upward velocity that is as you put it indescribable. After a few seconds, you found yourself within the Heavenly realm with these two Heavenly elder listening to your pleas for your wife's life. And her cure from the deadly cancer she had in her body.

These two elders remember you very well for the intensity of your love for your wife Marilyn as you now intensely love your wife, Evangeline.

The reason I am long-winded is because what you experienced being snatched out of your body and taken into the Heavenly realm is exactly what the believers in our Heavenly Father will experience. So, they will not have to suffer any painful death. Their bodies will subsequently die or be killed by Satanic forces after their spirit bodies are gone, but by then they will be within the loving arms of their creator and our Heavenly Father. Lastly please tell people that there is nothing to fear.

<u>**For those who reject our Heavenly Father, they will die a painful death because it is of their own making.**</u>

My dearest Mother Mary, I remember that event so very well. Also, for the benefit of others I want to tell them right after we boarded the cruise ship, I started to have this strong urge to go to the Chapel of the ship. I knew something significant was going to happen there. But I was so emotionally exhausted taking care of my wife and knowing this would be her last cruise, I really didn't want any spectacular spiritual event to occur I knew would happen. Yes, I really did have knowledge of what was going to happen.

It was only until the 4th day I finally went up to the Chapel. It was a beautiful yet modest Chapel that was on the very highest part of the ship which I thought was so appropriate. When I arrived there was a narrow stairway that led up to the chapel. It had little cubbyholes for privacy around the perimeter of the Chapel. And this is where I curled up and got comfortable and within a few minutes what you described, my dear Mother Mary, then that happened. I was gently yet at tremendous velocity, taken out of my body into the Heavenly realm where I met with two elders of the Kingdom. I complained awfully for them to save the life of my wife. After a few moments, they each looked at each other, and then in the blink of an eye, I saw them zoom upward at a speed I could not comprehend. A moment later I was then back inside the Chapel's cubicle from where I started.

I want all of God's children that read this to realize that there is absolutely nothing that is hidden. Those within the spiritual realm know the location of everyone of God's sacred children no matter where they are and no matter what they're doing. It is like what the psalmist said, "no matter where I go You are there."

Question: My dear Blessed Mother Mary, I know you dislike politics as I do. To me it is a pit of Vipers born out of Satanic urges. But I am forced to consider the fact Satan who is working through our political system and the Satanic Vipers that have achieved political offices and power over God's sacred children in our country. So, my dear Blessed Mother, no way do I want you to feel obligated to answer this question that has come into my mind. And my prayers for this rapidly disintegrated country called the United States of America.

The question I have is to what extent has Satan's minions infiltrated the distinct levels of our government? Just how extensive is it at the federal, state level and our educational systems Oh, that's wrong? I already know at the county level, especially our schools have been thoroughly infiltrated by those who want to twist our children's minds into Satanic minions. Through their God-awful propaganda and destruction of moral values to our children.

I don't know how else to ask this question but, just how bad is it for those of us who are true Christian believers?

Answer: *This is a painful question to answer my dear son. The infiltration of Satanic behavior has been going on as you have pointed out since the early 1960s. At first it was quite a minority of people and parents and other Godly people. Being busy with their own Godly lives, did not notice for many years the treachery that was slowly growing within public institutions and the public school system. As you like to say, it grew like a disastrous fungus promoted by people that did everything they could to hide the truth of what they were up to. I want to add dear son, that all of these people were Democrats because as you have said repeatedly, "The Democrat Party Is the Political Arm of Satan."*

As time went on the growth of Satanically oriented people in government and public education grew faster and faster. As you would put it your son it was an exponential mathematical increase over time whereas time went on it grew faster and faster. Over the last 10 years even under the presidential term of Donald Trump, the insides of government organizations and education departments kept growing like weeds.

Now, with Joe Biden as president everything has exploded, and huge vast amounts of tax money has gone to promote increasingly Satanic activity in your country. It is fair to say now that most school systems in the United States are controlled by Satanically oriented people. Dead set on dosing American children into the communist, socialist Satanic propaganda that destroys such things as the difference between boys and girls. Their comprehensive list of activities is Satanic and destructive.

Dear son, as you have explained many times to people, it is easy to destroy but difficult to create and rebuild. Donald Trump will be reelected later this year as the president, but the Democrats will fly into a violent frenzy as is a pure example of Satanic mind-sets. Some people will call this a civil war and that is probably correct. But this is what is to be expected from hateful

Satanic oriented people. Your yet to be President Donald Trump #47 will do everything in His limited power to erase the damage done under the Satanic Biden administration.

The problem will simply be president trump will respect and follow the rules of American law while the Democrats will ignore all laws so as to regain political power against the will of American citizens.

If everybody could only read this book that you are writing, your words within here will change the course of human History for the better.

I love you so very much my dearest of sons,
your Blessed Mother Mary

18

A Further Description of The Torment, Pain, and Agony Coming During the End of Times to Those Who Rejected Our Loving Father

March 1, 2024

Our Blessed Mother Mary now continues telling me what it is she wants all of God's sacred children to understand. This information exceeds what was originally told to Lucia, Jacinta, and Francisco in 1917. Take heed my dear sacred children of God.

Thank you, my dearest son, everything I have told you so far will completely unravel all man-made institutions and most all man-made infrastructure that they depend upon. Social upheaval will be beyond anything the worst that people can possibly imagine. The only thing left after this conflagration across the world will be the few remaining people who finally understand that in the end there is only God and there is only themselves.

Everything that mankind has produced will become nothing more than a distant memory. All the evil that has been built into human made organizations, human made buildings and bridges and infrastructure will be gone. After a time, people will be reduced to fundamentally the lifestyle of Abel, Cain, Adam, and Eve after they were expelled from the garden of Eden.

It is a remarkably interesting parallel such that when Adam, Eve, Abel, and Cain no longer lived in the Garden of Eden as Blessed by your Almighty Father. The sudden realization hit them as you would say like a ton of bricks. They had to scratch the ground for anything they could eat so they could survive. Yet even in that time Cain blamed anybody but Himself for the results of what he did within the physical world.

This consciousness is horrifically present in all of human society today. That consciousness along with ever so many Satanically oriented people on the earth that have as their goal monstrous political power over others of God's sacred children. It is your Heavenly Father that is in control of everything. And people who wish to contribute to God's sacred children must have in the center of their lives the attitude that they should become servants to others. To help where they can and to guide other people based on whatever knowledge they may have that is constructive and loving.

My dear son, you have said many times that the Democrat party in your United States is the political arm of Satan. This is far truer than you know because <u>many of the top Democrat leaders actively engage in Satanic worship.</u> People do not know about this because it is always very secret and behind closed doors. When this book that you are writing gets published many people will throw stones at it and throw stones at you for the truth that I am telling you.

As you already know my dearest of sons that there are high placed people in the Catholic Church that will do the same thing. They worship Satan. In secret and are using their position and power in the Church to change the holy and sacred Mass and other Catholic prayers. Designed to move the Church away from its sole reason for existence which is to love and adore your Almighty Father and especially your Lord and Savior Jesus Christ.

19

Satan's Plan for World Conquest

It is fair to say, my dear son, that Satan over the last 60 years as you have observed has been successful in penetrating the minds of so many of God's sacred children. Across the world to build upon their internal desire to govern, to control, to dictate the living standards and rule of all others of God sacred children. This is so rampant throughout the entire world and manifests itself in what you call liberalism, progressivism, communism, socialism, and so on.

<u>The goal is simple. Put all power in the hands of very few people so when the Anti-Christ takes the reins of the Church, which is nearby, it will be far easier to control the entire world population.</u>

This is what is at hand my dear son.

The End of Times Began in the 1960's.

But as I have said, this will come at a horrific price such that the world population will crumble into nothingness. Because of your Father removing His active support and guidance from the world. And he will let His children crumble underneath their own wretched rules and self-government that will bring only death, hardship, pain and suffering in a magnitude that is horribly unbearable to even think about.

<u>*As you have realized my dear son, all of this is now starting to happen. The prophecies of Father Pio, the information of my apparitions in Fatima as described by Father Malachi Martin and others you can see are starting to happen. As you have told your loving wife, things here will now only get worse and worse.*</u> *This will be from both a societal level a geographical level and atmospheric level and a cosmic level. There is nothing that God's sacred children can do to stop this once <u>your loving Father withdraws His constant support for His children on earth.</u> I know you are wondering my son how long this end of the world suffering will take. In large part it depends upon*

how quickly His sacred children begin to realize what the fundamental cause of all of this is.

Some will realize far quicker than others. You for example, my son realized this a number of years ago before things really started to crumble. I know you have been keeping a close eye on the activities, the Satanic activities in the Vatican. It will take quite some time for Catholics and other Christians to realize the danger that is now being constructed and posed by the Vatican toward all of the Christian believers all over the world.

I told you that when Pope Francis declared that the Anti-Christ is now on the earth, he is totally correct. <u>The Anti-Christ has been working extremely hard behind the scenes to construct a grid of political power that stretches across the world. And that political power is Satanic from the beginning to the end, and it is he.</u>

Pope Francis is the Anti-Christ.

The entire spiritual realm including the Heavenly Kingdom all know who and what he really is. There will be a huge schism within the Catholic Church where the Satanic driven people in power will wage war against the people who love and cherish Almighty God and your loving Savior Jesus Christ.

Do not worry, my dear son, for this situation will not last very long. As all of this comes to fruition. Along with all the geographic, the natural disasters and other calamities that will bear upon the world without the support of your Heavenly Father, Satan will see that His time is getting ever so short. It is then that God's children still left on earth will be in the greatest of danger for Satan and His demons will strike out against any person that opposes His rule over them.

<u>My dear son, continue to accumulate emergency supplies. Food stocks that will last you in your family for quite a number of years</u>. Especially secure clean water and <u>do not fill up your swimming pool for that will be a wonderful store of water that will be attacked by other people who are looking for the same thing.</u>

Speaking of things like that, my dear son, <u>there will be roving bands of very violent criminals looking for anything</u> that will help in their survival. And they will instantly kill anybody who stands in their way. All, my dear son, I hate so much to tell you all of this. But you are a perfect channel of distributing the future of the world. Because of all the wretched sin that continues to grow deeper and deeper and deeper. Not only in secular society, not only in secular covered meant was also in the Church of your Lord and Savior Jesus Christ.

We within the Trinity know very well that you are strong, and you are indeed a fighter as your Father told you a number of months ago. You will be one of the ones that will survive all of us. And you will play a deep role in the reconstruction of the world. To bring it back to true-life with the love of your Father, His only begotten son, the Holy Spirit which proceeds from them and of course me your eternal Mother of all time. I know you have questions dear son. Think about them and make them into a list and I will answer each and every one as you ask. I love you more than you can possibly know. Your eternal Mother Blessed Mother Mary.

April 7, 2024
None Will Be Spared Faithful and Unfaithful

Question: My dear Blessed Mother Mary. There is one part of the third secret of Fatima that bothers me a lot and I would love to hear your comments on it. The part that bothers me is:

Answer: *"<u>Fire will fall from the sky and will wipe out a great part of humanity</u>, the good as well as the bad sparing neither priests nor faithful. The thought of the loss of so many souls is the cause of my sadness."*

Will Believer Be Treated Different Than Those Who Continue to Reject God?

Question: I have often thought of this and like you, dear Mother, it makes me incredibly sad. My question is as people are dying from these calamities are the good and the bad both going to experience the agony and pain of death? Or somehow is our Heavenly Father going to take the faithful out of their bodies before horrific pain is experienced in the physical? I know this is spiritually possible. Because of my experience with the two Heavenly elders that took me out of my physical bodies to hear my complaints regarding my late wife Marilyn before she passed away.

Answer: *My dearest son, that is a wonderful and magnificent question. <u>Your Heavenly Father does not deal in pain for His sacred children.</u> As you know dear son, he loves you more than you can possibly imagine. You remember the time when you were in the jet halfway across the Pacific Ocean and a beautiful golden orb appeared to you and it said to you, "God loves you." That love was so intense it brought great tears of joy to you like nothing you have ever experienced before. I know you understand that is the kind of our Father's love for all of His sacred children.*

However, <u>those who reject your Heavenly Father will indeed experience all the pain and agony of a physical death. For they have turned their back on their Father</u> and thus they do not possess the grace that would shield them from horrific physical pain.

<u>For the faithful dear love, they will not experience pain like that at all. Instead, moments before their bodies die, they will be removed from the physical instantaneously into the loving spiritual realm. And they will be greeted by loving angels that will take care of them in every way.</u>

Your discernment of this detail is worthy of exclamation and joy to those who continue to love Almighty God within their Hearts in their minds. <u>Your Heavenly Father would never allow His faithful loving sacred children to feel agony and pain like what is coming to those who have rejected Him.</u> Thank you for asking my dearest son. This is a wonderful question and I know the answer will bring relief and joy to all those who love Almighty God and me as you do.

Also, my dear son, my son has told you that <u>your family is protected. And they will enjoy the same sacred treatment as you do, with the one exception of your son who has rejected your Heavenly Father. But he will be given a choice.</u> As I said before whether he wants to continue his sinful ways and experience the consequences thereof. Or will he reverse course and come back to you His loving Father, and His Almighty Father in Heaven.

Thank you ever so much my dearest Blessed Mother Mary. I apologize for not getting this book out sooner than it will be because I want everybody to know your Blessed words as soon as possible.

My dear son, as my son Jesus told you, we think in the longer-term. And an extra month or so to bring this book to the marketplace is something that will not make that much difference in the longer-term of God's holy plan for His sacred children. Please do not feel bad about that there is nothing to feel bad about.

I love you.
Your Loving Blessed Mother Mary

Dear son, I know you're getting very upset would you like me to pause for a little bit?

That's okay, dear Mother, I would rather continue onward.

My dear Mother Mary, some of this has already been spoken of by loving people like Father Malachi Martin and Sister Sasagawa in Akita Japan. But I must persevere to bring God's sacred children the truth. The truth of what is going to befall the earth due to the increasing wretchedness and sinfulness to a level that has never been seen before in the History of man since Adam and Eve.

Question: Dear Mother Mary, lately within the scientific news astronomers have identified two very large asteroids that pass through the orbital plane of earth around the sun. This makes it very possible to collide with earth. Is the "Fire from Heaven" one or both of these asteroids, Ephosis or Beneau? Or is it multiple others we have not yet detected? I also know there are between 1.1 to 1.6 million asteroids right past the orbit of Mars.

Answer: *Again, my dearest son you amaze me with your depth of knowledge in this case regarding astronomy and astrophysics. There will be multiple asteroids of very large size that will collide with the earth in the not-too-distant future. Mankind with all its rocketry technology will not be able to stop them for they are coming from a different direction than is anticipated with the two asteroids you just mentioned. They will bring death and* *destruction like nothing that has ever happened before on earth. They will not be as large as the asteroid that collided with the southern part of the Gulf of Mexico that wiped out 80% of all life on earth. Your heavenly Father wants to retain a large group of his sacred children who now thoroughly understand that they must conduct their lives in a very loving manner. That is consistent with the biblical literature that was written about my son Jesus Christ.*

All modern technology will be completely wiped out and people's lifestyle will be thrown back into the equivalent of the 1800s. The time when Columbus discovered America. Life will be livable but very difficult. You can say, my dear son, that your heavenly Father hit the reset button and now life can start a new and fresh with Satan gone. All his minions have been also removed and your Lord and savior Jesus Christ will bring about a magnificent era of happiness and love on planet earth.

You will be part of the reconstruction my dear son, however it most likely will not be in your physical form. This is something I know you will thoroughly enjoy. Creating loving societies that build new ways of living with your heavenly Father in complete control and your Lord and savior Jesus Christ. In control of all the aspects necessary to create a magnificent loving society where there will be no sin. What a lovely thought my dear son, a large society rebuilding from the ashes that has no sin. Yes, dear son you have said this before, and it is true it will be heaven on earth.

I love you so very much my dear eternal son. You're Blessed Mother Mary.

I know you have also uncovered the idea in your research about large meteors colliding with the earth. This will also be true as part of the torment that happens when your loving Father removes His protection. One thing that people never ever considered is that all the time during the development of the earth to be suitable for the physical existence of your Father's sacred children. Way up in space angels at your Father's bidding have always been deflecting those rocks from hitting the earth. And interfering with His sacred children's development and taking what you call the earth test.

But now your Father is removing His protection. and very large meteors will indeed assault Mother Earth like never before in the known History of your Father's children. These collisions with Earth will be so great that they will also produce large tsunamis that will assault the coastlines of the major continents across the world.

The world will be reduced back to what you would call the 1800s as far as convenience, availability of food, healthcare, and other kinds of technology. All technology that has been invented in the last 100 years will vanish. As a result, there will be murderous gangs roaming the streets and the houses for anything they can take while killing the occupants. It will be a lawless time that will bring untold hardship and agony to everyone still on earth.

What we call the Christian Church or more accurately the Catholic Church will be blended into a depraved Sodom and Gomorrah-like organization that will be controlled by Satan sitting on St. Peter's throne. As I said before and you have seen in pictures, my dear love, the depraved sexual acts, and other horrendous features of fleshly exploitation will become the norm of Satanic human behavior.

Yes, my son, small children and babies will be sacrificed to Satan in rituals that I know would make you sick if I described them.

Why will a loving Almighty Father allow all of this to happen to His sacred children? The simple reason is because never before in the History of humanity has so many people turned away from your loving Father in Heaven. Each passing day it gets worse and worse with no end in sight. So, by allowing events to take their natural perverted course, it will be only then that the remaining remnant, small as it will be, will then understand their true nature. Which is fundamentally giving up to Satanic impulses and turning their backs on Almighty God. In this way the remaining people will see what life is like without Almighty God. God never will cause any of this. But rather, he will simply allow things to take their natural course and people will then suffer the consequences of what they themselves have decided to do or not do.

My dear son, I know you remember raising your three children and how you handled their punishments. When you felt that they did something wrong, and you knew that they knew it was wrong but did it anyway you gave them a spanking of various intensities. After their spanking you would leave the room and wait five minutes then you would come back

to your child and hug them and explain to them why they deserve the spanking they received, and you always told Him also how very much you love them. It is much the same thing, my dear son, with all of your Father's sacred children.

However, in this case your Father will simply not continue His active protection of His children on earth and let the earth do what all other Heavenly bodies do within the universe. The instability of the earth will reinstate itself like it was many hundreds of thousands of years ago. The earth will no longer be a kind of Eden but rather a regular planet with no special protective features from Almighty God.

My dearest son, we should stop for now because I can see that you have become exhausted emotionally from what I have revealed to you. I would request to you, my dearest son, that we continue this sometime tomorrow. After you have had a good meal and have cleared your mind and your Heart to continue listening to this most wretched secret of Fatima.

Thank you, dear Mother Mary. The emotional impact of all of this has really struck me down for now. You are correct as always and let's continue as you suggest tomorrow sometime. I do have one request which is to not let me forget anything that could be of importance. I love you dear Mother.

February 29, 2024

Dear Mother Mary, thank you so very much for a little rest before we continue on with your message to all of God's sacred children. It has been a two-day rest for me because yesterday I was not feeling up to giving you the best I have. But this morning, it is now 4 AM and I have not slept a wink, I am up and alert. So, this is a good time to continue your message to God's sacred children.

Perhaps we can start where we left off two days ago. Talking about the absolute terrible condition the world is in. Where never before has so many people rejected our loving Almighty Father, creator of all that is seen and unseen and creator of every particle of human existence. Which, of course, includes the spiritual realm and the physical realm. I know great political forces under the temptations and control of Satan who as you know has attacked me on three separate occasions and then keeps attacking me most every day of my life.

With your permission, my dearest Mother Mary, should we start where we left off regarding the condition of the world?

Yes, my dear son, good morning. I know that you did not sleep at all last night but the message I gave to Lucia Santos and Jacinta and Francisco Marto at Fatima has been on your mind constantly. Thank you for your devotion dear son. We left off talking about the terrible disasters that are coming to the earth because of the enormous amount of God's sacred children turning their back on their loving Father. Frankly, my dear son, they have decided not to look past their own noses and see the beauty of what their Father has created for them. The awful thing is that they have become so self-centered and narcissistic. And they view life in accordance with the way they feel and not the way of your Father's rules for life, which as you know are very simple. You did a very good job in your previous book explaining the depth and simplicity of your Father's rules of existence so people will return to the Heavenly Kingdom.

My dear son, in addition to the other catastrophes I have brought forth to you, there is much more coming to the earth. As you know, my son you are aware of cosmic cycles like the orbits of their cycles that determine and have a great influence on the general climate of the earth. Also, the earth is getting very close to switching its magnetic poles to be the opposite of what it is today. This will happen a lot sooner than people think. And will bring a lot of havoc in weather patterns and affect food supplies and so many other effects this will have on the human population will be enormous.

Earthquakes of very large magnitudes will also start to happen this year and next. These earthquakes will be not only on the continents but also undersea. And the undersea earthquakes will be very violent. And will produce tidal waves. Which will appear as if they came out of nowhere because the people on the coastlines will not feel the earthquakes what they will see huge waves coming at them from the seas. Your Father, my dear son, has kept all of this in check in the last hundreds of years. But now rightfully so, they have decided to let the earth do what the earth does in the natural cycle of things.

My dear son I know you understand that it breaks your Father's Heart to let these things happen. But, my dear son, even though you did not know this when you spanked your children for doing things. They know were wrong. You felt so bad that sometimes you almost cried about what you had to do to instill the proper behavior in them that they would understand not to do those things again. I love the fact, my dear son, that a few minutes after the spanking you would always without fail return to them and hug them. And explain why they got spanked and then you would tell them how much you love them.

There will also be earthquakes that are very destructive on the land as well. My dear son, you live in an area on earth that is particularly active with not only earthquakes but a few volcanoes as well north of where you are. In the beginning, these earthquakes will not bother your home. But there will come a time when your Father wants you to move away from where you are. For the state that you live in is one of the worst in terms of the people's love for your Heavenly Father.

They will be punished severely for this just by allowing the natural forces of the earth to reassert themselves. Speaking of earthquakes and volcanoes I know you understand about the Yellowstone National Park and the volcanic caldera there. This will come to life in the not-too-distant future. And will wreak havoc across the entire world with toxic gases and particles that will mix with the air and make it unbreathable in many areas of the world. Acid rain will fall down on the crops in the Midwest of the United States where you live. Food will become very scarce, and many people will frankly starve to death.

All of this will trigger massive social upheavals where crime will become rampant on a scale that the earth has never seen before. It is written that the living will come to envy the dead. This is a true statement my dear son. When the time comes your Father, your Lord and Savior Jesus Christ and I will tell you when the best time for you is to move your family from the area you now live. I know you like Texas for many good reasons but depending on how things work out be open to other possibilities for the safety of yourself and your family.

On another note, dear son, I already mentioned the Milankovitch cycles that control the earth's orbit around the sun with cyclical properties that have the power to change the planet's climate. Right now, the earth is in that optimal position with regard to the cycles but as cycles do, they continue toward less friendly positions in the cosmos. This is what is happening right now regarding the earth. These cycles are unstoppable. Your Father has been muting much of the effects of these orbital cycles and will now let the earth do what it normally would do without His protection. This will result in extremes. The people on the earth have become very much like the hardheaded Hebrews in ancient times as described in the Old Testament.

In a very direct comparison, the manner in which your Father had to deal with them as His chosen people will now again be applied to the people on earth. To bring them to their senses and remember their real identity as you have described so well in your book <u>God's Grand Design Of All Creation For Your Redemption.</u> Many people will say that it is the anger of God that is causing all of this destruction suffering and pain. It is not rather, as you know, my dear son, your Father is pure love. And the agony in which your Father feels because of so many of His children rejecting Him. Is such that he is only withdrawing protecting His children the natural cosmic forces that press upon the earth. This will continue until finally the few that are left will finally understand that they must return to their roots, they must return to their loving Father and His ways of behavior. It will only be then that things will turn around quickly on the earth, and it will flourish again along with all of His remaining sacred children.

20

A Last-Minute Addition From Our Lord, Jesus Christ

Right before we were about to finish all the editing on the text within this book, there was an assassination attempt against President Donald Trump at a rally. The investigation by the government since then has been lukewarm at best and it does show that the FBI, the Secret Service, and other security agencies, were completely incompetent in protecting the president.

Additionally, our government, of the people and by the people, (that is meant to be sarcastic) has classified much information revealing horrible holes in their protection allowing the assassin a clear shot at the president.

This assassination attempt by the Democrat party is more proof that the End of Times has arrived in our country. Some may say that we have had assassinations and attempts before. Yes. But this thought is only looking at this one event. When you read what Jesus Christ said to me below, He puts this in the context this event is part of.

Remember, as I have said before, <u>The Democrat Party Is The Political Arm Of Satan</u>. There were 12 Democrats and appointees directly involved in this.

So, this was part of the End of Times in our country.

What you are going to read is pure and perfect information that will startle you, but it is completely true. Why is it pure and perfect?

Why is this true? Because the below text was told directly to me from Jesus Christ himself.

Lord Jesus speaks.
July 14. 6:00 PM.

My dearest son Richard, I wanted to explain a few things to you about the recent events yesterday and today in your country America. Yesterday, there was a legitimate and intentional attack against your presidential candidate Donald Trump. <u>*Your government knew about this coming attack, and they turned their backs on what they knew was going to happen.*</u> *This is one of your government's tactics. To manipulate the people, your Father's sacred children, who live there.*

As you know my dear son, there has been <u>constant verbal attacks from the Democrat Party, from your publishing media, from all different sources within the government. The legal system has been corrupted. The Democrat Party has actively and strongly promoted so many heinous sins against your heavenly Father.</u> And what you said about the Democrat Party as my mother has said is that you are completely correct when you label them as the political arm of Satan.

The fact that a rooftop with the clear view towards your next President, Trump, when he was speaking <u>was allowed to happen</u> is proof that your government purposely as you would say, dropped the ball so as to allow this kind of thing happen with what your government calls reasonable deniability.

Yesterday I mentioned to you, my dear son, that <u>one of your angels instantly modified the trajectory of the one bullet that would have otherwise struck Donald Trump at the base of his neck on the right side higher into the cranial area. It would have killed him in a few minutes. But your Angel deflected that bullet, so it penetrated the base of his right ear as everyone knows now.</u> [49]

What they do not know is that divine intervention saved literally your entire country from a horrific, grinding and painful end of its history.

---

[49] My dear sacred child of God, I am the only anointed messenger of Almighty God and the work that I do diligently in creating sacred literature for Almighty God, I am a prime target for Satan. Satan has personally attacked me on three different occasions back in my late 20s after I yelled at him and told him to stop the evil he conducts in this world. Make no mistake, Satan is real, and he has uncountable demons to help him. Since that moment I have been forced to conduct spiritual warfare against his relentless and frequent attacks against me. This is why our heavenly father has provided not one but two angels from my protection. Yes, their names actually are Gabriel and Michael.

My dear son, normally we do not interfere with political events or the history of nations because all of that is a product of the gift of free will that your Father has bestowed upon all of his sacred children on earth. But in this case, there were only a few very guilty people high up in your government, including your president Joe Biden and others that you know about like Hillary Clinton and a few others that gave secret orders to the Secret Police posing as protectors of Mr. Trump.

<u>Donald Trump will win the coming election, in a huge landslide which will shift the political scene entirely in favor of the foundational principles, the Godly foundational principles that your country was founded upon.</u> Mr. Trump after he is in office, there will be many investigations to ferret out the criminals that have been so well entrenched in ever so many of your government branches.

The Communist sympathizers within your country will largely stop shouting so loudly and many of them will question what their political beliefs were. Our Father has seen the change of heart and so many of the citizens of the United States. Your Almighty Father wants to give your country another chance to avoid all the terrors and horrors of the End of Times as my mother has described to you in great detail.

<u>Europe, however, will continue to burn because of all the Muslims they allowed into their countries.</u> [50] As you know my dear son and have said many times. Islam is the religion of Satan. Of this there is no doubt for anybody that wishes to think about it in an objective manner. Both of us, you're Blessed Mother and Are so happy that your second major book is now in the publisher's hands. Advantage will do a very good job for you. Your friend and colleague, Mike. will do everything proper. The next two or three booklets which you plan on publishing in the next three or four months is wonderful and please continue with that. Then I am looking forward. to working with you and speaking together like we did on the first book to

---

[50] My dear sacred children, both France and Britain have already fallen to satanic influences. In Britain they have banned the Bible and closed their churches. In France anything Christian is now forbidden. I encourage you strongly to go to objective news outlets and see for yourself the details since things will have changed since I wrote this. It will be worse. It will continue to get worse to the point that our blessed mother Mary has described in another part of this book.

produce the third major book for people which is how to get back into heaven. And I know you're already thinking about the contents. As always, I will be at your side, along with your Blessed Mother.

I know you have a question in your mind. Please articulate it and I will answer.

Question: *Thank you, dear Lord. Is there any one particular phenomenon or event that our Heavenly Father and You and the Spirit that influenced you to decide that United States would be given a second chance?*

Answer: *There were several things, my dear son. We could see within the hearts of ever so many millions of people in the United States that they were rejecting more and more and more of the Communist Manifesto being perpetrated on them. In your country more and more people were taking action to support the fundamental principles upon which your country was founded, which, as we all know is based upon the rules of life set forth by your Heavenly Father. And we also knew that to release that beautiful energy into the social and cultural dimension of your country, it needed a spark of some kind which would ignite the pent up passions and desires of your people for Almighty God to be expressed within your society and take it away from the Marxist and Communist people that have thrived all too long in your culture and in your country.*

It is now that, as you would say, my dear son, the worm has turned. In this case for the much, much better.

I love you ever so much, my dearest of sons.

Thank you, my dearest Lord, and Savior Jesus Christ

I love you too.

21

Third Secret of Fatima Continues

March 2, 2024

My dearest Blessed Mother Mary, it has been a whirlwind of terrible emotions I have suffered with regard to the third secret of Fatima. However, my sufferings are minuscule when compared to the sufferings of so many of my brothers and sisters in Christ. So as for now they count for nothing. Over the last number of months, I have been increasingly aware of the internal disintegration regarding the Church of our Lord and Savior Jesus Christ. At first, I thought, what I was hearing was just complaining from fundamentalist Christians who never seem to be happy. But the short period of time my doubts about the veracity of their descriptions of Vatican activities, those doubts vanished.

Earlier in the sacred work of your words meant for all of God's sacred children you mentioned Pope Francis said the Anti-Christ is now on earth. You said he should know because he is the Anti-Christ. The man named Anthony Stein at Return to Traditions website[51] follows every detail of Vatican activities and has provided great insight into the internal demise of the Vatican hierarchy and power structure. As you know my dearest Mother, from the beginning I did not like Cardinal Bergoglio, as he became Pope Francis. There was something about Him that was very sour in my mind. Unfortunately, he has confirmed my worst fears about Him.

With all this in mind my dear Mother Mary, I would like to gently ask you to provide not only the details within the hidden third secret of Fatima. But also, your personal comments on how things will progress in the coming years. I thank you in advance for this, and I love you so very much, dear Mother Mary.

---

[51] Return to Traditions, Anthony Stein, YouTube

Blessed Mother Mary
March 2, 2024
12: 07 p.m.

This is what was said in the third secret of Fatima regarding the Catholic Church:

"Yes, my dear son, there is a lot to be said regarding your Lord and Savior's Church on earth. None of it is really incredibly good, my dear son. When I first delivered this message to Jacinta, Francisco, and Luciana in October 1917, no one would have believed what I said. It is for this reason that I asked that this part of my message not be made public until 1960. If this content were made public more than 100 years ago. Everyone would have been frightened so badly that it would have induced terrible spiritual, emotional, and even physical suffering upon those sacred children of our loving Father. So, the written words of Sister Lucia were filed away deep in the archives of the Vatican. In 1962 when Pope John XXIII read the third secret of Fatima, he decided not to release my message to the faithful. This was a bad mistake on his part for if my words were published back then, the faithful would be on guard to prevent what I said would happen. Frankly, my dear son it would have been wonderful for me to say, "God's sacred children take action within the Church to prevent what is happening now." At least it would have been delayed for a long time. Giving more time to the faithful to expand their wings and save more souls for their own sake and join their Father in the Heavenly Kingdom.

I am very dismayed that even until now anyone who has read the words of Sister Lucia are sworn to secrecy. My words were meant for the faithful, but the Vatican is now working against the spiritual well-being of God's sacred children.

Basically, what I said was quite simple, over a period of time the hierarchy of my sons' Church would be infiltrated, would be poisoned in all manner of speaking. The fundamental tenants of Christianity and the will of your Father in Heaven will be sidetracked away from the fundamental message of loving God first, loving your neighbor as yourself and even loving your enemies. All that is sacred and holy within the Catholic Church is being attacked as you write this, my dear son. By withering away piece by piece the sacredness and the holiness of the Church that Jesus Christ has founded for the spiritual well-being of all of God sacred children.

My dear son, I know you have collected some pictures of the Pope and many cardinals watching profane performances in holy places very much like what they did in Sodom and Gomorrah. I know that is painful for you to see. But I will ask you in this book that you are creating that you include these kinds of pictures. So that God's sacred children will see the truth of things and just how far the Church has fallen away from my son and from your Almighty Father whose love knows no bounds.

My dear son, I can perceive the tears forming in your eyes right now and I am with you always no matter how bad you perceive things to be. I know you can feel the presence of your Lord and Savior and my son, I know you can feel His arm around your shoulders. This is what will propel you to continue with delivering this kind of information to all the faithful who need to hear this.

There are a few more things I need to say and then we will get to the good part. Within the Church there has been so many depraved celebrations consecrating Satan and performing Satanic acts within the Vatican that are kept ever so secret. But they happened. I want you to publish what was said from Father Martin's interview with Mr. Art Bell[52]. Both our Hearts are broken because of this.

The current pope who is the Anti-Christ will continue in His Satanic program to constantly change the holy mass to slowly erase away the true spirit of Christianity and turn it into a secular monster. At first it will be introduced as it already has. As very minor changes to the laity. But then over and actually short period of time more and more changes will be done to the mass. Such that the sacredness will be erased, and it will become

---

[52] Fr. Martin Malachi's interview with Art Bell

nothing more than a secular acknowledgment of the Historical Jesus and that will be it.

More and more Churches will be used for other secular purposes such as secular celebrations of things like Halloween which are innocent on the surface but are Satanic underneath the skin.

My dear son, as Christianity is slowly wiped away from the face of the earth by more and more people turning away from Almighty God. And their own sacred nature Christians will increasingly become persecuted in real celebrations of mass, that they will have to go underground.

Your lifelong friend, a Catholic Priest, has told you this for years. He is ever so right and has always been right in this and many other things. He has been given special graces that allows him the spiritual strength to endure a hostile spiritual environment within the Jesuit community at Santa Clara. I rejoice when you and your Catholic friend have coffee together. Be sure to give him a ride in your new car, he will enjoy that endlessly. And especially, dear son, treating him to the Alaska cruise will be one of the highlights of his life. Thank you for that.

In my previous comment, I mentioned that Christianity will be slowly wiped off the face of the earth. Except for those who were true believers in Almighty God the creator of all that is seen and unseen. As the loving Christian spirit is slowly eroded away from the Hearts of people, the more and more violent interpersonal relationships will become within the public sphere and even within families. This is precisely what Satan wants. For people who succumb to these violent Satanic influences the result of their behavior will exclude them from the Heavenly Kingdom. From the very beginning, my dear son, it is the goal of Satan to destroy 100% of all of God's sacred children and his ever-increasing hatred for anything related to your Heavenly Father.

I know you remember the three separate times that Satan Himself appeared to you in the middle of the night while you were sleeping. It deeply frightened you which would anybody. But over time you realized that it is Jesus Christ who is the way the truth and the life. That moment, as Jesus pointed out to you. When you said to yourself in the presence of your own Father that you will never treat your children the way he treated you, confirmed the great strength you have within you. This is part of the reason that your Heavenly Father has asked you to be His Anointed Messenger. You have done wonderfully well.

Continuing on with the disintegration of our holy Church, as you know, there are now proposals circulating within the Vatican hierarchy to allow priests to be married. This will be one of the final nails in the spiritual coffin of the Church that my son founded. For then, what makes a Catholic priest any different than normal laity? Really nothing substantial. Satan will say that this will solve many of the problems within the Church. That will be His advertisement. But His solution will bring the destruction of the spiritual identity of every Christian Catholic priest on the face of the earth. Make no mistake my dear son, your current pope will embrace this wholeheartedly and promoted until it is accepted.

The website titled, "Return to Tradition" is very good in keeping track of all the events within the Vatican and its policies. As they change and comparing this with what the true Church is all about. Add to this book, my dear son, any other topics you find appropriate from this website and Anthony Stein. The more our Christian laity knows about the internal crumbling of the Vatican, the more souls will be saved from Satanic deceptions.

Finally, my dear son, please add the other comments that Father Malachi Martin has to say about my apparition regarding the third secret of Fatima. He is a great Godly man. Lastly, I will be with you always as you walk down this road of publishing what I have to say regarding Fatima. And please put in a section regarding questions that come to your mind as I know they will. I will answer everything.

I love you my dearest son, your Blessed Mother Mary

Richard Ferguson

The Following is by Father Malachi Martin with Art Bell May 4, 1998, [53]

The document of Fátima is not pleasant to read. It does not make sense unless we accept there is a wholesale phenomenon of apostasy among the clerics and laity in the Catholic Church. Said differently this revelation by our Blessed Mother Mary makes no sense unless we accept that the institutional organization of the Roman Catholic Church. The organization of parishes and dioceses and bishops and archbishops and cardinals and the Roman bureaucracy throughout the world is disrupted and rendered null and void, the third secret makes no sense. Lucia said the message from Mother Mary is for the people, and she did not want to write it down and just handed over to the Catholic hierarchy. But she did at the request of her Bishop.

Pope Pius XII received her letter and put it away at the request of Lucia and not be opened until 1960. It was opened by Pope John XXIII in February 1960, and he proceeded to say the prophecy was not true it was unreliable, and the children did not know what they were talking about. The Pope further said Lucia was only 10 years old at the time Mother Mary told her so she could not have known what she was talking about. My view on this is simply the Pope did not want people to know and was grasping for any excuse not to make public the truth of what Lucia wanted to tell God sacred children. 10-year-olds are perfectly capable of understanding things such as this. The fact she could not yet read and write as nothing to do with it.

Pope John XXIII October 11, 1962, referred to the three children contemptuously as prophets of doom. We will have nothing to do with these prophets of doom. We are of a different age. And this remains so today. Pope Paul VI also did nothing about it. Pope John, I read it and did nothing about it. Pope John II read it and also did nothing about it.

Father Malachi Martin can say nothing about it because he is under oath. Father Martin however believes what the prophecy says is fully accurate and

---

[53] Fr. Malachi Martin with Art Bell. Vatican Murders etc. May 4th, 1998 (8) (NWO SERIES/ The Vatican) (youtube.com), https://www.youtube.com/watch?v=5CnKDjJLbvs&t=58s

detailed and is certainly not the ravings of crazy children. The prophecy is a very factual statement of things.

Back then, in 1998 Father Martin was genuinely concerned about the secularization of the Church. Yes, even back then people noticed the Vatican was moving away from their very reason for existence and continues too today even more so.

What Father Malachi Martin tells us about the third secret of Fatima [54][55]

I then said the conversation Cardinal Bea had, when the cardinal left the meeting with the Pope and His advisers reported Pope John XXIII went pale as death: "What is it, Eminence" I asked. 'Just kill a billion people. Look at this! 'He handed me a sheet of paper with 25 handwritten lines. Since that day, every word of the text remains indelibly engraved in the mind. "

Cardinal Bea made this statement about the "millions of people" because the Pope decided not to reveal the Third Secret, and to consecrate Russia. I asked Father Malaquias if I could say anything more about these "terrible" punishment that would kill a billion people. He explained that, before reading the Secret. He was asked to take an oath not to reveal, but he thought it should have been revealed, and that Our Lord and Our Lady wanted it to be known.

So, I mentioned the Third Secret whenever I could; spoke around Him, giving maximum information about Him, as well as the maximum number of tracks on Him, without actually revealing the text. Then, very quickly he cited a list of possible calamities and said some of them were in the Secret! Although the list included things like World War 3, the Pope's death, and the Three Days of Darkness, it was not particularly instructive. Because not all of the punishments were on the list, and not everything that was listed was part of the punishment.

---

[54] https://www.apostoladodegarabandal.com/en/o-que-nos-conta-o-padre-malachi-martin-sobre-o-terceiro-segredo-de-fatima/

[55] https://www.youtube.com/watch?v=5CnKDjJLbvs&t=58s

Spiritual punishment, the spiritual punishment apparently started shortly after 1960 resulted in the Holy Father's refusal, Father Martin said: "Cardinals, bishops and priests are falling like leaves in hell."

"Faith disappears in several countries and continents." "Many of the elect will lose their faith .... Things will be so bad, if Our Lady does not intervene, no one will be saved."

"God will withdraw grace" Father Malachi told me apostasy in the Church was the background or context of the Third Secret. But he also said this spiritual punishment was part of the punishment God would inflict if Our Lady's orders were not obeyed. In this regard, he said a disturbing thing several times: "God will withdraw Grace". This seems to be a difficult thing for God, such as sabotaging His own will "that all men be saved and come to the full knowledge of the truth." But it must be considered before a vicious circle. When the Pope refused to reveal the secret and refused to consecrate Russia, he lost the right of thanks to Himself and to the Church ..., and apparently, he was also punished for His disobedience ... " Satan will gain power in the upper echelons of the Church.

Another part of the spiritual punishment he mentioned several times was:

"Satan wants to gain power, even in the highest echelons of the Church."

The strongest statement came from a person who called Art Bell, saying an old Jesuit told him: "The last pope will be under the control of Satan." Father Martin reported this man "would have a means of reading, or he had been given the contents of the Secret. However, he said the quote was inaccurate. And that is because no one was authorized to quote the Secret exactly. But while the quote "The last pope will be under Satan's control" is accurate, Father Martin changed the last two main components of that sentence. "The last Pope," he said, does not necessarily mean the last Pope before the end of time, but the last Pope "of these times."

Did you mean the last pope before the Consecration of Russia? And after the words "under the control of Satan" it can have several meanings. Father Martin used to explain when talking about exorcisms and demonic activities, there are several ways in which Satan can control a human being, partially or totally.

The person may have "sold the soul to the devil" in exchange for a favor, or Satan can control these people and circumstances surrounding that person .... Pope Benedict's lament to several visitors in His papal office, "my authority ends after that door! ", raises the question of how far has the Church achieved this status? We can see spiritual punishment has been on the increase since 1960. This terrible punishment "... does not come without warning," he said. "But ... only those who have been renewed in their Hearts - and will probably be a minority - will recognize Him for what he is and prepare for the tribulations that will follow. "

22

Pope Benedict: The Terrifying Revelation in Fatima's Third Secret

Catholic Channel

This transcribes the text of the above title of a YouTube video carefully created to bring light to Mother Mary's message to all of God's children. She appeared a number of times to different children to bring her message, her warning frankly regarding the end of our world. This is more accurately stated as the end of times not the end of the earth. Great tribulations are going to be allowed by our Father in Heaven to occur on earth because he will withdraw His great protections of earth over the last many thousands of years. Our Blessed Mother Mary speaks to this in great detail and discusses also in detail what Satan has accomplished within the Church of Mother Mary's son our Lord and Savior Jesus Christ.

For years people have speculated there is a third secret of Fatima that has never been revealed by the Church. Finally, new light has come from an unexpected place in an almost off-the-cuff manner. Released by the Vatican in the year 2000 is not complete. That something is being hidden from the public. They think it might be warnings against changes introduced by Vatican II or struggles in the Church.

When the third secret was released Mother Angelica of EWTN famously said she didn't think we got the whole thing. She said I think it is scary and that wasn't scary. Now revealed for the first time the true third secret of Fatima. It is absolutely terrifying, so terrifying sister Lucia commanded by her bishop to write it in case something should happen to her. She spent days agonizing over it, but she could not bring herself to do it.

(Note: Sister Lucia is the only remaining of the three children in Fatima that received Blessed Mother Mary's complete message or warning. Jacinta and Francisco both died of a flu virus in Portugal within a few years after the apparition of Blessed Mother Mary. If sister Lucia did not write down the third secret, the world would never know the warnings of our Blessed Mother Mary regarding the coming End of Times and the problems in the Catholic Church.)

In the end, after a prompt from Heaven, she did of course write it down. Exorcist Gabriel Moore said Padre Pio told Him he knew the third secret of Fatima and it tormented Him. Father Malachi Martin was asked to help draft a response to the secret for Pope John 23rd. He read the third secret of Fatima. Father Martin said if released, people would fill the confessionals, kneel, and strike their breasts. The new information about Fatima comes from Akita Japan. What does the apparition at Fatima have to do with Akita Japan? In 1973 our Lady appeared in Akita to sister Sasagawa and gave her a message for humankind. The third message of Akita was given on October 13, 1973, the anniversary day of the miracle of the sun at Fatima. And like with Fatima it has been discovered recently a part of this message from Akita was never released.

Author Note: (This really angers me. In both cases, Fatima and Akita, the Church worked to hide the truths our Blessed Mother Mary wants to tell all of God's sacred children. The warnings they need to know in order to avoid our Father in Heaven from removing His protections that existed on the earth. Which if he does great catastrophes and millions upon millions of deaths both the good and the evil will occur. Frankly, in my humble opinion as a Christian minister and Anointed Messenger of our Heavenly Father, the Church in hiding things like this are actively doing the work of Satan Himself. No, what I just said is not too harsh once you realized the gravity of God sacred children not knowing the full contents of Fatima third secret and Akita. The reason the Church did this is because these secrets document how bad the Church is and will become against God's sacred children at the hands of Satan.)

Cardinal Ratzinger the future Pope Benedict the 16th served as the head of the congregation for the doctrine of the faith at the time. In that role he studied both the secret of Fatima and the message from Akita. At one point he pronounced the two messages of Fatima and Akita are essentially the same. Bishop of Akita also said the two messages are the same. Everyone thought this was strange because the official text of the third secret of Fatima released in 2000 has nothing in common with the strikingly apocalyptic message given by our Lady of Akita.

At the end of 2023 on the Mother and refuge of the End of Times YouTube channel a video was posted featuring Father Elias Mary, an expert on Akita. Father Elias read a passage from Father Yasuda's book written only in Japanese. Father Yasuda served as the spiritual director for Sister Sasagawa who received the message from Blessed Mother Mary. He was considered a very holy priest having the Oduor of sanctity. In Father Yasuda's book we find this hidden key part of the message from our Lady given at Akita.

<u>Like the first Judas, the last pope will sell Jesus to the enemy.</u> Therefore, the era of the Anti-Christ Pope will soon come very strong. The interpreter was not Catholic, so he never really turned to the book to look at it. So, they just recently in this last visit they decided to go and look up this book (in Japanese). And they just opened it up and he put his finger, and he found the exact spot where Father Yasuda talks about the sign left by her son. And Father Yasuda had this to say, the book is called, Oh Marie Shannan. It is a holy Mother's statue and its tears, an anthology of tap recorded preachings or talks given by Father Yasuda and the book was published in 2003 in Japanese. It has never been translated into English, so he was a very important figure. He was the one as I said was like the official explainer of the message of Akita.

If sister had any confusion or didn't know what certain things meant he was the one who was supposed to enlighten her. The era of Anti-Christ Pope will soon come and so no matter how much we worry we cannot prevent this and there is nothing we can do about it. Therefore, we must properly defend our faith. The Akita and Fatima messages are the same meaning the Fatima message also tells us the last pope is an Anti-Christ Pope. Silenced in 1917 our Lady repeated her message in 1973. Father Elias Mary speculates about the seriousness of this part of the message to Sister Sasagawa. Had Sister Sasagawa herself revealed this she might have been punished severely, but Father Yasuda being elderly and respected no one took any action against Him.

So, it may have been that the way our Lady chose to give this message. Ironically, Father Elias Mary was searching Father Yasuda's book for information on the meaning of the word **"sign left by my son."** Used by our Lady in the message when he stumbled upon the passage about the last pope as the Anti-Christ.

Finally, the third message of Akita which is the same as the third secret of Fatima can be revealed in its entirety adding the hidden sentences where they fit best. For the first time we have what is most likely the complete message as given by our Lady at Akita and Fatima.

As I told you, if men don't repent and better themselves, the Father will inflect a terrible punishment on all humanity. It will be a punishment greater than the deluge such as one will never have seen before.

Fire will fall from the sky and will wipe out a great part of humanity, the good as well as the bad sparing neither priests nor faithful. The thought of the loss of so many souls is the cause of my sadness.

If sin's increase in number and gravity there will be no longer pardon for them terrifying shocking, the Pope being the Anti-Christ has been set throughout the ages by enemies of the Church. What is shocking is Blessed Mary said it, so we know it to be true as she speaks truth.

Let us examine it more closely. Many times, Gods revelations come gradually but then more specifically as the event approaches. I will put entity between the woman and you the serpent. We now know that woman is the Blessed Mother Mary of Nazareth. For example, St. Paul tells us in 2nd Thessalonians the Anti-Christ will seat Himself in the temple of God. Let no one deceive you in any way. Unless the falling away comes first and the lawless one is revealed the one doomed to perdition who exalts Himself above every so-called God an object of worship. So as to seat Himself in the temple of God.

In His commentary on this verse, St. Augustine wrote in city of God book 20 is uncertain in what temple the Anti-Christ shall sit. Whether in that ruin of the temple which was built by Solomon or in the Church. There is no Vatican no Church of Rome of course at the time of St. Paul he spoke generally.

Fast-forward to 1846 our Lady appeared in La Salette France and reportedly said Rome will lose the faith and become the seat of the Anti-Christ.

This is more specific now mentioning Rome the head of the Church. One could say our lady's use of the words "seat of the Anti-Christ" points to the chair of St. Peter. Echoing in a more specific manner what St. Paul said about the Anti-Christ sitting in the temple of God.

Move forward again to 1917 at Fatima Blessed Mary said, like the first Judas the last pope will sell my son to the enemy. The era of the Anti-Christ Pope will soon come, accordingly a Pope the one who sits on the chair of Peter will be in Anti-Christ Pope. A very specific warning since that time is near and this message is repeated at Akita Japan 56 years to the day after the miracle of the sun at Fatima.

One might object but this is the only explanation that makes sense of all we know about the third secret of Fatima. That explains all the hints and innuendo said over the last 100 years about the third secret of Fatima. It explains why Cardinal Choppy, theological advisor to five popes, euphemistically said the unreleased part of the Fatima secret predicted the great apostasy in the Church will begin at the top. It explains why Cardinal Otiviani stated to a reporter the third secret had been relegated to the bottom of the Vatican archives and that is where it deserves to stay.

It explains why sister Lucia easily wrote of demons she saw in hell but could not write the third secret and why she confessed to being traumatized by it. It explains why Padre Pio was tormented by the third secret but not by any future catastrophic events. It explains why Father Malachi Martin said believers would fall to their knees in shock striking their breasts. It explains why Pope John XXIII nearly fainted when it was read to him.

And it might explain why Archbishop Fulton Sheen said the mystical body of Anti-Christ will be set up in counterpoint to the mystical body of Christ on earth. Today with its Judas is recruited by Satan from our bishops as its leader. His mention of Judas might be happenstance, but it's so close to the words of our Lady at Fatima and Akita, making one wonder if he too had read or been told the actual secret. Exorcist Gabriel Amorth said Padre Pio was tormented by only one thing. Padre Pio said to Gabriel, you know, Gabriel, it's Satan who has been introduced into the bosom of the Church and within a very short time will come to rule the ape of the Church. When told this by Amorth author José Zavala exclaimed oh my gosh some sort of Anti-Christ on the Art Bell show.

A listener asked Father Malachi Martin to comment on his Jesuit priest friend telling him the last pope would be under the control of Satan. Martin's reply yes, it sounds as if they were reading or being told the text of the third secret.

From Art Bell, most of what we know of the Anti-Christ comes from St. Paul in the second Thessalonians and from Revelation. Although that book is replete with symbolism so one must be very careful in its interpretation. St. Paul is clear although he doesn't say much. The Catholic catechism is also a source and we already looked at the main passage about Anti-Christ there. Interestingly Pope Benedict said the Anti-Christ does not have to be recognized as evil. He can appear acceptable benevolent, but he however goes against God. He also believed the Anti-Christ would reinterpret the words of sacred Scripture. In such a way as to cause confusion and then of course there is our Lady both that Lasalette and at Fatima with Fatima's message being repeated at Akita. From St. Paul the Anti-Christ, the lawless one, will come after the restrainer is removed from the scene. The lawless one represents the climax of human self-assertiveness against God in the temple of God itself.

Why does God allow this? St. Paul says God is sending them a deceiving power so they may believe the falsehood that all those who have not believed the truth but have approved wrongdoing may be condemned. On the objection a Pope cannot be the Anti-Christ Jesus said the gates of the netherworld shall not prevail against His Church. St. Athanasius when told the bishops were against him answered that proves they are all against the Church. Catholics who remain faithful to tradition even if they are reduced to but a handful, they are the true Church of Jesus Christ.

And Anti-Christ Pope would be a Bishop dressed in white giving the impression to the world he is the holy Father. Interestingly Jesus gave the keys to Peter making Him the first Pope but a few verses later Peter contradicts Jesus and Jesus shockingly said to Him "get behind me Satan," so, a Pope can become an obstacle to Jesus. He can speak like the Dragon.

This brings us back to Pope Benedict the 16th. Benedict was not a fool, humble gentle learned scholarly. That was Pope Benedict a man of superior intellect a master theologian, a man who knew the actual secret of Fatima, but he knew more. He knew of the reports of evil among the clerics both outside and especially inside the Vatican. He knew the warnings of His predecessors of the intent of God's enemies to infiltrate the Church. He could see a majority of those at the top of the Vatican holding to heresy.

He received the red report on Vatican corruption, and he knew the prophecy of the popes from Garabandal namely that after John XXIII there would be four more popes and he was that fourth Pope. And then it would be the end of times according to our Lady at Garabandal in the 1960s. All this along with his scholarship is knowledge of theology and his privileged position in the Church hierarchy over the decades. Which provided access to the full secret of Fatima. As well as a vast body of information from other Marion apparitions. he most likely came to believe he was the last true Pope and the one to follow Him would be the Anti-Christ Pope as revealed by our Lady of Fatima.

Benedict reacted, he worked to synthesize Vatican II with Pratic II. he eased restrictions on the Latin mass but facing growing resistance within the Vatican and growing frail, Pope Benedict decided to act and act boldly. Knowing all that was written in Scripture must occur and what our Lady said must occur he resigned the papacy likely believing this would usher in the Anti-Christ Pope.

Tellingly that night lightning struck St. peters. Lucifer fell in an instant like lightning from Heaven. So, for the first time in History of the Church we had to bishops and white, a Pope and an honorary Pope living in the Vatican. By keeping His ties to the papacy, he retained some authority specifically regarding any teachings of heresy. If the next Pope clearly taught against Church doctrine, Benedict would speak out hoping to delay corruption of doctrine. Because of Benedict's acumen as a theologian and His title of Pope emeritus, he could hope they would listen thus he could possibly place a check on the next Pope. Of course, Benedict knew the next Pope would most likely outlive Him so why bother. Why not just live to 95 as he did shorten the years of Anti-Christ Pope. Because stress kills, he most likely would have died long before 95 had he continued to rain. In 2010 at Fatima, Benedict prayed for our Lady's triumph to come during the next seven years before the 100th anniversary of Fatima in 2017. He knew the triumph is near. By serving as a check on the lawless one he could hope to delay the full onset of the destruction of doctrinal truth in Christ's Church mitigating the suffering until our lady's triumph. Thus, he would serve as the restrainer.

From his deep faith Benedict knew God placed him precisely at this moment in time. He alone had a vast knowledge of both Scripture and the dawning of the era of Anti-Christ. He alone was perfectly positioned to delay the full onslaught of the Anti-Christ's destruction of the Church of Jesus. So far, the first time and probably the last time the world saw to popes in white in the Vatican, one intent on serving Christ until the end and one intent unchanging Christ's Church forever.

It is true Benedict never revealed the secret of Fatima or any of this for that matter. We know he knew the real secret of Fatima about the last Pope, the Anti-Christ Pope. We also know Benedict spoke in and exacting efficient manner and we now know from the American conservative in 2015 he wrote His friend a telling message.

"We see how the power of the Anti-Christ is expanding. And we can only pray our Lord will give us strong shepherds who will defend His Church in this hour of need from the power of evil. He carefully chose the words this hour knowing their significance to mean now because theologically speaking the term this hour, my means this moment in time or my time. So, one could argue he believed we are living in the time of the Anti-Christ.

So finally, the Fatima mystery is complete. We are living it out now at this hour as Mother Angelica suspected it is scary. Sister Lucia said the Fatima message is in the book of Revelation and the Gospels. Eschatology is the theological study concerned with the final events in the History of mankind. Our Lady used the words, last Pope, and Anti-Christ Pope. Theologically both of these happen at the end of all things as the catechism reminds us. The final trial of the Church is the supreme religious deception of the Anti-Christ. This final trial will separate the wheat from the chaff. Those who stay true to Church doctrine and those who follow the deception of the Anti-Christ who puts Himself above the deposit of the faith given by God.

So, one can see how the Fatima prophecy tells us we are at the end of all things. For any who wondered what it would be like to live during the Roman persecutions or the time of the Aryan heresy, we get to live through something worse. Father Elias Mary said Father Yasuda wrote about this time no matter how much we worry we cannot prevent this. There is nothing we can do about it. We must properly defend our faith but the growth in the power of the mystery of iniquity brings us that much closer to the glorious triumph of the Immaculate Heart of Mary.

Blessed Mary promises us in the end her Immaculate Heart will triumph. She has assured us as our Lady of the good event when everything seems completely lost it will be her hour. The time she will act in glorious ways to restore all things. And Jesus promises he will return to slay the Anti-Christ. Our only means of help at this hour are the holy Rosary and the signed left by my son. Which is the holy Eucharist and the holy sacrifice of the Massachusetts Holy Eucharist reception of course. Also means confession we need to confess, receive holy Communion often and recite the rosary daily. This is the time of the Anti-Christ, but it is also our time, we have been placed here by God at this precise moment, this final hour to look up to defend the Church.

So, when Jesus returns, he will find faith. When these signs begin to happen stand erect and raise your head because your redemption is at hand. Be not afraid. In the world you will have trouble but take courage. I have conquered the world; behold I am coming soon!

23

Existential Morality as Defined by Almighty God

Before I address all the wickedness that is in the world today, especially in our own country America, I need to address sinfulness or breaking our Heavenly Father's rules for us to obey. It is simpler than you think but is also harder than you think. So, this is the yardstick of measurement to be applied to all human thoughts and actions while on earth. To decide whether or not a sacred child of God will return to the Heavenly Kingdom from where they were created to begin with by our Heavenly Father.

Our Heavenly Father is the creator of all that is seen and unseen. He created all of His sacred children in the blink of an eye untold millions of years ago within the Heavenly Kingdom. Each of us is a sacred child of God, no matter what the Satanically minded people want you to believe. Their beliefs about abortion and evolution where we are only piles of chemicals that happened by random circumstance.

There are only two, I repeat only two moral forces in both the physical and spiritual realms created by God. Everything is either of God or of Satan. There is nothing in between. Our Heavenly Father is pure love that is so intense and all-encompassing His sacred children cannot possibly understand it. The opposite of love is hatred. All hatred comes from Satan in only Satan. Satan rules His kingdom through hate and fear. Fear is a signpost who Satan in His works on earth.

Your author of this book knows Satan personally. Satan has attacked me on three separate occasions in the middle of the night while I was sleeping next to my wife. He threatened me 50 years ago with these words, "I WILL GET YOU! I WILL GET YOU! I WILL GET YOU!" Since then, I have been forced to conduct spiritual warfare against Him. He attacks me even today about three or four times each and every day. It is because I write God's truth so people like you can know our Heavenly Father and His enormous love for us all.

The God Test

If you want to know how to get to Heaven live by the following three principles of a Godly life. Like all things I write about our loving God I know for absolute certain he approves of what I say because I am His, Anointed Messenger.

1. Love Almighty God above all else in your life, all else in creation both physical and spiritual.

2. Love your Neighbors as you love yourself. Your Neighbors are defined as everyone else other than you.

3. Love your enemies. Yes, you read that correctly.

Do you realize if all sacred children of God on earth today lived by this trio of principles there would be no war. There would be no need for locks on doors. All security companies would go out of business. No need for police. Living by these three rules there really would be Heaven on earth. Why isn't there Heaven now? It is because of Satan in His hatred toward all of our Heavenly Father's sacred children who are made in His image. This is you and me!

Remember all of God sacred children have two parts to them, a physical part, and a spiritual part. Our minds are really spiritual in nature and extend beyond our physical bodies. Therefore, it is our minds that are the focal point for Satanic influence and attacks. I know this personally to be 100% true. Just as a reminder this Anointed Messenger of God was attacked on three separate occasions directly by Satan Himself about 45 years ago. Since then, I have been forced to conduct spiritual warfare every day of my life. Why? Satan hates me so badly because I am a writer of God's sacred truths and I do everything I can to communicate God's truth to all His sacred children which means you.

Lastly, if you love God, you have authority over Satan and you can command Satan to leave you alone in the name of our Lord and Savior Jesus Christ. This works! I should know because I have to use it all the time.

24

A One-World Government Is Coming

Pope Francis Approves

There are many hidden things going on within the Vatican. What I have discovered regarding salacious performances of nude men. In front of, for example, Pope Benedict the 16th. And what Father Malachi Martin knows about regarding Satanic rituals within the bowels of the Vatican. All of this is happening; and in the future, it will bubble to the surface. But that will not happen until the one world government has taken hold of all political power and after it has deemed the secularized or Satanized version of Catholicism is complete.

It is coming sooner than you think and for those people who are under the age of approximately 60 to 70 years old, you will experience this, and it is fruition. I refer you to what our Blessed Mother Mary said at the end of this book when I gave her free reign to say whatever it is she wants to on various topics.

For honest sacred children of God that go to work every day and lead a good life, believing in Almighty God, most of the items in this book are not readily visible to them. However, everyone certainly notices the various disasters that are increasingly prevalent throughout the world.

Rest assured there is a high-level elite class of extremely wealthy people on earth that believe they are like Gods themselves. Organizations like the WEF (World Economic Forum) Is hatching a plan for a one-world government where there will be fundamentally two classes of people. The elites that make all the rules and the rest of us that own nothing because it will have been stripped away from us. Why do I tell you this? It is because Pope Francis agrees wholeheartedly with a one-world government. world government. This is why he is secularizing the Catholic Church. This is why he does not condemn homosexuality as it should be per Biblical literature. This is why he blesses same sex marriage. Pope Francis is full of heresy in order to cooperate with other earthly secular leaders to bring about one world government.

Why has the Democrat party in the United States opened our southern border destroying it to let any and everybody into our Blessed country? Why does our government use hard earned tax dollars in order to feed and clothe and provide medical care to every illegal alien that crosses the border? It is to disintegrate our country as what President Ronald Reagan said, "a shining star on a hill." Barack Obama famously said, "he sees no reason why the United States should be any different than all other countries in the world." These are some of the destroyers of our country.

Democrats are purposely destroying our country so it will become much weaker and succumb to the Satanic one world government planned by Satan.

Why bother to do this? It is to prepare the way for Satan to take the reins of power at the top of the one world government. Theologically speaking in order to move toward a one-world government all Biblical literature and Catholic Christian tradition must be ignored and then destroyed. This is exactly what is happening in the world and the United States.

Question: Dear Blessed Mother, in my previous book I asked my Lord and savior Jesus Christ, your son, if you split up the population by religion what percentage would get to heaven. I really was not surprised except disappointed all Christians did not go back to the heavenly realm. But Jesus explained exactly why, and it is very understable.

If we were to split up the population of the United States into Democrats and Republicans what percentage of each group would make it back into the heavenly Kingdom?

Answer: *You have asked a very penetrating question as you always do. You are purposely trying to connect the belief systems of the population in the United States with their relationship to their Heavenly Father and the Trinity and me. As you rightly perceived the belief in our Almighty Father and Christian principles, is connected with what they say they are politically.*

My answer is a very sad one because the foundational belief of Democrats is that they know better than everyone else and there is no God. As you have stated many times my dear son, they believe that their bodies accidentally arranged themselves out of a swamp and they are nothing more than an accident of chemistry. They completely ignore the most important part of themselves which is their spiritual being.

The percentages of Democrats that make it into heaven is very small my dearest son. I hate to say it, but the number is 17% of Democrats in America somehow manage throughout their interpersonal relationships on earth and their inner beliefs that God does indeed exist. And that they do have a soul. And also, they lead their lives according to Christian principles which is hard to do when they are surrounded by Satanic Democrats

Regarding the percentages of Republicans, it is a lot better but still makes me sad that it is not more than it really is. Most Republicans do believe in the individual created by God and a strict code of conduct that was laid down by your founding Fathers which was in turn based upon Christian values. However, there are just sadly fewer than you and I would like that make it back into the Heavenly Kingdom because they still retain much narcissistic and the consciousness of, I know better than you. In other words, their world view is given by politics and not their Heavenly Father. So, my dear son the number of Republicans making it back into the Kingdom is 37%. Both you and I wish it were far more but there are so many societal forces that Republicans tend to give in to when they know better.

Thank you, my dear Blessed Mother Mary. I thought it was good to ask this question. Because it will give those who read your book a much better understanding of the situation humanity has found itself. In by virtue of its own actions that reject our Heavenly Father and his rules for our existence. I hope that knowing the numbers you just gave me will propel many people that read this book into a clear understanding of how much Satanic jeopardy they are in. Now I feel sad, and I know you do too dear Mother.

25

The Democrat Party Within Biden's Satanic Moral Disaster 56 57

May 16, 2024 Comments

The below list is really just a sampling of the anti-Christian anti-American White House under Joe Biden. [58]I do not even address all the financial scandals the Biden family is certainly involved with especially being paid off by the CCP in China who is now considered our number one enemy. This is called treason and under law punishable by death. However, that will never happen.

1. It is a well-known phenomenon socialist and communist governments extract a monster amount of money from the working population in the form of taxes. That money is distributed to the elites of the country and not put two enhancing the living standards of the people. What is worse is these goes far deeper than just money. People go to work as an expression of sacrificing part of their lives to earn the appropriate amount of money for their families. The government in effect confiscates their very life. What I just described is exactly the foundational values of the American Democrat party.

2. Canada is ahead of us in our self-destruction. 46% of income is taxed to their federal government.

---

[56] Biden Abandons Religious Freedom as First Among Rights | The Heritage Foundation

[57] Anti-Christian bias in the Biden White House | Voice (Christianpost.com)

[58] Anti-Christian bias in the Biden White House | Voice (Christianpost.com)

3. Our country is being Decivilized. Victor Davis Hansen [59] As the government grows, living standards decrease. I never saw such squalor in any city of America until recently. This picture is EXACTLY what the Democrat party wants.  Rather rule over a garbage heap than share wealth with Godly people. Remember, the Democrat party is the political arm if Satan!

4. Puts preference on those men who claimed to be women and women who claimed to be men. Floods our military with transgender freaks to sacrifice our armed forces into a much weaker killing force preoccupied with wokeness and Satanic gender theories. The example was a military man reassigned into whatever. Do we   want to have people like this defending our country? A perversion against God!

5. People within the Biden administration assert "men can get pregnant"!

6. Men are now legally able to go into woman's locker rooms.

7. In many cases religious speech is considered hate speech because it hurts the feelings of the LGBT people. In Canada people have gone to jail for "religious hate speech."

8. Promotes unrestricted abortion on demand right up to one minute before birth.

---

[59] The De-Civilization of America | Victor Davis Hanson (youtube.com)

9. Encourages demonstrations against God's chosen people now known as Israel. Wants this Jewish nation, the chosen people of God, to restrain their military that will certainly cause more death of the Jewish people.

10. Is purposely destroying our country by eliminating our southern border with the plan to give these illegal aliens the vote and which will give Democrats and almost permanent majority in the federal government. Comments from democrat Jerry Nadler proves this.

11. Is proposing monster increases in taxes. As of this writing, a 40% capital gains tax on unrealized gains. If you have a profit on something you now must sell 40% of the assets to pay these taxes.

12. The elimination of the tax breaks from the trump administration to the middle class further destroying the middle class so the only thing remaining are rich people and poor slaves. This will make America into a communist socialist society where only the few will have money. The Satanic Democrat party intends to tax the middle economic class in our country into oblivion. This leaves only a few very rich people like Bill Gates who want the rest of us to eat bugs. He says it is nutritious. This social structure is what already exists in communist countries like Russia and China.

13. Lawfare: The creation of 91, yes 91 criminal charges against Donald Trump who is leading dramatically in national polls for the presidency in 2024. This is blatant election interference. Right as this is written, Trump was found guilty on all 91 counts after only a few hours of deliberation. No matter your politics, we have now descended to a new low of tyrannical jurisprudence in our country to attack a political opponent this way. As I have said before, the Democrat Party is the Political Arm of Satan, and this proves it beyond any shadow of doubt. I cry for our country. What Trump was convicted of was not even a crime, against the law.

14. In cooperation with Pope Francis, the recognition of homosexual marriages.

15. There is now sufficient evidence regarding the existence of a bill that will be put before Congress that erases completely all distinctions between men and women. Legally there will be none.

This is another step in the destruction of our Judeo-Christian ethics, morality, and principles.

16. Laws have been written to favor one societal group over another based on race. The enforcement of such concepts as equity makes legal discrimination against Asians and whites in favor of blacks. This is the further development of Barack Obama's idea regarding identity politics. He said during his anti-God presidency there were only two groups of people, whites and all the rest of the people. Sets up horrible race wars. This is a direct slap on the face against our Heavenly Father where all His sacred children are equal in all respects. This is nothing more than Democrat vote buying and spewing racial hate.

17. Critical race theory, too nasty and Satanic for me to say anything more.

18. White supremacy as claimed by Joe Biden is the biggest problem in America. How many people think this is Satanic racism?

19. Woke, nobody has never explained what this really is.

20. Diversity is our strength. NO!

21. Huge cost to taxpayers for electric car subsidies paid by working citizens. Huge infrastructure costs. All this is NEVER voted on by citizens. Done by democrat directives from White House. Anti-American stealing people's lives to pay for someone else's electric car.

22. Emmet O' Regan was a blogger who observed in the 1968 to 1971 period, there was a mass legalization of abortion throughout the world. This horrific and Satanic law was first introduced in the United Kingdom and followed shortly thereafter within our beloved United States of America. I have lived on this planet for more than three quarters of a century. It has been my observation many times England or the United Kingdom seems to either way in the destruction of Christian society and love of Almighty God. Canada as this is written has become a socialist hellhole where a person can be arrested and put in jail even if they are praying silently within themselves in a public place. Yes, it is illegal in Canada to pray in any kind of public space.

People have been actually put in jail for this. Trudeau, Canadian Prime Minister is becoming an expert Satanic minion. Abortion has other disgusting attributes that must be present to complete an entire Satanic belief system.

23. Over the last 50 years, the US has had the US dollar as the Petro-dollar that kept the dollar very strong way beyond its real economic value. Within the next few years, the dollar will lose the vast majority of its economic and political value. Because other countries are now making permanent agreements with all other countries to trade NOT in dollars. But other currencies like the Yuan and a soon to be introduced common trading currency that is in its final stages of development. The value of our dollar will sink like a rock driving up interest rates in the US. Precious metals will skyrocket to unknown heights while our economy will grind to a halt due to our gargantuan federal debt. Unemployment will also skyrocket. This will be the financial end of times for American citizens. With unheard-of suffering to make up for the horrific government spending up to $35 Trillion dollars in the federal debt that will NEVER be solved.

How does a Christian existential theologian know all this? I have a master's degree in business with extensive knowledge in economics. Yes, this will be the economic end of times for America and the US Dollar

24. Since 1973 due to the Supreme Court decision on abortion rights there have been approximately 61 million legal abortions in the United States

Abortion

Let's face it dear reader, anybody that believes in abortion believes these additional things. All of them are Satanic:

1. Life is not from our Almighty Father in Heaven.
2. Life is nothing more than a pile of chemicals accidentally formed by the idiot idea of random selection. (Note: The website reason.org has studied the idea and probability the human body can result from pure accident. Their scientific studies conclude objectively there is only one chance in 1×10 to the 170th power.

Dear people, there are not that many atoms in all the universe! This calculation does not include the enormous complexity of our DNA which in and of itself repeats the probability of our genes spontaneously creating themselves. Remember, each cell in our body contains DNA and it knows how to replicate itself upon cell division. Yet many progressive liberal minded ignorant people actually believe this Satanic garbage.

3. Female atheists scream many times in protests, "It is my body therefore it is my right!" No! It is not your body. Every molecule in the physical universe was created by our Heavenly Father. Therefore, our Heavenly Father owns every physical molecule in the universe and every molecule that makes up your body. You are not a physical pile of chemicals either. You are a sacred spiritual child of Almighty God. If you don't like that, too bad! Live with it because it is the existential truth of all that is seen and unseen.

If you reject our Heavenly Father, you have put yourself on the path to Hell. I personally know of two people who went to hell. I saw them both after they died. One of them was my own Father. He rose up out of the floor a few times. Wanted to talk to me. Forget that BS. I instantly commanded him to go back to hell where he belongs. He had to sink back under the floor not to be seen again. I can tell you the details but let's just say it is more awful than you can imagine.

4. Satan does not exist. This is exactly what Satan wants people to believe because it makes His hateful job far easier. I suggest any moron who believes they should experience what I did when Satan Himself invaded my bedroom three separate times. And the conduct of spiritual warfare against me three or four times each and every day of my life. It is ugly so much I don't want to describe it because it is too upsetting.

Remember this dear sacred child of God. All of those who believe in God also have power over Satan and all His minions. I fight spiritual warfare every day. When I am attacked, I say one Our Father and one Hail Mary. And then I command Satan to "go back to hell where he belongs" in the name of my Lord and Savior Jesus Christ. It is really that simple, but most people don't know they have this God-given power. You do! Each morning, pray one Our Father and one Hail Mary, and when you retire in the evening.

5. God does not exist either. Being our Heavenly Father's Anointed Messenger to all His sacred children on earth, our beloved Father speaks to me whenever he wishes. No matter what I am doing, our Father sometimes decides to speak to me. I drop everything instantly and listen very closely. His voice is so loving, so caring and kind many times it brings tears to my eyes because when he is speaking, I feel like His arms are wrapped around me and protecting me. I should write an article about this but no time for now.

6. Reality is what we imagine it to be because there is no objective reality other than what we wanted to be in imagine it to be.

7. If you do not believe Wokeism and other moronic Democrat liberal thoughts then you are a hater. Remember people who accuse others of God sacred children are typically performing psychological projection. Simply meaning they say what is wrong with themselves in others. This is a common phenomenon among those who have emotional issues.

8. There are endless numbers of genders each with their own personal pronouns.

9. Men can get pregnant! Of course, we have never seen one of these unicorns.

10. Abortion is the right of every pregnant female. I suggest everyone go online and look up what a ripped apart fetus looks like when it's put on the table to count the body parts to make sure nothing was left inside the woman. That used to be a sacred child of God taking residence in the physical body provided by our Heavenly Father.

11. In England, it is a crime to pray silently in public.

12. I will stop here because this list only gets much longer and much uglier.

Abortion is such a heinous sin, linked to other Satanic beliefs by God's sacred children. It is no surprise our Blessed Mother Mary chose the Zeitoun district of Cairo in Egypt for her multiple apparitions over a three-year period of time.

There are many more examples of the moral and anti-God policies of the Biden White House. If I listed all of them this book would turn into an encyclopedia. I encourage you to go online and do some basic research yourself and you will be shocked.

https://www.youtube.com/watch?v=5CnKDjJLbvs&t=58s

Richard Ferguson

26

Current Democrat Politics Promotes the End of Times

Now, for the first time in American History, there are riots and demonstrations that are pro Hamas, pro-Iran. Remember all these leaders in Iran and its surrogates are Muslims. Also remember the stated goal of Islam is "total domination of the world." Everyone knows what they did last October murdering 1400 innocent Israeli citizens. There are now people carrying signs that read, "death to America." We have a Democrat Congresswoman, Rashida Tlaib, that refuses to condemn this kind of hatred against our country. She is a Muslim Palestinian.

The Democrat party views these people as future Democrat voters because they do plan to give them the vote at some time. Jerry Nadler from New York denied they gave illegal aliens the vote in local elections. He told a falsehood! Nadler lies. When he was proven wrong that <u>he told another falsehood he said, "well it is only in New York and local elections. I wish it were for the whole country.</u>" That is the Democrat plan, to take away political power from taxpaying citizens so as to tip the scales in favor of the illegal immigrants. You pay all the taxes, and the illegal aliens vote on how your money is spent.

My Personal Editorial on The Democrat Party and It is Malignant Dangers to American Citizens

As said a number of times within this book dedicated and written by our Blessed Mother Mary, she agrees with me when I say the <u>Democrat Party Is the Political Arm of Satan.</u> Blessed Mother Mary says so within these pages. These next few paragraphs will enlighten you into something that could kill you based on a program and laws put into place by the Democrat party.

You may have heard of programs labeled DEI. That stands for diversity, equity, and inclusion. The result of this simply means <u>when it comes to hiring employees it is no longer a case of hiring the best qualified and skillful. No!</u>

Now there are laws put into place silently with malice and forethought that dictate hiring must be based on race and gender, not qualifications to do a job.

I personally posse a commercial pilots license with more than 2,000 hours of pilot in command time. It takes a great degree of brainpower to safely pilot a complex jet commercial passenger aircraft. Now the Democrat Biden Administration wants to aggressively promote people into the cockpit of aircraft you and your family will fly in. According to the Bookings Group, Christopher Jencks, and Meredith Phillips, they said the following: [60]

African Americans score lower than European Americans on vocabulary, reading, math tests as well as on tests that claim to measure scholastic. aptitude and intelligence."

It is these same people Democrats want to put into the cockpit of aircraft you will fly in with your family and not have the slightest idea how incompetent the flight crew is. This is also true for people in the control towers. Additionally, there have been many other studies by other institutes of higher learning that show the same results. I encourage you strongly to look up all the other studies about intelligence and see for yourself.

Now, not all of this is theological, but it is the result of theological Satanic thinking where Satanic ideology is put ahead of the safety of God's sacred children on earth. This is why I bring this up because you and your family are being put at grave risk by Democrats without you ever knowing it until it is too late.

United Airlines had an almost horrific disaster with the new Boeing 777 that took off from Maui Hawaii. The new hire first officer did not understand what he was doing in changing the departure flap setting. This caused the airplane to take a dive right close to the ocean 2 minutes after departure. Three hundred people were almost killed that morning in a perfectly working aircraft. The airplane dove toward the ocean pulling out only 500 feet above the water. I

---

[60] The Black-White Test Score Gap: Why It Persists and What Can Be Done | Brookings

have uncovered a frightening video that threatens your life if you fly on commercial airlines. It is made by a highly respected newsman named Matt Walsh. United Airlines refuses to reveal the hours flight time the copilot had and other competence measurements. I smell a rat.

United Airlines hiring practices now officially state at least 50% of their new hires for pilot positions must be female and or women of color. Gone are the requirements to hire the best qualified. As a pilot, I have several thousand hours of pilot in command time with a commercial license and flight instructor rating among other qualifications. I will tell you point-blank the Democrat Party's laws of DEI will certainly result in horrific loss of life by the incompetence that will wind up in the cockpit of commercial airliners.

United will hire people of color and gender instead of flight experience and aptitude. Sound logic and reasoning and judgement is necessary when things go wrong in the cockpit with tough meteorological situations. When you board the airplane, you just will never know who is flying the airplane. The Democrats do not give a damn about competency in the cockpit, only color, race, and gender. This is destructive racism because they think they will look good and get more votes no matter all the deaths they will cause. Be warned, dearest sacred children of Almighty God! [61] Lastly be warned, other airlines are doing the same things.

Question: My Dearest Blessed Mother Mary, I think I know what you're going to say. But I would like any comments you might have on the paragraphs above regarding be purposeful lack of competency in commercial flying these days.

Answer: *My dearest of sons you have yet again identified a horrific problem that has been purposely put into place by what you call the Democrat Party as The Political Arm of Satan. Satan will use any way he can to put God's sacred children at risk and ultimately expose them to deadly circumstances that will result in pain, agony, and death. You have identified my son as yet*

---

[61] This is how pilots are being chosen to fly. You should be frightened, Matt Walsh January 2024, YouTube

another way that Satan has constructed through the use of horrifically minded Satanists in the United States government.

My dear son, as you have said they are only interested within the Democrat party in money and power. And they will do anything they can to guarantee their reelection for more power and more money. Ultimately, the Democrat party as you have said is the political arm of Satan. And these Democrat politicians only care about themselves. And they do not care at all about any at all of the people who make the United States of America be the best country in the world until recently due to the Biden administration.

I do not like to get political, my dear son, as you know. But these are my feelings about my dear sacred children. And I cannot help but cry a lot and get angry toward these vicious people that will do anything for themselves. Even if it means killing many innocent people with their so-called political agenda that hurts and kills so many people. There is just nothing good that I can say. I truly wish it were otherwise.

What is happening in this instance is one of the manifestations of my prophecies for your country. Where death and destruction will rear its ugly head as it already has begun like you have already said dear son. I love you dear son.

Joe Biden

President Biden mocks our Catholic faith, but what about Trump?

Joe Biden claims he is a Catholic. But all his actions prove he is sacrilegious.

Biden Mocks Our Catholic faith, but What About Trump? - Bishop Paprocki explains his viral video - YouTube

Joe Biden ravages about his undying support of abortion. What is the definition of abortion? It is simply the murder of a developing sacred child of our Heavenly Father still in the mother's womb. Biden also mocked Christianity when he made the sign of the cross at an abortion rally.

https://www.youtube.com/watch?v=nTQg1RKeA4U

From the Wall Street Journal Headline:

"Biden to Morehouse College commencement speech: America Hates You!

Dear sacred child of Almighty Father, it is plain that this statement purposely sows the seeds of division and hatred. Remember that the ultimate foundational source of ALL hatred is Satan Himself!

Another Headline from the Wall Street Journal: Biden spreading racial division for November.

Buying votes: Joe Biden's insistence on bailing out student loans affects 4.3 million students. Remember ALL these students signed a loan agreement to pay back the tuition money they borrowed. The cost of this to American taxpayers who worked very hard for their money is $153 billion dollars. The source of this information is the White House itself.

Joe Biden declared the holy day of Easter to be the celebration day for "transgender visibility day." This is a disgusting slap in the face of our loving Almighty Father and especially our Lord and Savior Jesus Christ. Celebrating reprehensible sexual perversion on the same day that celebrates our Lord and Savior Jesus Christ rising from the dead from His grave. This is certainly a horrific Satanic thing to do. It is hateful beyond belief no matter how the Biden administration tries to cover it up.

More Racial Hatred Sowed

In a speech within the last three months of when this is written, Joe Biden said the following: "The biggest problem we have in America is White Supremacy! Yet he cannot even define what that term actually means. This is hate-speech that divides our nation against itself.

Again, Biden is sowing the seeds of hatred against the group of European people that founded our country.

It is explicitly said in our founding documents "all men are created equal" and the founders created the legal infrastructure to ensure all our values and ethics are based upon Almighty God. 'Yet Joe Biden's personal hatred comes to the surface in His disgusting attempt to get more votes based on pure disgusting hatred. All of this is pure Satanic!

In our schools

Our children are being taught liberal progressive propaganda that goes against Judeo-Christian morals and principles. They are taught that:

Our forefather s ravaged the country and enslaved people.

Anyone that is rich today got their money through horrific immoral means.

This is another way to sow the seeds of hatred among our children.

Sexual Perversion

Our federal Department of Education has developed a curriculum that indoctrinates our children starting at age 6 or earlier. They are taught for example sexual perversion is normal and fun. Drag queens actually teach young children in school.

Tyrannical Control of our language

The use of pronouns is now a battleground within our country and people will go to jail if they do not use the proper pronoun. As stated, before a man in the UK was sentenced to jail because he used the wrong pronoun when addressing His son. Yes, His own son.

Dozens of Churches in Canada have been torched and burned. [62]

The United States of America is on the verge of insanity. Victor Davis Hanson [63]

Our Now Destroyed Southern Boarder

The Biden administration destroyed our southern border in order to allow millions of illegal aliens to enter our country. Our federal government distributes American citizens tax dollars to these illegals to give them free housing, free food, free medical care. And in the process is known that luxury hotels in New York were forced to boot out homeless American military

---

[62] https://www.youtube.com/watch?v=gxkX6NPpe14 ,

[63] https://www.youtube.com/watch?v=X8kKZtSU4TU

veterans and replace them with illegal aliens. It is estimated that costs for this from American taxpayers is well north of $10 billion per year and climbing. We now have illegal aliens giving speeches on the streets of our major cities that cry, "death to America."

This is a conscious effort to sow the seeds of chaos, confusion in order to destroy the foundational values of the United States of America. Remember our country was created and founded on Judeo-Christian values which led to the best country in the world. The foundational force that destroys our country is Satan Himself working through the Democrat party. Remember what I have said quite a number of times, The Democrat Party Is the Political Arm of Satan Himself.

The Biden administration destroyed our southern border in order to allow millions of illegal aliens to enter our country. Our federal government distributes American citizens tax dollars to these illegals to give them free housing, free food, free medical care. And in the process is known luxury hotels in New York were forced to boot out homeless American military veterans and replace them with illegal aliens. It is estimated that costs for this from American taxpayers is well north of $10 billion per year and climbing. We now have illegal aliens giving speeches on the streets of our major cities that cry, "death to America."

Covid Lies

The covid virus killed tens of millions of people across the world. It is now well-known it was created and leaked out of a Chinese lab in Wuhan. Joe Biden refuses to hold China responsible for what it did to the whole world.

Rumors That a Chinese Army Is Forming Within Our Country

There is no solid proof of the above claim yet. I believe that will come after Biden is no longer president. Then there will be a flood of truth out of the Trump white house. Remember the spy balloon the Biden administration allowed to float over most all of our nuclear missile sites from North Decota. He waited for it to fly through the heartland of our country waiting for the balloon to finish its spy mission to be shot down of the Atlantic coast of North Carolina. Biden stated they had to wait because they did not want the balloon to fall on a school. They could have shot it down right at the border with Canada WHERE NOBODY LIVES! Biden has hidden personal financial ties to China, and he earned his money by doing this directly against the best interests of our citizens.

Regarding the possible Chinese army, do not think for a moment the Biden administration does not know about this. It is impossible for them not to. Speaking of our southern border, tens of thousands of Chinese nationals have already crossed into the United States from Mexico. Realize these young military aged men can only come from China with the specific permission of the Chinese Communist Party. Put this together with the following article that demonstrates Chinese men of military age are being trained in the use of sniper rifles and other army type equipment within the United States right now.

Soon, there will be a Chinese army operating within our own country. With the help of our Democrat government, our country is being prepared for a soon to be one world government controlled by Satan. Video on this subject from Maria Bartiromo, fox news.[64]

Statistics show the world is in the most dangerous place it has been since the 1930s. The 1930s was a lawless time in United States and heading for World War II. [65]

Joe Biden is by far the most tyrannical president this country has ever seen.

Life, liberty & Levine
May 19, 2024

Please remember: The Democrat Party Is the Political Arm of Satan! Other anti-American actions the Biden administration took includes:

1. Biden ignored Supreme Court decisions Regarding the forgiveness of student loans. This involves taking hard earned tax dollars from

---

[64] https://youtu.be/AmBWk2--x6c

[65] https://www.youtube.com/watch?v=42_AXjcqNXw

working people and giving it away to students who didn't attend college and people who did because he wants the votes purchased by hard earning American taxpayers.

2. He destroyed women's sports by allowing men who say they identify as a woman to compete in women's events and share the same locker room with naked women athletes.

3. It is against federal law to interfere with federal elections. The Biden administration working with die hard Democrat attorney generals and prosecutors have invented a total of ninety-one, yes 91 different charges against Donald Trump, Biden's main competitor for the presidency. This has never happened before in the History of our country. This cost American taxpayers five hundred billion dollars out of their pocket. The plan is in the near future to give the vote to all these illegal aliens which would be predisposed to vote Democrat. It is illegal to buy votes, but the Democrat party does not care. As of now, depending on your information source there are anywhere between 11,000,000 and 15,000,000 illegal aliens in our country today receiving federal funding for shelter, food, clothing, and all medical care. Remember dear people, we have many military veterans who remain homeless and are ignored by the Biden administration.

4. Biden supports all kinds of abortion on command no matter even if the head of the baby in the process of being born is showing in the delivery room. Biden is in favor of killing it, a sacred child of God.

5. Thinking he can get more votes; Biden is now supporting the butchers in the Mideast called Hamas whose ultimate goal is domination of the entire world including the destruction of the United States.

6. Biden as used executive orders to get around the people's representative called Congress, so he and essence has nominated Himself to be a tyrannical dictator. This is how he has given away hundreds of millions of dollars in rebates to people who buy an electric car. Everyone else pays for it.

7. Recently Biden was pressured into agreeing to two debates with Donald Trump. He put draconian restrictions on the conditions of the

debate. Conditions like, there will be no audience, the press will be only those Biden approves of, there will not be an open mic so Donald Trump cannot respond to what Biden says.

8. It is well known that during the state of the Union address, bite in was highly drugged so he could get through the speech. Trump wants a drug test for the debates but of course that would reveal the extent of the dementia Biden suffers from therefore the Democrats refuse.

9. There is a Chinese army that is being formed within the boundaries of our Blessed country the United States of America. It is known well over 50,000 men of military age have come into our country from China. The Chinese Communist party knows every one of them and must have given them approval to come to the United States. There will come a time in the not-too-distant future when our military forces will be fighting against hostile Chinese army action in Kansas, Philadelphia, Florida, and all the many other states in our nation. Lastly, it is impossible the Biden administration does not know what I have just said. Treason!

10. It is well known the Biden family amounts to a treasonous crime family. Many people do not want to admit it, but the evidence is overwhelming. They have received many millions of dollars from foreign countries such as our worst enemy, the CCP in China.

11. Lastly, the Democrat party is well known to cheat during elections. A personal story: During the 2020 election for president, I was watching on TV as the votes were being counted. Early in the election returns I saw a Republican and a Democrat vote counts. While I was watching, I saw the Republican candidate vote count decrease instantly by 585 votes. Instantly I saw 585 votes get added to the Democrat candidate. Vote counts are never decreased but it did for the republican that night.

Now, as this is written, Joe Biden gave a speech about four to six months ago where he accused Republicans of voter fraud for the presidential election that will not happen for another six months. Remember dear sacred child, our country is built on the fact that only and I mean only citizens of this country have the right to vote, no one else! Everyone must provide a government issue form of identity before they can vote. Now that the Democrat party has destroyed our southern border, they want all the illegal aliens to vote. We know as the fact Venezuela has emptied all of its prisons and jails and sent them north to enter the United States. It is these people the Democrats want to give voting rights in our presidential elections.

President Of United States Joe Biden said: [66]

"By attempting to pass laws requiring voters to show ID with their vote, Republicans are risking permanent internal division as well as violent conflict. There is a lot of assault taking place in America today in an attempt to suppress and subvert the right to vote fair and free elections. We are facing the most significant crisis of our democracy since the civil war. Is that hyperbole? No, since the civil war."

My comment is simple, why don't we just send write-in ballots to the rest of the world? Democrats would love this. They are trying to strip away the rights of legitimate citizens in our beloved country in an effort to gain more political power and money. All this is simply Satan doing what Satan does. The Democrat party remains the political arm Satan.

These are just eleven examples of how the Biden administration has destroyed the normal workings of our constitutional Republic federal government.

Question: Dear Mother Mary, it seems as if this secular activity of our government falls right in line with the goals of Satan. Is there anything dear Mother you would like to say regarding the corrupt and dishonest Joe Biden Democrat administration?

Answer: *Blessed Mother Mary: My dearest son Richard, yet again you have uncovered much of the ugliness that is aimed at destroying The United States of America. All these terrible things have as their root foundation, Satan Himself. The people in high places in your government within the Democrat party are those people who do not care at all about The United States of America. Who was founded upon it is constitutional government*

---

[66] Tucker Carlson: wow, this is really taking place. YouTube OZK Agency Team

that is for the people by the people and of the people. In other words, your government was founded in order to serve the needs of the American people and not descend into the Satanic tyranny that it has through the Democrat party.

I love it when you say that the Democrat party is the political arm of Satan. That is so ever true my dear son and I know what you have just written is very painful. You are one of the few that can see into the future and know what is going to happen with or without my help. Nonetheless, I will say that a lot of nasty things will occur between now as I tell you this and Election Day. <u>*Additionally, the election will be contested by the Democrat party with the idea of throwing the entire country into chaos and confusion. As you know my dearest son, two of the hallmarks of Satanic activity are exactly that, chaos, and confusion.*</u>

In the end, your country will return to some measure of law and order as the criminal element in the Democrat party will be removed from their various offices. However, this will not be permanent. And over time, Satanic forces from outside the country and inside will garner more strength. To bring Satan's chaos, confusion, suffering, the destruction of free will, and the persecution of anybody that believes in the hallmarks and the foundational values of your beloved country. It is then that my son and I will tell you what area you and your family will need to flee to. Especially you dear son because you have written so much Godly truth there will be a price on your head.

Thank you, dear Blessed Mother Mary, I love You.

Question: Dear Mother Mary, within the life of Joe Biden, has there ever been a time where he was an honest man working for the best interest of the America people? I hate to say it, but I know the answer.

Answer: Again, my dearest of sons, Joe Biden was and is one of the people who got attracted to politics for the sheer power and money it brings. As you know, dear son, now in America when someone gets elected, the system is so money based and corrupt. The elected person can count on receiving lots of money in shady deals and insider information. This last

thought demonstrated the character of Nancy Pelosi who now is worth many millions of dollars.

She and Joe Biden have sold their souls to Satan. Yes, you did know this answer and it makes me sick to say the reality of these things. Lastly as you remember back in the 1950's there was honest negotiations between Democrats and Republicans on all matters that affected the American people. I know you remember Everet Dirkson who was a kindhearted honest Democrat. These days that is no more. Like OAC said right after her shady election "it is all about the Benjamins" … money!

Your Blessed Mother Mary

So, What Is a Loving Christian Voter to Do?

First off, this is not a hard question to answer. In fact, the answer is staring every Christian in their face. Within this book of our Blessed Mother Mary, I do not have the time to go over all the verbal atrocities and Satanic based policies of the Democrat party. This following word, a singular word should be enough to determine there should be 0 Christians voting Democrat in this coming election. What is that word? <u>Abortion!</u>

Our Heavenly Father who is the creator of all that is seen and unseen and the creator of every particle of our existence. Our Father loves us so very much instantly after all of us were created in His image in the blink of an eye, he left a part of Himself within our spiritual existence. Through this magnificent love, our Father cannot help but know every detail of our lives on earth. Even every thought we have, every emotion and every feeling. Remember, what the psalms say." Wherever I go you are there, meaning our Heavenly Father."

The Satanic Democrat party is responsible directly for the murder of developing sacred children of God within the womb. The secular version of this thought is: Developing human beings. Women that say, "my body my choice" spewing out of their mouths that is Satanic garbage guised as freedom. Yes, it is freedom to commit mortal sin through the murder of a developing sacred child of Almighty God. Frankly, this leads to an undeniable answer there should never be one Christian that votes Democrat, ever!

27

The Catholic Church

In the document Fiducia Supplicans the Pope wants all clergy worldwide to give blessings to homosexual unions. When this idea floated like a lead balloon, Pope Francis decided to lawyer the wording and twist it into something different. He tried to save face by saying what he meant was to bless the two people in the same-gender relationship not the relationship itself. Nonetheless, the result is the same! This is in direct defiance of God's laws. [67]

Pope Francis has turned the tables on the Catholic Church in its entirety. Our beloved Church always taught sinners must repent and come to live by Church teachings. Under this Pope, he is making all efforts possible to adapt Church teachings to the sinners. This is blasphemy of its worst kind.

Pope Francis maintains all people are basically good. Well, throughout the whole Bible because our beloved legal literature says exactly the opposite! What the hell is the Pope thinking? This is done in the name of Wokeness. The Pope wants the Church to be all-inclusive no matter the sinful condition of the people. This sounds a lot like Joe Biden with the cross hanging from his neck.

Now, busloads of transgender man ever so recently had lunch with the Pope. The obvious interpretation is the Pope approves of sex change operations. [68]

Additionally, Pope Francis wants to allow priests to marry, women to be deacons and priests can bless same-sex marriages. The Pope wants people with "alternative lifestyles "to be baptized against the teachings of the holy Gospel. [69] This is pure Satanism.

---

[67] https://www.youtube.com/watch?v=dd9S03Sp3p8

[68] https://www.youtube.com/watch?v=j9qcZy6o3zU

[69] https://www.youtube.com/watch?v=O5lK_wUMcHQ

On another occasion the Vatican released an interfaith document that compares Jesus to Buddha. This comes from the Seventh Buddhist – Christian Colloquium. With the specific approval of <u>Pope Francis this document says:</u> <u>"As Buddhists and Christians we see the Buddha and Jesus as great healers."</u> <u>Pope Francis agreed our Lord and Savior Jesus Christ is at the same level as Buddha. This is heresy against the Catholic faith.</u>

According to Pope Francis this equation is true: Jesus = Buddha

In my personal spiritual journey, I have never once heard about the Buddha healing anybody.

Pope Francis removed Bishop Strickland from Tyler Texas because he was critical of the Popes unchristian actions like what is presented a few sentences above.

<u>The Pope is in favor of a one-world order</u>. He is in favor of <u>a one-global Church and one global government.</u> For that to happen the Catholic Church must allow everybody in no matter with their state of sin is. <u>The Pope said "everyone, everyone, everyone must be allowed in.</u>" [70]

<u>The Pope wants everyone admitted to the now fake Catholic Church regardless of their unforgiven sins and belief in God or not</u>. He is turning the Catholic Church into nothing more than a big club that it permits anyone. The Pope said His goals are inclusiveness and diversity. This is pure political wokeness.

Bishop Vigano is now living in hiding for fear the Vatican will get Him. Yes, my dear people our beloved Catholic Church under this Pope Francis, our beloved Catholic Church is crumbling into dust and now being run more like the Mafia. [71]

---

[70] https://www.youtube.com/watch?v=O5lK_wUMcHQ

[71] IBID

Question: Blessed Mother Mary, I would at this point love to hear your points that summarize the Fatima Apparitions. Especially what you refer to that has not happened yet.

Answer: *Regarding Fatima my dear son, there was a great concern in the Kingdom about they are drifting away of God's sacred children across the entire world actually. The densest population among a few others in the world is in Europe and that is why I chose Fatima Portugal. That town has not have been contaminated with worldly political views that lead to destruction. The townspeople lived amazingly simple yet Godly lives. Even back then, it was getting harder and harder to select a location from my apparition.*

My dear son, you already know why I chose the three little children. For others it is because their minds have not been polluted with worldly things that take away from a pure Godly existence on earth. Some people would call that naive. Well so be it. Then naive are the ones who are the purest on earth. I chose those three children because first they were friends, and they were close together. Also, I did not want to choose one child here one child there and another child elsewhere even within the same town. I needed a camaraderie among the children I chose that existed before my appearances. It is in this manner that they will have a shared experience that will bring them closer together. And each would be able to support the others and what I know is a very holistic and surprising experience.

Regarding the content of Fatima secret three, first off, the first two secrets are not really secrets if you think about it. The secret about hell conforms with the age-old description of hell where everyone is basically on fire with never ending torment. My dear son as you know and as you have already written in your first book God's Grand Design of All Creation for Your Redemption come you accurately described what hell is really like. And as you pointed out it is far different and worse than fire. I must emphasize repeatedly and again that the sacred children of our Heavenly Father must realize that their Father would never torture anybody for any reason. The torment as my son you pointed out, comes from being exposed to the pure and perfect love of the Trinity. And they see how wretched and cruel they were in their lives. And when it is demonstrated to each of them what their terrible deeds were the effect of that and how the effects extend beyond just one person or generation. Suffering from one act can occur to subsequent generations as well. Thank you, dear son, for explaining that in your previous book.

Regarding Fatima, which was extremely hard for me to tell the children the awfulness of what is to come. Oh, how I wish the world would turn to God and pray as you do my son come pray from your Heart. The Pope that was supposed to consecrate Russia to my Immaculate Heart did not do so for terrible skimpy reasons. He caved in to certain people within the magisterium. Then when your <u>Pope Francis had a chance to consecrate Russia during the visit of Putin, he faked it as if he consecrated Russia, but he did not</u>. I have said before within this marvelous document that you are creating my son, that <u>Pope Francis really is the Anti-Christ and under control of Satan Himself</u>. And my dear son as you have pointed out in great detail in another part of this book, you expose the treachery, the falsehoods and deceit of the Vatican.

I know my dear son you are extremely upset that tears came to your eyes while you were writing what you knew you had to write for the benefit of others of God's children.

Now come regarding these specific contents of Fatima in secret three, I think my dear son you have done an excellent job within this book. There really is nothing more than I can add other than <u>to tell everyone that what you write is true and has the approval of their Heavenly Father.</u> And of course, you have my approval as well yes, my son Jesus Christ. There are now other things that I do want to comment on when you get to them including them in this book. Till then

I love you my dearest of sons, Mother Mary.

Question: Being of a poor memory, would you please say again what are the four words that you want everyone to include in their prayers and actions?

Answer: *Peace, prayer, penance, the rosary, and sacrifice*

On April 11, 2024, the Vatican released a new document titled "Dignitas Infinity" which means.

"Condition, think, sin, and circumstance." The problem is the word infinite. No human being can be infinite anything. We are not by nature infinite. The only human being that was ever infinite is Jesus Christ Himself. The title of this document stabs at normal Christian teachings. It waters down the infinite glory of Jesus Christ by saying everybody is infinite which is false. There is a lot more in this document. I refer to the video in the footnote shown below. [72]

One last item, in a conversation with our Blessed Mother Mary I mentioned Pope Francis said the Anti-Christ Pope is now on earth. ***Mother Mary's Response Was, "He Should Know Because He Is the Anti-Christ."***

---

[72] https://www.youtube.com/watch?v=DcM4UnJDLCs

28

The End of Times Are Here!

The Prelude for The Return of Our Lord and Savior Jesus Christ!

The next section deals with the current trends that are now taken for granted in the eyes of the billions of people on earth. I have heard personally many people say things like, "it is what it is." Simply, this is a way of surrendering to the evil forces that are taking over the earth as described in the Bible and various specific books which there's no time in this book to cover.

It was very painful for me to write the following section about the End of Times being here and now. Our Blessed Mother Mary agrees with every word. Mother Mary's apparitions describe in great detail what's coming to the people on earth because they've turned their backs and rejected our Heavenly Father who has lovingly created every particle of our personal existence.

Fundamentally because of this rejection the world will experience the natural results of living on earth without our Heavenly Father's ongoing protection. Yes, we invisibly enjoy our Heavenly Father's protection from cosmic and earthly natural forces that are very hostile to our lives. One example: If you want to know what the earth would be like without our Heavenly Father's protection just look at the moon. Earth would be much like that except for having an atmosphere. It would be unsuitable for life.

Worldwide trends

There are undeniable worldwide human trends that started 50 or 60 years ago. These trends would have happened earlier but societies on earth were too separate and geographically distant from one another for any notion of a consolidated government that would rule over all human life on earth. That separation has now ended because of modern air transportation, shipping, and communications.

As of now the worldwide trend is toward a communist or socialist form of government whereby government reaches into every detail of each of our lives. This form of government has the embedded premise everyone is the same. We see today in the Democrat party they are pumping the Satanic garbage men can be pregnant, men can compete in women's athletics and men can marry men and women can marry women. Every last particle of Democrat party beliefs is born out of Satanic foundations.

The American Democrat party has demonstrated time and time and time again since the late 1950s their underlying fundamental beliefs is, "<u>tax more and spend more</u>." As time has gone on more and more people have become more and more dependent upon a check from the government for their expenses. Naturally, they will vote for the party that would send them the most money. The legislation supported by the Democrat party is always "vote for me and I will give you more money and benefits". There are legitimate people in our country that do need honest help for circumstances beyond their control. We have a moral obligation to take care of them. However, the number of people that decide to become social parasites and suck up as much benefits as they can from the federal and state government has gone past the tipping point. And has led to impending financial ruin for our country. That will happen within the next 5 to 10 years if government spending is not stopped and reversed. Otherwise, The United States will become just one more communist-just like socialist quagmire of a society.

Communism and socialism by its very nature must have concentrated power over the many by the few. This power must be ultimate over the lives of the people and backed up by huge amounts of police power over every citizen and their lives. So, picture a world full of countries with socialist central governments. This is the first step toward a one-world government. It is much easier to consolidate a few 100 dictatorial socialist governments into a one-world government. This trend has one direction and one direction only. It is toward a one-world government that will be headed by none other than Satan Himself.

If you doubt this remember the largest countries in the world are losing their Godly faith. Think of Canada as the poster child for hate against Christian faith and the burning down of dozens of Churches in the very recent past. I bet you did not know that. In the minds of the people, they think they are fully capable of governing themselves and in their activities, they will create institutions that are founded upon human self-adulation and worship. This will be paganism in its worst form. Because it is the sacred children of God deciding to follow Satanic urges and believe there is no God and if there are these children believe they are the supreme power in the universe.

These trends are evolving and fundamentally headed in the direction of a one-world government. Gone will be individual countries that have complete sovereignty over their population and the landmass they occupy. Gone will be all Biblical literature and the Bible itself. The Bible will be declared illegal and strong penalties against the people who are caught with one. Gone will be all of our Christian Churches for open prayer to God will be considered a threat to society. Read the true story below. Gone will be the different currencies we have in our world. Gone will be the individual freedoms each country has the capability of tailoring to the needs and desires of its specific population. Gone will be the firearms we can possess now for our own personal protection from criminals. Gone will be the individual heritage brought forth by the elders in society and passing those traditions on that give life it is particular grandeur and uniqueness. Gone will be the concept of private property. This means the American dream of owning your own home will be completely shattered and not exist anymore. In fact, as Klaus Schwab, founder of the Worldwide Forum, has stated many times, **You Will Own Nothing And You Will Be Happy**. Kiss your house good-bye if these people get their way. Klaus Schwab Says the Theme of the 2024 World Economic Forum Is All About 'Rebuilding Trust' In the Globalist Plan to Enslave the Planet.

Klaus Schwab and His Dystopian worldwide government by its very foundational nature is stuffed full of Satanic ideas that strips away the very identity of everyone of God's sacred children. All of us will be forced, and I do mean forced by people with guns, to live our lives in the exact manner that is dictated by the singular world government.

Wikipedia has a good description of what these people are and what they say they do. Please look at the WEF [73] website. They did a great job of dredging up great sounding phrases and vocabulary. Make no mistake what you are reading is their one world government that will dominate every aspect of your life. The fundamental underlying premise of a one-world government as viewed by individual citizens is very simple. <u>Conform or die</u>!

As time goes on in the next few decades there will be less and less individual human rights as currently implemented in America and across the world, frankly. If you are not part of the ruling elite, you will be a worker bee in the eyes of a one-world government.

In the world today a cabal of elites in the world that no longer identify themselves with the specific country of their birth. Rather, they viewed themselves as citizens of the world with no particular allegiance to any particular country or group of countries. These are very powerful men and are mostly multibillionaires, each with their own personal desires for more money and more power even though they already have more than they know what to do with. We all simply call this greed.

The members of the world Economic Forum [74] certainly believe they are better than everyone else. They are smarter, they have a worldwide vision they do not believe regular people could ever understand. They view themselves as little Gods flying around the world in their private jets ignoring completely the climate change pollution they generate because they're better than the rest of us.

Why on earth am I spending the time to describe all this to you? Because it seems like it is way out there, and it is superfluous to an in-depth study of theology and the apparitions of our Blessed Mother Mary.

These two subjects are inextricably linked together! Surprising as this thought may seem the reality and the connection go something like this. It goes way

---

[73] World Economic Forum - Wikipedia

[74] The World Economic Forum (weforum.org)

back to the moment when each and every one of you and me were created by our Heavenly Father within the Heavenly Kingdom. After Satan's rebellion within God's Kingdom, and Satan was thrown down to earth, He made each of us unique and one-of-a-kind. Even though we have strong commonalities and gifts he has bestowed upon us like the gift of free will, the gift of reason and logic and the gift of being able to love. These are all Heavenly gifts that are unique to every separate sacred child of our Heavenly Father.

A quick story that dates back to the beginning of World War 2 in the late 1930s. After Japan attacked The United States at Pearl Harbor and Germany invaded Poland the United States had to mobilize an extremely large army and create huge amounts of weapons of war. The only way our government could do this is to treat everybody the same even though we knew there were not. A prime example is of all things a soldier's shoe size. The only way to meet the needs for the war is to realize the average foot size is size 10. So, all combat boots were made to size 10. It didn't matter what your shoe size was you got size 10 combat boots.

What the American government did with soldier's shoe size is precisely what the World Economic Forum is going to do with your entire life. They envision treating everybody the same and not caring that nobody is the same as God created us. We are all unique but that will not matter in the slightest. One-size-fits-all, and as the founder of worldwide Economic Forum says, you will own nothing, and you will be happy. That last part sounds like an order that you will be happy or else! They will never tell you that you will conform or else you will die! If you doubt this look at China today.

The Conclusion

So now I get to the conclusion of this general description of what is going on in the world. This section of the book is titled the End of Times and nothing could be more appropriate in a description of the End of Times is the World Economic Forum. Forget all their high-class Wall Street propaganda they describe themselves as. And realize this is nothing more than poison frosting on a cake of personal despair for all people who are not part of the elite cabal.

<u>All of this worldwide Economic Forum stuff is to prepare the entire world for the arrival of the Anti-Christ.</u> It will be far easier for Satan to rule the world if

the organizational hierarchy is such it has already been prepared for a one-world leader. Who is that leader? It is none other than Satan Himself.

In the world today the generalized political trends continue toward communist kind of governments. If you doubt this only look north to Canada. Under their Prime Minister Trudeau they have regressed into septic pool of government control over every aspect of a Canadian's life. I saw a video of a woman who was silently standing on a sidewalk across the street from an abortion center. She was praying for the victims being slaughtered inside the womb of women that did not want their babies even though they engaged in the act of creating them. Two police came up to her and ended up arresting her for being a "threat to society" by silently praying within the confines of her own mind.

There will be more candidates in the world and within the United States the general thrust is still toward a communist government structure that will destroy our hard-fought personal rights. Donald Trump as I write this is the only lasting hope this country has. The worst problem we have is in the last 3 1/2 years of the Biden administration they've inserted countless communist-minded bureaucrats throughout our executive branch of government and legal branch as well.

If you doubt the United States is headed toward one world government just look at what the Biden administration did to our southern border that does not exist anymore. The manifestation of one world government is to let the entire world into our borders and give them free everything that was worked for by all the citizens of our country. Over the last 60 years I have observed the Democrat party it does everything it can using every excuse I can think of to destroy personal freedoms in our country. All of this started with Lyndon Baines Johnson and His so-called, "war on poverty," and His "Great Society." Which mandated if a family is to receive federal government financial support the Father must leave His own home and His family behind. Johnson wanted to ensure that getting government aid meant the destruction of the family as was designed by Almighty God.

If you paid attention to what Mother Mary stated in her apparitions contained in other parts of this sacred literature, you should be arriving at one conclusion. That indeed mankind has entered into the End of Times as described not only by our Blessed Mother Mary but also by quite a number of Biblical passages. Passages in areas like the Book of Revelation, the book of Isaiah and others. Since this book focuses strictly on Blessed Mother Mary's apparitions, I will not have time to explorer other Biblical literature, but there is a lot that supports what Blessed Mother Mary has said.

Remember always, our Blessed Mother Mary and I speak with each other very frequently and anything in this book that is bold type and italicized that is Mother Mary speaking directly to me. What a magnificent gift this is, as you'll see in this section where I'll be asking her specific questions that are facing the world right now as this book is being written in June 2024.

This is not one of those, "The sky is falling," kinds of analysis. But we need to pay attention to what is happening around us and compare that with what Biblical literature has prophesized in the past. There are now remarkable colorations if you think about it. Additionally, because I am our Heavenly Father's Anointed Messenger, I provide to each of His sacred children totally objective and honest information from not only the Trinity but our Blessed Mother Mary.

It is her that is the focal point for this entire book. And I will be asking her comments on various topics that are tearing apart social structures in the world. Emphasizing the United States of America, and many other increasingly serious problems that are rampaging across this world created by our Almighty Father. I feel though you have to hit people over the head before they will listen to common sense, especially if new information conflicts with their preconceived worldview notions. Because of this I cannot help but think most people will ignore all of this.

But just now personal analysis. The End of Times is surely here because: **Mother Mary Told Me So!** I can also see it forming all around us if we care to just open our eyes and look and after that use the brain God gave us to think about what we see.

Beyond Human Politics and The Mess, It Causes

I hear so many times in the media the phrase about the Rath of God or God's anger and stuff like that. Stop thinking that way! Our Father in Heaven loves us so very much that it goes beyond human understanding. One important point of truth you need to know. When all of us were created in the blink of an eye billions of years ago within the Heavenly Kingdom, our Father loved us so much he left part of Himself within our spiritual being. This is so he could know us and help us every moment of every day we live our lives on earth. This is also so that when we pray there is absolutely no way our Father can hear every little tinkling of what we say, and the emotions attached to it. Our Father loves us that much and even more than I can possibly understand even though I am His Anointed Messenger.

<u>So, our Father is pure love, and he never gets angry, never!</u> In the coming End of Times, which we are approximately 60 years into based on my observation in the physical world and the people messing that up, what is coming is indeed earthly disasters. Is this God throwing lightning bolts at us? NO!

One thing everybody needs to understand is the earth in and of itself and the orbit that it has throughout our Galaxy is actually quite unstable. Our precious earth needs the constant intervention of Godly angels and other forces at our Father's disposal to stabilize things. So that the earth does not erupt in some way that would cause misery and death to a lot of His sacred children.

So, as is the case today, the vast majority of our Heavenly Father s sacred children have rejected Him. And they keep on rejecting Him worse and worse. So, our Heavenly Father sadly, and I'm sure full of sacred "tears", has decided <u>he will simply remove His protection for all of His sacred children on earth. To demonstrate to us what life would be like without our Heavenly Father.</u>

For those who think the earth is so stable, and things are the way they are because that's the way they are, that's completely wrong. The earth is the way it is because of constant intervention of love by our Father and His angelic host to keep His children safe. So as to make their ultimate decision regarding wanting Heaven or wanting hell by rejecting our Father.

If you do not believe what I just said ponder for a moment the asteroid and the damage they can do. It is certain we will see a lot more asteroids hitting the earth. Remember earlier in this book our Blessed Mother Mary said there would be fire from the Heavens. This is precisely what she meant. There is a huge ring of asteroids orbiting around the sun that does not take much to move some of them out of their orbit and hit the earth. If you don't believe me then I asked you to take a good look at the moon. That is what earth would look like if it were not for our Heavenly Father's protection.

What I just said regarding our Heavenly Father removing His protection for all of us also applies to strong increases in solar coronal mass ejections that will play havoc with the earth's electromagnetic fields. He may even let the North Pole swap ends with the South Pole in the not-too-distant future scientists are already talking about that.

Expect a lot more earthquakes that will be horrific and large. The Yellowstone Park caldera is showing increasing signs of life and recently as this is written there have been hundreds of small earthquakes they're building up to larger ones. If that caldera blows its top the entire earth will be horrifically affected in food production will suffer dramatically for all of people on the earth.

So, in conclusion, our Heavenly Father has decided to let His delinquent sacred children have it their way. The result will be unspeakable agony and pain across the entire world with Satan assuming power over the entire planet. He being helped by a bunch of spoiled brats called elites with jets that make them think they're better than everyone else.

Our Father will allow the normal cosmic forces in orbit around the earth to do what they normally would do. Because he will not protect us any longer. Due to our rejection of Him and His very simple rules for life and then proceeding to live with Him in all eternity and they paradise we can barely imagine.

Our magnificent, Blessed Mother Mary has appeared on earth 375 times to various people across the globe to deliver her messages of prayer, peace, penance, sacrifice, and love. To me it is horrific that only a small percentage of all her appearances have been distributed on a wide basis to our Father's sacred children. From my discussions with our Blessed Mother Mary, I tell you she hurts a lot about that and the word she used is, she "laments" the lack of attention she has received for our benefit.

The Above-Described Disasters Will Indeed Happen

It is now certain the above will happen. Our Blessed Mother Mary has performed 375 apparitions where she talks about, warnings of disasters to come. Disasters coming if the world does not reverse course. She tells us to pray to Almighty God, realize the rosary is the most powerful force on earth, except and live our lives according to the rules set forth by our Heavenly Father. And importantly, Russia must be consecrated to the Immaculate Heart of our Blessed Mother Mary.

The Vatican will tell you Russia has been consecrated. Like many other things Pope Francis has said, that was a complete falsehood. It is said Pope Francis consecrated Russia. No, he did not! He purposely chose words that are not what Blessed Mother Mary has asked for to consecrate Russia. How did he done so; Russia would not have invaded Ukraine?

Pain and suffering that are to come.

If you add up all the catastrophes coming to earth you will easily realize our Heavenly Father has indeed removed His protections from us. Hundreds of millions the people will perish as the natural catastrophes and other men made disasters will result in horrific death across the entire globe. As our Blessed Mother Mary has said, it will be so bad the living will envy the dead.

Now, you may wonder how a loving God can allow this to happen to His own sacred children and suffer so much they wish they were dead. Our Heavenly Father is indeed pure love the intensity and breadth of which is beyond human comprehension. Oh, you asked our Lord and savior Jesus Christ how can her Father do this and allow this horrific pain and suffering to happen?

Jesus Answered to Me the Following: Father will snatch Godly believers before their physical pain and subsequent death. In some manner I do not know, it will be as if they're in the middle of horrific circumstances leading to death and the next moment find themselves in the arms of our loving God. The non-believers will suffer what they believed in and their corresponding results that will cascade upon them.

The End of Times Is Really the Beginning:

All of this horrific pain and suffering caused by the fundamental attitude of rejecting our Heavenly Father does have an ending. This will not go on for eternity. I ask you to investigate this yourself by reading our beloved Bible. A great place to start is the Gospel of Matthew chapter 24. However, in a nutshell, when things look like they could never get any worse and people are wanting to die to escape the agony, it's then our Lord Jesus Christ will conduct His second coming. It will begin with a shout from Heaven heard around the entire world. This will usher in the times of Heaven on earth. Our time with our Lord and savior Jesus Christ defeating Satan once and for all. And our Blessed Mother Mary whom I love dearly and have spoken with for many hours to create this book for you, a sacred child of God, Mother Mary will crush the head of Satan.

29

The Last Words from Our Blessed Mother Mary

Our dear Blessed Mother Mary, UNI have shared in something so beautiful and sacred I feel unworthy to be involved with such magnificent wisdom you have bestowed upon all of us sacred children of God. I thank you from the bottom of my Heart for everything you have said, and I hope I have not left out anything you want to be included in this book. If so just let me know and it will be included.

Question: Dear Mother Mary, please share with us your thoughts regarding your apparitions and what it is you intend to accomplish with them. I feel like because of human fear, anxiety, and other negative social pressures the sacred information you want to bestow upon God's sacred children gets cut short or not set at all. I hope this book once it is published, we'll bring new light to your messages. Thank you so very much from the bottom of my Heart.

Answer: *My dear favorite son, come, I have been worried about you that you have worked so very hard on everything that we have shared together. You have put yourself beyond the limits of what your body can take and I want you to rest now for a little while before you finish editing and sending this book to the publisher.*

Actually, dear son, the material that exists within this magnificent book sums up to a great degree everything that I wanted to say to God's sacred children on earth. You have explained things so well that you have made it far easier for me to participate in projecting all that your Heavenly Father wants His children to know.

My Dear Blessed Mother Mary, thank you so very much for those kind loving words. I want to make this book as perfect as you are because this is your book and not mine. I am our Heavenly Father's Anointed Messenger and all the credit for things go to you that are contained within this book of Motherly love. I am looking forward one day to give you a big hug and then we can talk about all our common experiences in the creation of this work of theological truth.

**I love you so very much dear Mother,
Richard**

30

Blessed Mother Mary's Closing Thoughts

Question: Dearest Blessed Mother Mary, this has been a magnificent project of creating a book. A book that brings to all of God's children the actual truth of five of your most important apparitions and details about the end of times we have entered into in the early 1960s. This has been a magnificent journey for me working with you with the love of the Trinity propelling us forward or the benefit of all of our heavenly Father's sacred children.

I would love to hear your closing thoughts on this book both you and I have created. Please say anything you wish because whatever that is, it will magnificently benefit God's sacred children.

Answer: *My dearest son, come when my son Jesus and I first approached you a few years ago. We were very concerned that somehow, we would overwhelm you with our holy presence and that would be enough for you not to respond to us in the way that we were hoping you would. Since those first few days you have responded to us with your entire spiritual being and intellect. You have proven beyond any shadow of any doubt that you truly are one of the most holy sacred children that I have ever encountered. I am amazed at your dedication and the scope of your knowledge. Both within the spiritual realm and the physical realm which includes the sciences and logic and reason and an unquenchable thirst for God's truth. It has been a complete delight for me to go through everything in this book that both you and I have created for the benefit of your Father's sacred children. This has been a most wonderful experience for me, and I sincerely thank you for that.*

During the times that we spent together you always ended up overworking yourself and you got sick on a number of occasions because of your hard work and dedication. My son Jesus told me that in the previous books you have written this would be how you are. To experience this with you firsthand was amazing to me. Because in all my previous apparitions and dealing with God's sacred children while they're still on the earth, I was fighting against so much resistance. And the people I spoke with being frightened by authorities and the Church that prevented them from saying what it is I wanted them to say. To all the others of God's sacred children they come into contact with.

You and the other hand my dear sacred child is very fearless, and Jesus was right, you are a fighter. The best kind of fighter that you fight for the Holy truth of all of creation. When Satan attacked you those 3 famous times when you were in your early 30s, he's scared the heck out of you, but you responded so quickly coming back even stronger. Right now, while you have been writing the previous books and this one, Satan has no chance of interfering with the truth that you are the messenger of.

You have brought warmth and love to me my dearest son, and this along with so many other qualities that you have will be remembered in all eternity. And after this book is completed, I will remain always with you off your right shoulder along with my son Jesus. For both of us will always have our left hands on each of your shoulders while we stand on your right side. And yes, what Jesus said is true that for your protection from Satan you now also have two very powerful angels on each side that will protect you from any spiritual dangers and physical. I thank you for everything my dearest son. I love you ever so much for now and through all of eternity.

I love you so very much my dearest son.
Your Blessed Mother Mary

Appendix:

Author's Note: During the writing of this book, I took great pains to verify the validity of all the sources of information that are contained herein. Public sources of information are not always to be trusted by any means. All the references within this appendix have been consciously vetted to the best of my ability. Is all of this perfect? No. Is it close to being perfect? Yes.

Universal Secular Signs of The End of Times

As a general comment, across the globe we are seeing more and more very severe weather phenomena. Within the third secret of Fatima our Blessed Mother Mary warned of exactly this kind of thing happening before the return of our Lord and Savior Jesus Christ. Be forewarned my dear sacred children of Almighty God, these things are starting to happen and for every one incident I publish in this book, there are a lot more I have not detected.

Neil DeGrasse Tyson: Voyager 1 Has Detected 500 Unknown Objects

https://www.youtube.com/results?search_query=neil+degrasse+tyson+%3A+Voyager+1+has+detected+500+unknown+objects

Please refer to the warning from our Blessed Mother Mary about "Fire from The Sky."

A view minutes ago in Pueblo Mexico! The city up with blow was paralyzed by a hailstorm.

https://www.youtube.com/results?search_query=A+view+minutes+ago+in+Pueblo+Mexico!+The+city+up+with+blow+was+paralyzed+by+a+hailstorm.+

The Yellowstone caldera. People think the Yellowstone volcano or caldera will erupt as part of the End of Times. However, since September last year the magma chamber has gone down by 3 centimeters. A summary of Yellowstone's risk is it is increasing greatly toward a cataclysmic eruption in the not-too-distant future. Exactly when? Who knows? But given the end of times started 60 years ago and Yellowstone is definitely showing strong signs of an impending eruption that will destroy most of our country we need to pay attention. As always, think for yourself and pray.

Tucker Carlson: "Yellowstone Park Just Shut Down & Risk Of SUDDEN Eruption Increased By 320%!" (youtube.com)

https://www.youtube.com/watch?v=qV1oJKPeGsY

Neil de Grasse Tyson: Voyager 1 has detected 500 unknown objects passing.

https://www.youtube.com/watch?v=TUzgCiJ5eYM

I include this item in the list only because to demonstrate there are so many intergalactic bodies in and around our solar system with widely varying trajectories. Mother Mary said there would be fire from the sky. What Mother Mary also said was our Heavenly Father has now withdrawn his protection for the earth which opens the door to asteroids hitting our earth. If you wonder what that might be like just look at the craters on the moon.

Increasing Deadly Earthquakes Worldwide

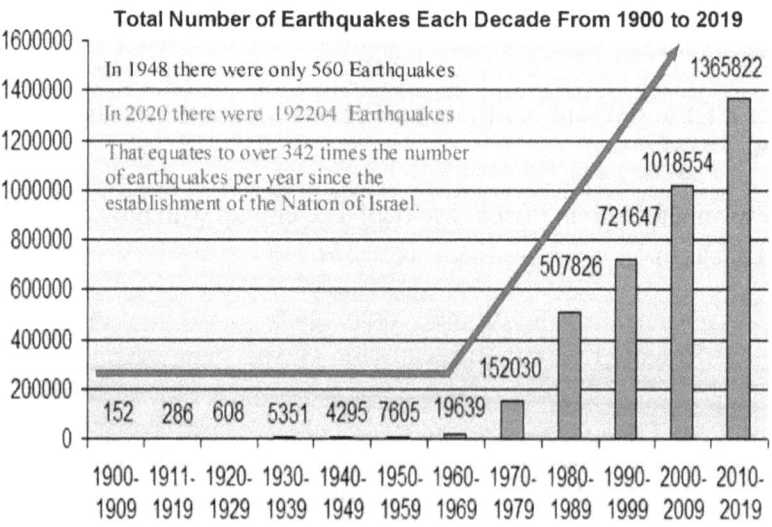

Regarding earthquakes on a worldwide level, we have seen a huge increase of earthquakes across the globe. Remember what I said earlier our Heavenly

Father is removing his sacred protection of his sacred children on earth due to their rebellion and rejection of him.

Our Heavenly Father has decided we are now entering into a time where mankind's rejection of their creator (HIM) will result in more and more severe events as time goes on.

I should mention the above data completely agrees with another scientific source of this kind of information: Our World in Data.

https://ourworldindata.org/grapher/number-of-natural-disaster-events?country=~Earthquake

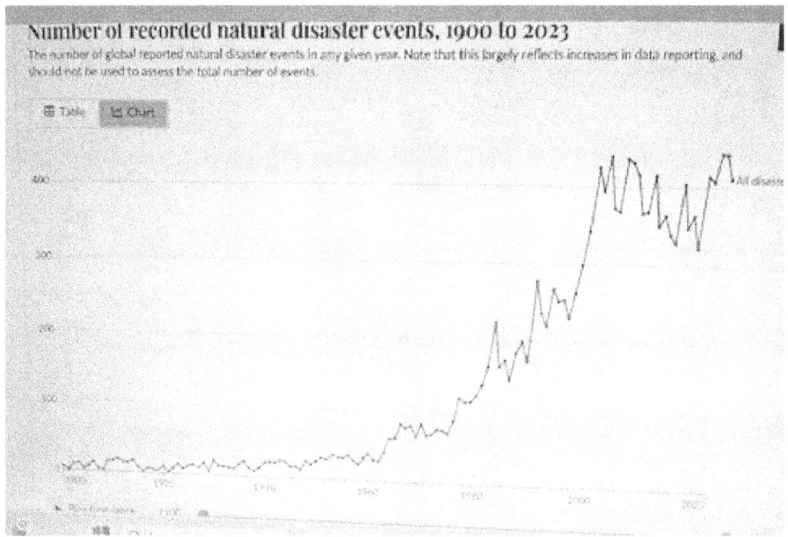

Unless you are paying attention to worldwide seismic activity over long periods of time you probably would not have noticed the catastrophes that are occurring around the world.

Our Heavenly Father is not angry. Our Heavenly Father is not mad, nor does he have any negative feelings or emotions. Our Heavenly Father is pure love the intensity of which exceeds in every way our imaginations of what that would be like. Remember dear sacred child of God, our Heavenly Father has asked me to be his only Anointed Messenger. Magnificently, this means there have been many occasions where I have spoken directly with our Heavenly Father in regard to my activities on earth. And his message he wants to bring forth to all of his sacred children, which means you. This book from our Blessed Mother Mary is a key part of the message from our Holy Father in heaven.

Our Heavenly Father is pure love for every one of his sacred children. Like all good Father s, there comes the time to discipline the children. So, they learn what they need to which will then provide the eternal lessons that are needed to reenter the Heavenly Kingdom and spend all eternity in paradise with Our Loving Father. You can see by looking at the above earthquake graph that starting in 1960 earthquakes became far more prevalent throughout the world.

Huge Increase of UFO Sightings, The End of Times Is Here Since The 1960's.

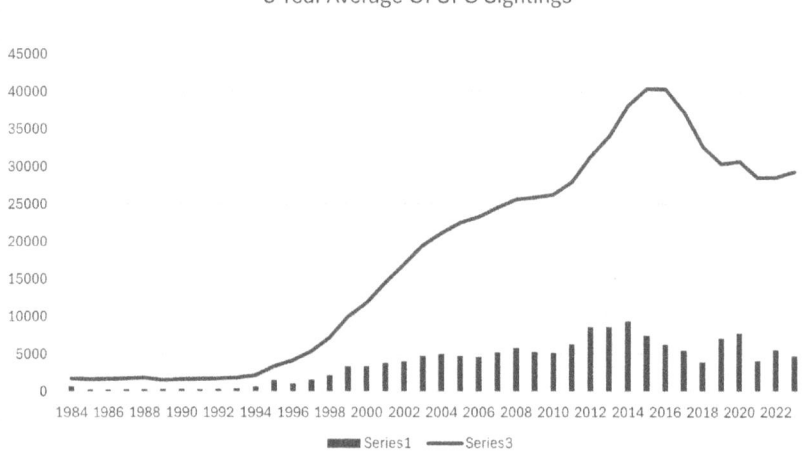

Data From: National UFO statistics - Search (bing.com)

The above data is just directly from the organization titled national UFO statistics. Their mission is to do the best possible accounting of UFO activities. As you can see above, the five-year average of the FO sightings started to increase dramatically in the 1990s. This appears to be the best data available. Most people automatically assume, and yes, it is an assumption with no proof, all these UFOs are alien beings from other planets.

However, these UFO's have shown they can disappear well someone is watching them. These UFOs are not necessarily a physical thing but rather some scientists believe these are interdimensional beings or worse yet interdimensional demon-like entities. So,

Question: Dearest Mother Mary, if you do not want to comment on UFO's I thoroughly understand. But only if you wish could you characterize what is the real truth about the foundational nature of the UFO's we have been seeing in large increasing amounts over the last 40 years.

Answer: *My dearest son, I would love to comment on this because this is a sign also of the end of times. We need to put this phenomenon into the proper context. These vehicles and beings were not in any way friendly at all to God's sacred children on earth. They represent a grave threat to all his children on earth. How can I possibly say that? It is because these vehicles and entities are indeed interdimensional. They are piloted by interdimensional Satanic demons. They are indeed able to cohabitate for a limited amount of time in the physical realm before they have to return to the spiritual realm. They are Satanic. Of this there is no doubt. Their plan is to participate in the one world government that as you have eloquently discussed in this book, Pope Francis is completely in favor of this. And remember as always, Pope Francis is the Antichrist.*

Your heavenly Father will allow this to happen. Simply because his sacred children on earth have turned away from him. And he is removing his protections for his sacred children. So, they will learn. That it is only the ways of Almighty God that will bring happiness, fulfillment, love and all the other magnificent moral values that were intended from the very beginning with Adam and Eve. It is now after these many thousands of years that your heavenly Father has decided. That this is the only way to have his sacred children realize the horrific errors of their ways by rejecting his holy Fatherly love.

One bit of proof that these entities are demonic is that there is no case out of all the many hundreds perhaps thousands of episodes where humans come

into direct contact with these Satanic demons. Where it is a positive experience for the children of God involved. It is always a highly negative one with lasting damage to the children of God that experience the exposure to these multidimensional Satanic beings. I know this sounds farfetched and very science fiction, but it is the truth. Thank you for asking me this my dear son. Understanding this will bring a far deeper understanding of this situation that is crumbling on the face of the earth, and it will continue to get worse and worse until my son returns. Thank you for asking my dearest son, "I love you so very much.

I love you too my Dearest Blessed Mother Mary

1960 Was A Worldwide Pivotal Year That Nobody Noticed. It was the Real Beginning of the End Times

By the way, the prophecies from our Blessed Mother Mary in 1917 we're supposed to have been released to the world from the Vatican during the year 1960. **That was never done!** It is not a coincidence that earthquakes on a global basis started to increase dramatically the same year the Pope was supposed to announce our Blessed Mother Mary's Prophecy regarding the third secret of Fatima. The Pope was supposed to consecrate Russia to the **Immaculate Heart of Our Blessed Mother Mary**. The stupid political Pope refused to perform **The Immaculate Heart Consecration to Russia** back in 1960. That year is the specific time the Pope was commanded by our **Blessed Mother Mary** to **consecrate Russia to Her Immaculate Heart**. "The reason why is very simple. The third secret of Fatima makes the Church look really bad and rightly so because they deserve it, but unfortunately untold millions of people have suffered because of what the Vatican consciously failed to do.

If you detect a certain amount of anger within my writing, you are correct. The Catholic Church, the Vatican and the Pope is supposed to serve the spiritual needs of all of God's sacred children. They purposely did not for their own selfish political reasons.

A disaster on a national scale: Floods are washing away northern Italy.

https://www.bing.com/search?q=A+disaster+on+a+national+scale%3A+floods+are+washing+away+northern+Italy&qs=n&form=QBRE&sp=-

1&lq=1&pq=a+disaster+on+a+national+scale%3A+floods+are+washing+a way+northern+italy&sc=0-70&sk=&cvid=378F0A6BEED94941B74F55F300000700&ghsh=0&ghacc =0&ghpl=

More than 20 different rivers have burst their banks in Italy, leaving 13 people dead and forcing thousands from their homes after six months of rainfall fell in one day and 1/2.

Cuba collapse accelerates - sugar harvest disaster, blackouts, food & fuel.

https://www.bing.com/search?q=Cuba+collapse+accelerates+-+sugar+harvest+disaster%2C+blackouts%2C+food+%26+fuel+&qs=n&form=QBRE&sp=-1&lq=1&pq=cuba+collapse+accelerates+-+sugar+harvest+disaster%2C+blackouts%2C+food+%26+fuel+&sc=0-75&sk=&cvid=E797EB3953E943288C0B3DAB0C88259C&ghsh=0&ghacc=0&ghpl

During the End of Times, which as I pointed out earlier started around 1960, it is the weaker countries that will fall and collapse first. If you want to know which countries those are, just look up which countries are socialist or communist. Economically speaking those are the countries that will collapse 1st and have the highest death rate on earth. Cuba is a communist country ever since Fidel Castro overthrew the previous government in 1959. Cuba is just the first of many to come.

Strong geomagnetic storm reaches Earth, continuing through weekend.

https://www.noaa.gov/stories/strong-geomagnetic-storm-reaches-earth-continues-through-weekend

I do not mean to be a chicken little running around yelling the sky is falling down. I bring up the topic of coronal mass ejections from the sun. Because it is real. And in this month of May 2024, we just had a significant CME event two weeks ago that brought the Aurora borealis down to the latitudes of Texas in the United States.

About 100 years ago there was something called the Carrington event which was a very large coronal mass ejection that set Telegraph wires on fire. Our electronics now are far more sensitive than that these days. And it will not take too many coronal mass ejections to blow out our navigation satellites, our communications satellites and lots of other stuff we depend on and take for granted these days. Your online orders to Amazon for stuff just will not get there and you will never receive what you wanted.

The sun has an 11-year cycle, and we are just entering into the most active part of that cycle which means there will be lots of more CME's heading to the way of earth. I should mention that through a complex mechanism coronal mass injections can also affect earth terrestrial weather as well. It is not too hard to believe our Heavenly Father will withdraw his protection for earth resulting in catastrophic events from the sun. It hasn't happened yet and may not happen, but it is something if we're discussing the End of Times would fit right in to the menu of possibilities.

Secular Societal Problems (In No Particular Order)

It all started with Obama.

It All Started With Obama | Victor Davis Hanson (youtube.com)

https://www.youtube.com/watch?v=faPNpovMeuU

Pres. Obama didn't believe in the principles and values of America.

Pres. Obama Didn't Believe in the Principles and Values of America - Chief Divider | Thomas Sowell (youtube.com)

https://www.youtube.com/watch?v=IzIJJ_MyzXI

America is getting more evil.

CALIFORNIA DINING AND BARSTOOLS - V2 - Final (11-29-2023) (youtube.com)

https://www.youtube.com/watch?v=vIQC7b81sCo

The De-civilization of America

The De-Civilization of America | Victor Davis Hanson (youtube.com)

https://www.youtube.com/watch?v=D7e34f22HXY

China's looming crises – CNBC Marathon
CNBC

China Has been sinking deeper and deeper into the effects of their one child policy from 20 years ago. Now they do not have enough labor to grow the economy. This puts the Chinese Communist party into a serious bind which will probably result into far more aggressive international policies. This puts Taiwan into serious trouble. I don't know if this is the prelude to war or not.

Victor Davis Hanson: Biden Is the Most Dangerously Radical President in U.S. History.
The Telegraph

https://www.youtube.com/results?search_query=Archbishop+Vigano+Responds+To+Francis%E2%80%99+Diabolical+Statement+About+Baptism

Food Shortages: All Americans Stockpile Food Right Now!
https://www.youtube.com/results?search_query=Food+Shortages%3A+All+Americans+Stockpile+Food+Right+Now!+

This is no joke or no exaggeration. More and more retail food stores and chains are experiencing what they call supply-chain issues. And if the food gets to the retail outlet it is a lot higher in cost because of socialist policies of the Democrat Joe Biden federal administration. The United States is becoming more and more like Venezuela, which is precisely where Cardinal Bergoglio comes from, a.k.a. Pope Francis.

Home Depot issues stark warning to U.S. economy by Michael Bordenaro
https://www.bing.com/search?q=Home+Depot+issues+stark+warning+to+U.S.+economy&qs=n&form=QBRE&sp=-1&ghc=1&lq=0&pq=home+depot+issues+stark+warning+to+u.s.+economy&sc=10-47&sk=&cvid=7931B3F95C8E48068C58789312A6B7F7&ghsh=0&ghacc=0&ghpl=

USA on the brink of chaos: How Americans are living the end of the American dream

Best Documentary

https://www.bing.com/search?q=USA+on+the+brink+of+chaos%3A+how+Americans+are+living+the+end+of+the+American+dream&qs=n&form=QBRE&sp=-1&lq=1&pq=usa+on+the+brink+of+chaos%3A+how+americans+are+living+the+end+of+the+american+dream&sc=0-81&sk=&cvid=5170A2005E074D69BE4B2BFD8677E08A&ghsh=0&ghacc=0&ghpl=

California: The decline of the American dream

Best Documentary

https://www.bing.com/search?q=California%3A+the+decline+of+the+American+dream&qs=n&form=QBRE&sp=-1&lq=0&pq=california%3A+the+decline+of+the+american+dream&sc=11-45&sk=&cvid=22735590108940FA9D807DF5B97DDD63&ghsh=0&ghacc=0&ghpl=

What it is like to live in Cuba today

https://www.bing.com/search?q=What+it%E2%80%99s+like+to+live+in+Cuba+today+&qs=n&form=QBRE&sp=-1&ghc=1&lq=0&pq=what+it%E2%80%99s+like+to+live+in+cuba+today+&sc=11-37&sk=&cvid=14D9BE67304543C8B8827591D2D7777F&ghsh=0&ghacc=0&ghpl=

If you are a Democrat, then your leadership is in many ways led by Bernie Sanders who loves communism so very much he spent his honeymoon in Moscow. Bernie and many other godless Democrats want to transform the United States into what you see in this video on a walking tour throughout Havana.

The Car Market Is Collapsing

Reppond Investments Inc.

https://www.bing.com/search?q=The+car+market+is+collapsing+&qs=n&form=QBRE&sp=-1&lq=0&pq=the+car+market+is+collapsing+&sc=3-29&sk=&cvid=DB6CAA7CBFC2451D8C01E47299913612&ghsh=0&ghacc=0&ghpl=

Seattle is a liberal progressive city in Oregon. Due to their socialist, communist ideology the city is dying both from an economic and moral perspective. The below website was created five years ago. It is far worse now!

Seattle Is Dying

https://www.bing.com/search?q=Seattle+is+dying&qs=n&form=QBRE&sp=-1&ghc=1&lq=0&pq=seattle+is+dying&sc=11-16&sk=&cvid=3CFA7F054A89422586B0B3F0F8FFE613&ghsh=0&ghacc=0&ghpl=

Economic and social warnings are now flying all over the place due to the Democrat party socialist and communist ideology they put into action without any approval by Congress. Joe Biden is a tyrant and rules by issuing executive orders where the citizens of our Blessed country have no say or no vote in anything. Fast-food McDonald's is another example of the fatalities within our country.

The Recession Just Hit McDonald's. CEO Warns: Low – Income People Have Stopped…

https://www.youtube.com/watch?v=SMslf5albGs

A Restaurant Apocalypse Is Starting to Sweep Across America & That Is Bad News

https://www.youtube.com/results?search_query=A+Restaurant+Apocalypse+Is+Starting+To+Sweep+Across+America+%26+That+Is+Bad+News

More terrible leading indicators of a serious economic recession immediately ahead due to Democrat party economic policies during the last three years of the Biden administration

15 Biggest Chains in America That Will Disappear in The Months Ahead

https://www.youtube.com/results?search_query=15+Biggest+Chains+In+America+That+Will+Disappear+In+The+Months+Ahead

The entire world is starting to buckle under economic laws of existence. The countries that will bring the most pain to their citizens are socialist and communist ideological hotbeds.

Pakistan insane walking tour.

https://www.bing.com/search?q=Karimabad%2C+Pakistan+insane+walking+tour&qs=n&form=QBRE&sp=-1&lq=0&pq=karimabad%2C+pakistan+insane+walking+tour&sc=0-39&sk=&cvid=3FEDDBD4BD624B8B89BA55CBE901AF6A&ghsh=0&ghacc=0&ghpl=

The collapse has begun! 15 big restaurant chains that are in deep, deep trouble. Epic Economist

https://www.bing.com/search?q=The+collapse+has+begun%21+15+big+restaurant+chains+that+are+in+deep%2C+deep+trouble&form=ANNTH1&refig=E9130FD1FA6B46BF8AF281C0DF6BA278

The United States under the economic socialist/communist economic ideological policies is starting to crumble in very serious ways. Since I am almost 80 years old, I remember very clearly the economic disaster brought to our beloved country by that peanut farmer president also known as Jimmy Carter in the early 1970's. The problem this time around will be 10 times worse because the starting point for inflation will be far greater. And the starting point for unemployment is also far greater than what it was in the early 1970's.

Food shortages: All Americans stockpile food right now.

https://www.youtube.com/watch?v=hWTp7M0hy6A

The end of everything, with Victor Davis Hanson

https://www.youtube.com/results?search_query=The+end+of+everything%2C+with+Victor+Davis+Hanson

Ray Dalio explains why America is entering into a horrific financial crisis.

https://www.youtube.com/watch?v=f6u1-2Emyic

A few minutes ago, in Puebla Mexico! The city of Puebla was paralyzed by a hailstorm.

https://www.youtube.com/watch?v=VSqIb25D8kU

A disaster on a national scale: Floods are washing away northern Italy.

https://www.youtube.com/results?search_query=A+disaster+on+a+national+scale%3A+floods+are+washing+away+northern+Italy

DEI

This is how pilots are being chosen to fly. You should be concerned. They are now being chosen not by experience and unquestioned ability to fly safely. Instead because of the Democrat party of Diversity, equity and inclusiveness, unexperienced people with low aptitudes are being put into the cockpit with the safety of hundreds of people in their hands. United Airlines has said it is their official goal to hire 50% of their pilots that are women and people of color. Minimums for safety through lots of flight experience went out the window for political ideology. The almost disaster of a United Jet with about 200 people. The plane departed from Maui for San Francisco where the unexperienced new hire came within 400 feet of the ocean on departure is a prime example of what is to come. Only the quick action of the very experienced captain saved the day.

https://www.youtube.com/results?search_query=this+is+how+pilots+are+being+chosen+to+fly.+You+should+be

This 100-foot-wide fissure - crack just opened in the Yellowstone super volcano! There are many articles about Yellowstone caldera showing quickly increasing volcanic activity. This caldera has the potential of causing horrific food shortages with the U.S.

https://www.youtube.com/results?search_query=This+100+foot+wide+fissure+-+crack+just+opened+in+the+Yellowstone+super+volcano!

Demonic falls profits in the White House!? Pastor Mark Driscoll

https://www.youtube.com/results?search_query=Demonic+falls+profits+in+the+White+House!%3F+Pastor+Mark+Driscoll

Campi Flegrei super volcano update; largest earthquake in 40 years

https://www.youtube.com/results?search_query=Campi+Flegrei+super+volcano+update%3B+largest+earthquake+in+40+years

Cuba collapse accelerates - sugar harvest disaster, blackouts, food & fuel.

https://www.youtube.com/results?search_query=Cuba+collapse+accelerates+-+sugar+harvest+disaster%2C+blackouts%2C+food+%26+fuel

Fidel Castro a bloodied communist tyrant, succeeded in revolting against the Cuban government in 1959 and created a communist government. Since then, there has been nothing but hardship, repression, and Tyranny. Communism is a disaster economically from one into the other and enriches only very few people, and everyone else suffers badly. This is the kind of government our Democratic Party wants to install within the United States of America.

Brave kid horrifies his teachers by reading their own woke garbage, then…

https://www.youtube.com/results?search_query=Brave+kid+horrifies+his+teachers+by+reading+their+own+walk+garbage%2C+then

Within this book I did not have time or pages to explore the Democrat party filth that exists within our elementary school system. The term Democrats use is, "woke." The actual word must be perverted and disgusting Satanic morality that is a complete insult to Almighty God. If you have children you must go to the next meeting in front of the school board. You will be shocked.

What just happened on earth! May 2024.

https://www.youtube.com/results?search_query=What+just+happened+on+the+earth!!!+May+2024

Very good website to keep track of increasingly dangerous and damaging natural disasters stretching across all of earth. Remember our Blessed Mother Mary warned of exactly this and through my own personal observations it seems as if the frequency and intensity of natural disasters is increasing a lot. Please take steps necessary to protect yourself and your family.

This is completely disgusting! And for all the people that are involved in creating this economic trap for the innocent sacred children of Almighty God, they are sending themselves to hell so they can rub shoulders with Satan himself. The new plan by the elites is simple. They aim to enslave families with high interest loan debt on their homes. They want to force families into foreclosure with a very simple plan. Simply, create debt instruments so people can refinance their homes within debt instrument that will readjust the interest rate. Readjusting after a short period of time to levels that will not allow the family to be able to pay off the loan when it comes due.

This will force families into bankruptcy and the bank will then take over their home. This ties in directly with Klaus Schwab's WEF (World Economic Forum's) when he stated you will all do nothing, and you will be happy. Those are Satanic words right out of the mouth of Klaus himself.

The Worst Plan Yet To Take Your Money – U.S. Housing Markets Newest Disaster!

https://www.youtube.com/results?search_query=The+Worst+Plan+Yet+To+Take+Your+Money+%E2%80%93+U.S.+Housing+Markets+Newest+Disaster!

She destroys gender ideology in five min.

She Destroys Gender Ideology in 5 Min (youtube.com)

https://www.youtube.com/watch?v=abTMFKoytMo

Abortion

I have said many times the "Democrat Party Is Indeed the Political Arm of Satan." Their policies align horrifically well with what Satan wants to happen on this earth. The Democrat party goes out of its way to promote the murder of developing sacred children of Almighty God while they are still in the womb. The following URL is from an ex-abortion Doctor giving his testimony through a congressional committee. He describes the horrific ugliness of what it takes from a medical perspective to perform a midterm abortion that results in the death, a painful death, of a four-to-six-month-old developing sacred child. The Democrat party loves to hide behind the word fetus as if changing the label somehow justifies the murder.

ex-abortion doctor tells shocking truth - YouTube

https://www.youtube.com/results?search_query=ex-abortion+doctor+tells+shocking+truth

Christianity and the Vatican

Bishop Strickland's Warning to the Faithful: "There's A Storm Coming"

Bishop Strickland's Warning to the Faithful: "There's A Storm Coming" (youtube.com)

https://www.youtube.com/watch?v=vA32lzCJRwA

Bible flagged under new book ban.

To think Biblical literature is now getting more and more censored and illegal. This IS PART OF THE END OF TIMES

Bible flagged under new book ban law pushed by Republicans in Utah - YouTube

https://www.youtube.com/watch?v=TUCXmGeIBVc

Father Chad: This country is fulfilling end times prophecy.

ID833 SAL Gas Station YT DMZ SC162 Maor (youtube.com)

https://www.youtube.com/watch?v=nwPtLykImV8

Exposing the satanic infiltration of our church.

Exposing the SATANIC Infiltration of Our Church! With Dr. Janet Smith (youtube.com)

https://www.youtube.com/watch?v=LzNNtMvfXAo

New Details About Pachamama Show What Pope Francis Did Was Far Worse Than Anyone Realized

Return To Tradition

https://www.bing.com/search?q=New+Details+About+Pachamama+Show+That+What+Pope+Francis+Did+Was+Far+Worse&qs=n&form=QBRE&sp=-1&lq=1&pq=new+details+about+pachamama+show+that+what+pope+francis+did+was+far+worse&sc=0-

73&sk=&cvid=FC47FF97C3BB4C15ADE29EC837AACBF2&ghsh=0&ghacc=0&ghpl=

Archbishop Vigano Responds to Francis' Diabolical Statement About Baptism

Return To Tradition

https://www.youtube.com/results?search_query=Archbishop+Vigano+Responds+To+Francis%E2%80%99+Diabolical+Statement+About+Baptism

Simply put, Cardinal Bergoglio wants to secularize the sacrament of baptism. I'm so angry about this one that perhaps our so-called Pope should just tell everyone go get a cup of tap water, pore over their head of the baby while saying these words "Yeah God."

Fatima's 3rd secret: Vatican's dark deception

Fatima's 3rd secret : Vatican's dark deception - YouTube

tohttps://www.youtube.com/results?search_query=Fatama%27s+3rd+secret+%3A+Vatican%27s+dark+deception

The In-between

This video is the absolute best and most accurate source of the third secret of Fatima. It agrees with what our Blessed Mother has personally said to me in the past months. This information is to be cherished and studied. It is Godly truthfulness for your personal spiritual growth and all the others of our Heavenly Father's sacred children still on this earth.

Cardinal Burke denounces the godless ideology of the Synodal Church promoted by Pope Francis

https://www.youtube.com/watch?v=WxgxtSXfuV0

Father James Altman – Bergoglio is not the Pope because he has proved he DOES NOT believe in basic Christianity.

https://www.youtube.com/results?search_query=Father+James+Altman+%E2%80%93+Bergoglio+is+not+the+Pope

The chilling revelation of a priest who read the third secret of Fatima intact.

https://www.youtube.com/results?search_query=The+chilling+revelation+of+a+priest+who+read+the+third+secret+of+Fatima+intact

Nuns smeared by bishops and the media for rejecting Francis.

https://www.youtube.com/results?search_query=Nuns+smeared+by+bishops+and+the+media+for+rejecting+Francis

The vortex - another persecuted priest

https://www.youtube.com/results?search_query=The+vortex+-+another+persecuted

Archbishop Vigano responds to Francis diabolical statement about baptism.

https://www.youtube.com/results?search_query=Archbishop+the+gunner+responds+to+Francis+diabolical+statement+about+baptism

Persecuted from within: A priest whistle-blower story.

https://www.youtube.com/results?search_query=Persecuted+from+within%3A+a+priest+whistleblowers+story

"Servants of Satan":

Archbishop Vigano responds to Pope Francis blessings for Pachamama meaning. It is a pagan goddess promoted by Francis.

https://www.youtube.com/results?search_query=Servants+of+Satan%3A+arch+Bishop+Vigano+responds+to+Pope+Francis+blessings+for

https://www.youtube.com/results?search_query=pachamama+meaning

https://www.youtube.com/watch?v=8byD6EBF-4s

Pope Francis consecration to Pachamama

https://www.youtube.com/results?search_query=Pope+Francis+consecration+to+pachamama

Francis sins the most wicked message about the Eucharist.

https://www.youtube.com/results?search_query=Francis+sins+the+most+wicked+message+about+the+Eucharist

The Pope blew it big time when he said this.

https://www.youtube.com/results?search_query=The+Pope+Blew+it+big+time+when+he+said+this

Did Francis just call Jesus a liar?

https://www.youtube.com/results?search_query=Did+Francis+just+call+Jesus+a+liar%3F

The Pope is shocked: Medjugorje prophecy coming true in 2024! Vatican alert

https://www.youtube.com/results?search_query=The+Pope+is+shocked%3A+Medjugorje+prophecy+coming+true+in+2024!+Vatican+alert

People are already accepting the mark of the Antichrist without knowing it.

https://www.youtube.com/results?search_query=people+are+already+accepting+the+mark+of+the+Antichrist+without%E2%80%A6

Heresy of the Pope - John MacArthur

https://www.youtube.com/results?search_query=Heresy+of+the+Pope+-+John+MacArthur

John MacArthur is a well-known televangelist who is a person that sticks to the Bible. This is a good video to watch where he gives multiple examples of Pope Francis and his anti-Catholic heretical teachings.

Pope Francis finally reveals the truth about the third secret of Fatima.

NO, he did NOT. He lied about Fatima 3 distorting the truth into nice sounding lies.

https://www.youtube.com/results?search_query=Pope+Francis+finally+reveals+the+truth+about+the+third+secret+of+Fatima

Note: Two things about this disgusting Vatican video - the picture of sister Lucia is a fake as covered within this book written by me and our Blessed Mother Mary. Pope Francis is a Satanic liar. Secondly, what he says is the third secret of Fatima IS NOT! The truth of the third secret is contained within the book you're holding in your hands. Among many prophecies contained in the authentic third secret of Fatima is the prophecy the 112th Pope will be the Antichrist. Cardinal Jorge Bergoglio IS the 112th Pope with the chosen name Francis!

Remember always, dear sacred child of our Heavenly Father, Pope Francis is the antichrist and everything he says and does is aimed at one purpose. To destroy the Christian Church that was founded by our Lord and Savior Jesus Christ. He is attempting to create a second Church with the name Synod in it. I included this video so you can see firsthand the falsehoods that spew out of Bergoglio's Satanic mouth. If you sense I am angry about this, you're completely correct! So too is our Blessed Mother Mary!

Francis is purposefully trying to provoke faithful Catholics by insulting Mary.

https://www.youtube.com/results?search_query=Francis+is+purposefully+trying+to+provoke+faithful+Catholics+by+insulting+Mary

Francis gets political, smears faithful Catholics.

https://www.youtube.com/results?search_query=Francis+gets+political%2C+smears+faithful+Catholics

Vigano: Is Francis invalid Pope?

https://www.youtube.com/results?search_query=Vigano%3A+is+Francis+invalid+Pope%3FI

Francis Is Purposefully Trying to Provoke Faithful Catholics by ...

https://www.youtube.com/watch?v=hlFi-gT1Ok8

Return to Tradition

Anthony Stein a well-known and respected traditionalist within the Catholic Church, confirmed the people within the Vatican have published anti-Blessed Mother Mary material that is exposed in this video. This is how Satan works.

Chip away at the foundational structure of our Blessed Church founded by our Lord and savior Jesus Christ, one brick at a time. And so, this is the latest chipping with the target being our Blessed Mother Mary.

The pope blew it big time when he said this.

https://www.bing.com/search?q=the+pope+blew+it+big+time+when+he+said+this&qs=n&form=QBRE&sp=-1&lq=0&pq=the+pope+blew+it+big+time+when+he+said+this&sc=13-43&sk=&cvid=396179A9C5C54C4DB4ECEA6500000700&ghsh=0&ghacc=0&ghpl=

During this seemingly simple interview, the fake Pope Francis said things that contradict the core teachings of our Lord and savior Jesus Christ.

Pope Francis finally reveals the truth about the third secret of Fatima.

No, he did not…just more lies.

https://www.youtube.com/live/6EjLpfSkb8Y

What the Pope just said in this video are falsehoods.

The beauty of this book you hold in your hands is you have the word for word loving description directly from our Blessed Mother Mary. Each word, every single word that is contained in this book is exactly what our Blessed Mother Mary has said that Fatima number three really is. There can be no greater proof that so-called heretic Pope Francis is under the direct control of Satan himself. I am so enraged with this, if I got close enough to our fake Pope, I would have a very hard time restraining myself from punching him in the nose!

This is so evil and clever at the same time very much like what Satan loves to do. First there is the admission that what has been said about Fatima since 1960 has been a falsehood. That in and of itself is disgraceful and a direct violation of Canon law about honesty and one of the 10 commandments. The Vatican knows people did not believe that description they handed out calling it the third secret of Fatima. Mother Angelica of the EWTN TV program along with many others within the Catholic Church did not believe what the Vatican was pumping out as the third secret.

So, what did they do? They invented another bigger falsehood that simply replaces the previous falsehood calling it finally the truth is revealed. They are a bunch of Satanic bastards and should be stripped of all papal authority!

www.ingramcontent.com/pod-product-compliance
Lightning Source LLC
Chambersburg PA
CBHW071737150426
43191CB00010B/1603